WHACKED

HOW GM CAREENED INTO BANKRUPTCY AND TOOK THE INNOCENT WITH THEM

Thanks for Your Support.

Dennis Hayarek /12

D0488673

Cher François,

Ton support autant professionnel
que personnel m'est très
reconfortant.

Merci de demeurer dans
ma vie.

27/7/2012

WHACKED

HOW GM CAREENED INTO BANKRUPTCY AND TOOK THE INNOCENT WITH THEM

DENNIS GAZAREK

GSPH

GSPH

GENERAL STORE PUBLISHING HOUSE
499 O'Brien Road, Box 415
Renfrew, Ontario, Canada K7V 4A6
Telephone 1.613.432.7697 or 1.800.465.6072
www.gsph.com

ISBN 978-1-926962-47-4

Copyright © Dennis Gazarek 2012

Cover art, design, formatting: Magdalene Carson
Printed by Custom Printers of Renfrew Ltd., Renfrew, Ontario
Printed and bound in Canada

No part of this book may be reproduced, stored in a retrieval system,
or transmitted in any form or by any means without
the prior written permission of the publisher or,
in case of photocopying or other reprographic copying, a licence from
Access Copyright (Canadian Copyright Licensing Agency),
1 Yonge Street, Suite 1900, Toronto, Ontario, M5E 1E5.

Library and Archives Canada Cataloguing in Publication
Gazarek, Dennis, 1949-
Whacked : how General Motors careened into bankruptcy and took
the innocent with them / Dennis Gazarek.
ISBN 978-1-926962-47-4
1. General Motors Corporation--Corrupt practices. 2. General
Motors Corporation--Finance. 3. Bailouts (Government policy)--United
States. 4. Bailouts (Government policy)--Canada. I. Title.
HD9710.U54G47 2012   338.7'62920973   C2012-900635-1

The author and publisher have made every attempt to locate the sources
of photographs and written excerpts. Should there be errors or omissions,
please contact the author/publisher for correction in future publications.

This book is dedicated to all the good people who over many years devoted themselves completely to General Motors. Either through their labour, commitment, or emotional and financial investments, they made General Motors a great company. It is sad to see their many accomplishments overshadowed by the greed, avarice, and mismanagement of a few.

Contents

PART 2 General Motors Canada

Acknowledgments

Special thanks to the following individuals:

I want to especially thank Janet, my wife, who supported and encouraged me through the long months and years of angst and frustrations. Thanks to my family (and especially my brother and former employer, Jerry), many friends, dealers, and co-workers who shared my enthusiasm for this project and assisted through to its completion.

Thanks to Richard Szpin, Robert Knuckle, and Don Pazaratz whose guidance and advice was invaluable.

Finally, thanks to Jane Karchmar, who, as my editor, was a saviour and made my manuscript intelligible; and to publisher Tim Gordon, who made it all possible.

Preface

The Collapse of General Motors as Seen through the Eyes of a Thirty-five-year Dealer Employee

The title *WHACKED* was inspired by a dealer's remark regarding how General Motors dealt with any obstacles it perceived in its quest for billions of dollars in government funding in the years 2008 and 2009. "Whacked" is a Mafia euphemism for "destroy/ murder."

Hiding behind the shield of the Canadian and United States governments, General Motors ruthlessly destroyed the net worth of thousands of workers, dealers, investors, and customers in its desire to save itself with taxpayers' monies.

This book is about General Motors and its declaration of bankruptcy on June 1, 2009. The media has given excellent coverage of the downfall of GM. They even have tried to give some opinions as to why it failed. I found that most of these explanations were both superficial and simplistic: too many dealers, too many brands, the unions, the economy. In reality, a company like GM has to have leaders who are vigilant and able to react. In today's world, economy, and instant communication, events thousands of miles away can have a direct impact on the citizens of, say, Peoria, Illinois. When Saddam Hussein attacked Iran in 1980, it caused only a little ruffle in the U.S. economy; in 1990, when he invaded Kuwait, it impacted America for the next twenty years.

The reader should be aware that I might appear at times cynical, bitter, and full of resentment. I began writing this book as a

ɔf dealing with my grief at the loss of a lifetime of effort,
ɳent, and loyalty to, and on behalf of, General Motors.
ʂentful toward the actions of General Motors managers,
both on my account and that of the thousands of other individuals who were displaced. This book has helped me "get over" the
reality of the loss and move on with my life.

My goal here is to give the reader a better understanding of
the North American auto industry and, in particular, General Motors. I will also endeavour to offer some insights as to what happened in a small sector of the worldwide General Motors empire
of which most readers are not aware. After reading this book, if
you can say to yourself, *"I did not know that!"* I have succeeded.

Dealer Sales Tricks

After having spent thirty-plus years in the automotive business,
many of them as a used-car manager and appraiser, I would be
shirking my responsibility if I did not address the issue of "Dealer
Sales Tricks." One popular belief is that car dealers and salesmen
have a number of tricks they utilize to convince consumers to
buy something they do not need or want, or cannot afford.

My personal experience is that *people want to buy cars*; that
is why they go to car lots. As a salesperson, I did my very best
to present my car as the vehicle that best suited my customer's
needs. I am fully aware that automobiles have been misrepre-
sented and odometers have been spun, along with other nefari-
ous practices. These actions by unethical individuals were their
response to a customer who wanted a "good deal." Some individuals, a number who work in the automotive industry, will use unethical, immoral, and illegal tactics for their own financial gain.
If a customer wants to buy a car with low mileage for less than
the fair market value, there is always an unscrupulous person
who will sell that consumer a high-mileage car with an altered
odometer at a "good" price.

In my province of Ontario, dealers operate under very strict
controls and supervision, and most of the odometer tampering
was done by private individuals. People who were leasing vehicles with mileage penalties would regularly alter the odometer

to avoid the penalties. And customers who had desirable vehicles to trade in would have the odometer altered to secure a better trade value.

Remember, no salesperson or dealer wants to sell you a "lemon"; it is just plain stupid business to do so. The dealer/salesman has no way of knowing which car is going to be a lemon. The best way for you to avoid a "lemon," if you are concerned about getting one, is to buy all the extended warranty coverage you can.

In general, how does a consumer protect him/herself?

Rule Number 1: If the deal appears too good, be very careful. You would not drink French champagne that someone is selling for fifty cents a bottle, would you?

Rule Number 2: Spend less than you can afford. Be very careful not to buy too many options, accessories, and toys, as their value is hard to recoup at trade-in time. Your five-year-old Nippon Star-Trooper will not be worth much more than the next one even though you have a 50,000-watt stereo system, lifetime paint protection, and unlimited car washes. Of course, if you have lots of money, enjoy and spend away.

Rule Number 3: If you need insurance, or you think you do, always get a quote from an insurance agent. Sometimes the dealer's insurance price will be better, but it never hurts to check.

Rule Number 4: When you are buying a product you do not have great expertise in, you have to trust the salesman. I suggest that you ask friends and family for recommendations; or, discreetly ask the dealership receptionist whom *she* would deal with if she were buying a car. The dealer's receptionist is usually a long-term employee and knows who the incompetent salesmen are. In almost all dealerships, most salespeople will treat you fairly; you just want to avoid the incompetents that the dealer has not weeded out yet. The receptionists do not like them and will not recommend them.

Rule Number 5: Avoid buying big-ticket items like vehicles with Lines of Credit. On the surface, the interest rate might be lower than a fixed-term car loan; however, Canadian bank statistics demonstrate that most people (me included) do not have the self-discipline to pay the line off promptly and, as a result, end up paying more dollars in interest for a longer period of time than with a fixed-term car loan.

PART 1

GENERAL MOTORS CORPORATION

1

Centralized versus Decentralized Organizational Structures

There are many ways to structure the management of an organization. The Roman Catholic Church, the British Empire of the 1880s, Switzerland, Soviet Russia, General Electric Corporation, and Sony Electric all have (or had) management structures that are effective. Simply stated, organizational structures primarily vary by the amount of centralization versus decentralization that exists in the organization. The appeal of centralization is the apparent economic and financial advantages of central control, central resource allocation for maximum efficiency, and related economies of scale. The central planning systems of the former Communist states were examples of centralized planning at its best and worst.

Decentralized organizations have genuine control and responsibility issues; top management often does not know and would not approve of what is going on in the hinterlands. The Catholic Church based in Rome has suffered dearly as a result of the deviant behaviours of a few priests who were isolated from the Vatican by many layers of authority.

However, the decentralized organization of the Catholic Church has initiated and fostered Miracles and Saints who would have never flourished under strict, centralized authorities. Mother Teresa, Saint Francis of Assisi, Maximilian Kolbe, and Marguerite Bourgeoys are examples of individuals who far exceeded the expectations of their roles in their service to their fellow man and their church. These individuals and thousands of others acted without policy manuals, head-office memos, and similar accoutrements of today's organizational structures to achieve great things. Decentralization frees individuals to be the very best they can be within simple parameters and guidelines.

General Motors once was the greatest business organization in the world. It was one of the most decentralized as well, with a myriad of successful operating divisions. After the 1960s, top management made a determined effort to eliminate the independent divisions and brands, supposedly so as to create efficiencies and increase profitability.

It is my contention that any efficiencies and savings that accrued were illusory and short-term and resulted in an inability to produce cars people wanted to buy. Instead of having divisions and brands that were focused on producing automobiles and products people wanted to buy, top management became focused on maximizing profits through organizational rationalization and centralization. The end result was that on June 1, 2009, General Motors declared bankruptcy, costing millions of individual American and Canadian citizens billions of dollars directly and indirectly.

2

The Durant—Du Pont Years

When looking back at General Motors' history, you quickly realize that the company was the result of the efforts of a very small group of individuals. An individual would take control of the company and push it forward.

William C. Durant joined the Buick Corporation in 1904 and soon was the president. He saw the future of the booming automobile business and believed that not all of the hundreds of auto producers could survive. He set out on a path of acquisition and concentration of many companies into one. In 1908, Durant formed General Motors as a holding company for Buick and then acquired Oldsmobile. In the years following, Durant brought in Cadillac, Cartercar, Elmore, Ewing, Oakland (later known as Pontiac), Reliance Motor Truck Company, and the Rapid Motor Vehicle Company. Durant was also instrumental in establishing the dealer franchise system as we know it today.

Durant lost control of GM in 1910 to a bankers' trust, due to the large amount of debt (around $1 million) taken on in its acquisitions. Durant had been financing these acquisitions by debt, and he lost the confidence of the bankers in his ability to pay it back. (Incidentally, by 2009, GM was again financing operations by debt, but there were no bankers available to save it: the banks were broke, too, due to the U.S. bank failures of 2008.)

It should be noted as well that Durant was not a "car guy" but a financier. Unlike Henry Ford, Ransom Olds, William P. Chrysler, and numerous engineers, designers, and innovators who were the foundation of the early automotive industry, Durant had little mechanical expertise.

After being forced out of General Motors in 1910, Durant co-founded the Chevrolet Motor Company in 1911 with Louis Chevrolet. After a brilliant stock buyback campaign, he returned to head GM in 1916, with the backing of Pierre S. du Pont, of

DuPont Chemicals (DuPont was making millions selling military raw materials to England and France, who were fighting WW I). On October 13 of the same year, GM Company became incorporated as General Motors Corporation. Chevrolet entered the General Motors fold in 1917; its first GM car was 1918's Chevrolet 490. DuPont removed Durant from management in 1920 and replaced him with Alfred Sloan, a GM vice president. Sloan had owned Hyatt Bearings and, when the firm was acquired by General Motors in 1916, he joined the GM management staff. Various DuPont interests held large or controlling share holdings until about 1950.

In 1918, GM purchased the McLaughlin Motor Car Company of Oshawa, Ontario, Canada, manufacturer of the McLaughlin-Buick automobile since 1908 as well as Canadian versions of Chevrolet cars since 1915. The company was renamed General Motors of Canada Ltd., with R.S. "Colonel Sam" McLaughlin as its first president and his brother George as vice-president.

GM Chairman Alfred Sloan, Jr., right, and GM founder William Durant reunite at an event marking production of the twenty-five-millionth car in Flint in 1940. Durant was forced out of GM for the second and last time in 1920, while Sloan went on to become the first celebrity CEO and a management genius lauded for his brilliant stewardship of the automaker. *(Author's collection)*

3

The Sloan—Kettering Years

Alfred Sloan was elected president of GM in 1920. Under Sloan, GM surpassed Ford Motor Company in sales by the late 1920s. While Ford continued to refine the manufacturing process to reduce costs, Sloan was inventing new ways of managing a complex—and by now worldwide—organization, while paying special attention to consumer demands. Car buyers no longer wanted the cheapest and most basic model; they wanted style, power, and prestige, which GM offered them. Thanks to consumer financing via GMAC[1] (founded in 1919), easy monthly payments allowed far more people to buy GM cars than Ford, as Henry Ford was opposed to credit on moral principles.

Charles Kettering, the brilliant inventor of the electric starter motor, leaded gasoline, innovative paint finishes, and numerous automotive innovations, worked hand in hand with Sloan's leadership to initiate GM's foundation of R&D and technological leadership in the automotive world.

During the 1920s and 1930s, General Motors assumed control of the Yellow Coach bus company and helped create Greyhound bus lines. They replaced intercity train transport with buses and established subsidiary companies to buy out streetcar companies and replace these rail-based services as well with buses.

In 1930, GM also began its foray into aircraft design and manufacturing by purchasing the Fokker Aircraft Corporation of America (the U.S. subsidiary of Fokker of the Netherlands) and Berliner–Joyce Aircraft, merging both acquisitions into General Aviation Manufacturing Corporation. Through an exchange of stocks, GM took controlling interest in North American Aviation and merged it with its General Aviation division in 1933, but retaining the

---

1   General Motors Acceptance Corporation, a wholly-owned subsidiary of GM until 2006.

A Sherman M–4 tank is fitted with tracks at a Fisher Body plant in 1942. After the Japanese bombed Pearl Harbor in December 1941, GM converted plants for the nation's war machine with remarkable speed. Fisher Body factory #1 in Flint produced its last car body in January 1942 and sixteen days later started assembly of M–4s. The first tank was completed forty-seven days later.
(Author's collection)

name North American Aviation. In 1948, GM divested NAA as a public company, never again to have a major interest in the aircraft manufacturing industry.

General Motors bought railcar builder Electro-Motive Corporation and its engine supplier, Winton Engine, in 1930, renaming both as the General Motors Electro-Motive Division. Over the next twenty years, diesel-powered locomotives—the majority built by GM—largely replaced other forms of traction on American railroads. (During World War II, these engines were also important in American submarines and destroyer escorts.) Electro-Motive was sold in early 2005.

In 1935, the United Auto Workers labour union was formed, and in 1936, the UAW organized the Flint Sit-Down Strike, which initially idled two key plants in Flint, but later spread to half a dozen other plants, including Janesville, Wisconsin, and Fort Wayne, Indiana. In Flint, police attempted to enter the plant to arrest strikers, leading to violence; in other cities, the plants were shuttered peacefully. The strike was resolved on February 11, 1937, when GM recognized the UAW as the exclusive bargaining representative for its workers.

General Motors produced vast quantities of armaments, vehicles, and aircraft during World War II for both Allied and Axis customers.

GM's William S. Knudsen served as head of U.S. wartime production for President Franklin Roosevelt, who called Detroit "the Arsenal of Democracy." The General Motors UK division, Vauxhall Motors, manufactured the Churchill tank series for the Allies. The Vauxhall Churchill tanks were instrumental in the UK campaigns in North Africa (ironically often being used to attack German transport units then using GM Opel trucks). Bedford Vehicles manufactured trucks and logistics vehicles for the UK military, all important in the UK's land campaigns. In addition, GM was the top manufacturer of U.S. Army 1 1/2-ton 4x4 vehicles.

GM's headquarters were located in Flint until the mid-1920s, when it was moved to Detroit. Its building, originally to be called the Durant Building, was designed in 1919 and construction begun when Durant was president; it was completed in 1923 and officially dedicated as the General Motors Building in 1929. GM maintained this headquarters location, now called Cadillac Place, until it purchased the Renaissance Center in 1996 from Ford Motor Company on the Detroit riverfront.

General Motors made its first overseas acquisition in 1925, when it bought Vauxhall Motors of England. In 1929, GM went on to acquire an 80 percent stake in German automobile manufacturer Adam Opel AG. Two years later, this was increased to 100 percent, and the company remains the core of GM Europe to this day (after an aborted attempt to sell it in 2009). In 1931, GM acquired Holden of Australia. In 1926, GM created the Pontiac as a "companion" to the Oakland brand, an arrangement that lasted five years. The companion outsold its parent during that period, by so much that the Oakland brand was terminated, and the division was renamed Pontiac.

At one time, each of GM's automotive divisions in the United States was targeted to a specific market segment, and, despite some shared components, each distinguished itself from its stablemates with unique styling and technology. The shared components and common corporate management created substantial economies of scale, while the distinctions between the divisions created (in the words of GM President Alfred P. Sloan) a "ladder of success," with an entry-level buyer starting out with a "basic transportation" Chevrolet, rising through Pontiac, Oldsmobile, Buick, and ultimately to Cadillac.

From 1920 to the late 1960s, this concept was the foundation of the General Motors philosophy.

4

"Engine" Charlie Wilson

In terms of its revenues as a percent of GDP at this point in time, GM had become the largest corporation registered in the United States. In 1953, Charles Erwin Wilson, then GM's president, was named by newly elected President Eisenhower as Secretary of Defense. When he was asked during the hearings before the Senate Armed Services Committee if, as Secretary of Defense, he could make a decision adverse to the interests of General Motors, Wilson answered affirmatively—but added that he could not conceive of such a situation "because for years I thought what was good for the country was good for General Motors, and vice-versa." Later, this statement was often misquoted, suggesting that Wilson had said simply, "What's good for General Motors is good for the country."

At the time, GM was one of the largest employers in the world—only Soviet state industries employed more people. In 1955, General Motors became the first American corporation to pay taxes of over $1 billion.

(Courtesy of Wards Automotive Group)

By 1958, some of the divisional distinctions within GM began to blur with the availability of high-performance engines in Chevrolets and Pontiacs. The introduction of higher trim models such as the Chevrolet Impala and Pontiac Bonneville priced in line with some Oldsmobile and Buick offerings was also confusing to consumers. By the time Pontiac, Oldsmobile, and Buick introduced similarly styled and priced compact models in 1961, the old "step-up" structure between the divisions was nearly over. However, each brand had a unique and distinctive image with its loyal customers. It was not based on Sloan's step-up concept, but depended upon how the car meshed with its owners' personality and perception.

Chevrolet was the car for the family's "to see the USA" and performance cars. Pontiac was "wide-track" and performance. Oldsmobile was sophisticated, Buick classic elegance, and Cadillac was Cadillac! Each brand was very successfully satisfying different segments of the American market with distinct and different vehicles. Of course the step-up concept initiated by Sloan was still an effective marketing concept.

Since 1945 and the near-collapse of the Ford Motor Company, GM had been on a tremendous upward spiral. If it moved, it was probably built by GM. To get some idea of the vastness of GM's empire, here is a summary of some of GM's smaller subsidiaries.

- Euclid, and later Terex, which were competitors to Caterpillar in the earth-moving business

- Motor Coach Industries, America's largest bus builder

- Electro-Motive, builder of railway engines

- Detroit Diesel, builder of diesel engines for all purposes

- Allison Corporation, builder of aircraft engines

- GMC, heavy-duty trucks

- Car companies such as Vauxhall in England, Opel in Europe, and Holden in Australia

- Delco batteries, brakes, and suspension systems

- AC spark plugs
- Saginaw steering gear
- Muncie transmissions
- Hydramatic transmissions
- New Hyatt Bearings

GM even built home appliances through its Frigidaire division. Plus, they owned hundreds of other associated companies.

If it moved on land, on water, or through the air, chances were that GM made some or all of it. Of course, GM made products and equipment for the military.

GM was loved by the stock market and investors. Besides its history of growth and profitability, it had a history of great management. (It even had its own university, GMI, The General Motors Institute, to train the best high school students in America.) Because of its diversification, it weathered the economic storms that plague the consumer automobile market on a regular basis. GM stock was the perfect investment for retirees and pension plans.

GM had its own finance and insurance arms (GMAC and MIC), which were bigger than many U.S. banks and insurance companies. It was the evolution of the perfect business enterprise. All of these divisions that were not reliant on new car sales for profitability insulated GM from the cyclical nature of car sales, which was good for the GM shareholder.

So, as General Motors was entering the second half of the twentieth century, it was the dominant manufacturing company in the world. GM had six major advantages that would guarantee its long-term success.

1. **The divisional concept** whereby powerful, relatively independent division managers ensured a "creative tension" between divisions. For example, Oldsmobile management and leadership strove to be better than Chevrolet, Pontiac, and the other divisions in all areas: sales, profitability, owner loyalty, engineering. GM headquarters personnel acted as umpires and referees to ensure all divisions "played nice."

2. ***Divisional and corporate culture*** that fostered pride, effort, and teamwork in every employee and retiree. Workers knew they were not only employed by General Motors, they worked for Fisher Body, or Oldsmobile, or Hydramatic, or Chevrolet.

3. ***Loyalty*** to each division from customers, workers, and, more important, from the dealers. Owners, dealers, and employees earnestly believed that their brand was unique, significant, and superior to all others.

4. ***A history of success*** that attracted the best and brightest university graduates each year to want to work for General Motors in management

5. ***Huge design and technology departments*** that worked on future developments under the auspices of headquarters. Even though each division had its own design and technology sections, research into areas with long-term payoffs were not subject to the divisions' budgeting.

6. ***Economies of scale*** that no other automotive manufacturer in the free world could match.

By 1960, General Motors appeared to be the company that could not lose. Its competition was disappearing (Packard, Studebaker), it held 50 percent of the domestic car market, and life was beautiful at headquarters.

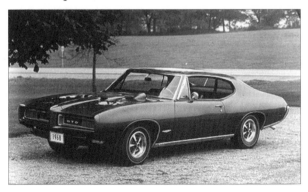

The 1968 Pontiac GTO: big, powerful engine in a small, mid-size body, the "muscle car is born." *(Photo courtesy of http://www.productioncars.com. Used with permission)*

The 2008 GTO. The original GTO was developed under John DeLorean's leadership at Pontiac Division. Thirty years later, Bob Lutz reintroduced the GTO—unfortunately, a little too late for GM.

(*Photo courtesy of http://www.productioncars.com. Used with permission*)

5

The Decline:
When Did It Start Going Wrong?

It has been said the value of a manager is based on the quality of the decisions he or she makes. Many decisions were made that resulted in GM's bankruptcy in June of 2009.

I believe the tailspin of decisions began in the 1960s, when America experienced a major social and cultural shift.

The 1960 election of John F. Kennedy signified a change in politics and life in America. His death by assassination, and subsequently those of Martin Luther King and Robert Kennedy, were further examples of traumatic changes in American and Western society. Prior to this time, Americans believed in big government and big business. Most people were aloof from the activities of both entities, took no interest, and felt they had little power. With the assassinations, society learned how much power an individual can really have. Race and protest riots showed that groups coming together for a unified purpose can have an even more powerful effect. Even in peaceful activities, individuals and groups became empowered and effected change. State and federal laws were changed; even the enforcement of laws radically changed, as evidenced by the U.S. Supreme Court's Miranda Warning ruling in 1966.

A great evolution in the American way of life was occurring. A popular slogan of the times was "Power to the People," and, in reality, people individually and in groups gained an ability to impact change in all aspects of society.

For the Big Three—GM, Ford, and Chrysler—the '60s were the glory days. The Baby Boomers were buying cars. Muscle cars, pony cars, and sporty cars like the Corvair, Mustang, Camaro, and Barracuda were the rage. There was even talk in the late fifties-early-sixties by the U.S. Federal Trade Commission that GM, at close to a 50-percent market share, was becoming a monopoly and should be broken up into separate, independent car companies.

There were a few other clouds on the horizon that would have ramifications that would impact the auto industry into the next century. I believe the 2009 bankruptcy of General Motors was the result of decisions made from the 1960s on. In the next chapters, we will see what crises faced the leaders at GM, and the decisions they made.

One of GM's great strengths was continuity of leadership. The men in this photo taken in 1960 had been either president or chairman, going back to 1923! They carefully nurtured the company to greatness.
(Author's collection)

6

Foreign Cars

Cars manufactured in Europe and imported into North America had always been a reality. The most popular were British sports cars, Italian Fiats and Alfa Romeos, and some French brands; but the only volume seller of any consequence was the Volkswagen Beetle from Germany. Marketed as a cheap, efficient, dependable, and sensible car, the VW was the best-selling import in America through the '50s and '60s.

One must understand that European cars and American cars were designed with very different expectations.

In Europe, the roads were smooth but narrow; the personal automobile was still exclusive to the more affluent citizens and therefore taxed that way; driving distances were relatively short; and fuel was expensive. As a result, cars were small and nimble, with fuel-efficient motors.

In America, the roads were diverse—rural gravel to Interstate smooth; since Henry Ford, the new car was a goal of everyman; distances were great; fuel was cheap. Cars were large and comfortable with large, powerful engines and supple suspensions.

The North American public still had no awareness of Japanese automobiles. The Japanese motorcycle industry, led by Honda, was making inroads in North America in the early to mid-sixties. Honda did not initially target the traditional motorcyclist who rode a Harley Davidson or an English motorcycle such as a Triumph, BSA, or Norton. Honda eased a new segment of millions of non-traditional consumers into becoming motorcyclists with the "You Meet the Nicest People on a Honda" marketing campaign.

Also, in these times, people were buying Zenith or Philco televisions (a division of Ford Motor Company); Kodak cameras; RCA phonograph players; and Remington, Underwood, and IBM typewriters. Nobody had ever heard of Sony, JVC, Panasonic, Toshiba, or Canon.

The Big Three monitored the VW sales and introduced competitors in the form of the Chevrolet Corvair, Ford Falcon, and Plymouth Valiant in the 1960s. These cars were basically scaled-down versions of their regular domestic product line and were price competitive with the VW. The Big Three were not too concerned with Volkswagen in the long run, as they believed that VW had no car for the consumer to move up to.

The marketing strategy of all of the Big Three manufacturers followed GM's: the consumer was always encouraged to move up to "better," more profitable models. Start with a Chevrolet, then up to Pontiac, then to an Oldsmobile or Buick. This was the natural progression of life from the Big Three point of view. If GM could get the first-time buyer to buy a Corvair instead of the Beetle, there was all the more likelihood that that consumer would be with GM for life.

Imported cars like the VW, the Mini, and the Fiat were always perceived as being a little quirky and unique: rear engines, air-cooled motors, four cylinders, floor-shift manual transmissions, front-wheel drive, emphasis on fuel efficiency. But to some North Americans, this quirkiness was perceived as advanced and sophisticated technology. GM with the Chevrolet Corvair emulated this unique nature in a North American body style.

Designed in the late 1950s and introduced to the retail market in January 1960, the Chevrolet Corvair came with an all-aluminum, six-cylinder engine mounted behind the rear axle, like the VW Beetle. The rear suspension design was also a basic copy of the VW design (the Beetle was originally a 1930s design by Ferdinand Porsche), while the front suspension was a more sophisticated North American design. The Corvair engine was quieter and smoother than the VW four-cylinder and provided much better performance. The car was boxier in shape than the VW Beetle, with a significant improvement in passenger space and comfort. The Corvair sold well and was soon embraced also as a sporty fun car. A Monza version was introduced, with better equipment levels, higher-output engines, and bucket seats. Another sales winner for GM, Corvairs were comfortable, roomy, and efficient and could be repaired anywhere in North America with regular tools. (Mechanics working on most imports needed metric tools.)

Corvair sales reached 200,000 annually. Life was beautiful! Except for Ralph Nader . . .

How things had changed
by the twenty-first century

Segment Size	2003	2004	2005	2006	2007	2008	Change
Compact Car	14.8%	14.6%	15.7%	17.4%	18.3%	20.0%	35.71%
Mid-size Car	17.0%	16.0%	16.0%	16.3%	16.1%	16.3%	-3.80%
Large Truck	14.1%	14.9%	15.2%	13.9%	13.7%	12.2%	-13.95
Mid-size SUV	13.2%	12.6%	11.7%	12.8%	13.6%	11.6%	-12.58
Compact SUV	3.9%	3.8%	4.2%	3.8%	4.1%	6.3%	61.65%

This chart shows the five biggest volume segments in the U.S. The volume #1, #2, and #5 segments are dominated by imports. The two big segments #3 and #4, which are shrinking rapidly, are dominated by the domestics.
(Edmunds.com)

7

Ralph Nader

Nader was a young, idealistic, and aggressive Harvard-trained lawyer who wrote a book called *Unsafe at Any Speed* about how dangerous North American cars were, both to the occupants and to pedestrians hit by those cars. His number one target was the hot-selling Chevrolet Corvair, with its swing axle rear suspension design (remember, it was a copy of the VW design) that in aggressive cornering situations could facilitate a rollover of the vehicle. (Please note that the 1961 Corvair models had an additional component called a *camber compensator*, which solved the problem; and later models introduced a fully independent rear suspension system that eliminated any increased risk of rollovers. VW did not make these suspension improvements until 1968.)

By their nature, Corvairs had handling characteristics that at the extreme limits were somewhat different than a conventional North American car. It was very important to follow the manufacturer's instructions on tire pressures and to exercise normal restraint on slippery roads. There were some domestic automobiles that had handling characteristics worse than the Corvair, but the Corvair was an easy target for Nader and the media. The precedent established at the Salem Witch Trials, where anything different than the norm should be persecuted, was applied in the court of Public Opinion.

Nader was correct up to a point: all automobiles could be designed and built to be safer for occupants. Unfortunately, by putting the emphasis on the vehicle design alone, he and others ignored the *vehicle operator* in the safety equation. It took another twenty to thirty years before the horrific impact drunk drivers had in contributing to 50 percent of all motor vehicle deaths and injuries was to be addressed.

Historically, the North American car buyer was not concerned about vehicle safety if it cost him or her time, money, or convenience. In the mid-fifties, Ford made a major safety initiative by standardizing and marketing safety innovations, including seat belts, in their new models. The effort bombed! The customers were not interested in reducing risk in their automobiles. Psychologically, Americans did not want to be made aware of the risk of death or injury in driving an automobile. To put it into context: over the course of the decade-long Vietnam War, some 58,000 U.S. soldiers died. In the same time period, 1963–73, there were 570,623 U.S. highway fatalities.

If you consider how the course of the American political process was impacted by those deaths in the Vietnam War, one wonders why 450,000 more motor vehicle deaths seemed to be so insignificant to the American public. The car makers were right: people did not want to know about risks and safety. As further proof of the American public's myopia regarding safety, Congress had passed legislation that mandated new 1974 vehicles could not start unless the driver's seat belt was connected. When buyers took possession of their new cars that year, there was such a hue and cry that within months, Congress rescinded the legislation, and the new car owners could drive without seat belts again! Even today, consumers pay $2,000 to $5,000 per new vehicle for mandated airbag systems because they refuse to wear seat belts!

Regardless of the public's lack of concern with auto safety issues, GM did not like Ralph Nader or his book. Their dislike increased when Congress decided to hold hearings into motor vehicle safety. GM decided that they had no effective rebuttal to Nader's accusations, so they hired private detectives to snoop into Nader's private life, hoping to find some facts with which they could discredit Nader. Rather than finding discreditable facts about Nader, they were caught invading Nader's privacy! This ended up with GM making apologies to Nader and Congress for their unethical behaviour. GM had lost all credibility in the eyes of Congress and the nation. Nader's book became a best seller. Congress used the hearings to initiate legislation that resulted in the formation of the National Highway Transportation Safety Board (NHTSB), which would mandate motor vehicle safety standards, and the Environmental Protection Agency (EPA), which would mandate motor vehicle emission standards and fuel economy standards.

From that point on, Washington politicians would tell the Big Three and their engineers in Detroit how motor vehicles would be built—necessitating a colossal change in auto design. Of course, the Big Three spent millions fighting every government mandate that Washington imposed on them.

The campaign against Ralph Nader and against safety and pollution standards was a bad decision for several reasons.

- By trying to discredit Nader and his book, GM gave Nader and his book more publicity and greater sales than it warranted.

- By fighting Congress (the elected representatives of car consumers), GM appeared to the nation as adversarial, arrogant, insular, and more interested in profits than people's lives.

- By utilizing delaying tactics (usually by filing lawsuits), GM and the other Big Three members appeared technologically retarded to the public. The public felt, "If we can put a man on the moon (1969), why can't Detroit build clean and safe cars?"

Honda specifically introduced cars that always seemed to meet or exceed the government standards, even ones that had not come into effect. Because of this, Honda and the Japanese gained the moral and technological "high ground" as builders of fuel-efficient and safe automobiles.

If GM had made the camber compensator standard on the 1960 Corvair models and reinforced to Corvair drivers the importance of maintaining correct tire pressure differentiation front to rear, Nader would not have had anything to say in his book about the Corvair. GM saved about $10.00 per car in 1960 by not installing the camber compensator, or about 2 million dollars. Bad decision!

LESSON: If the product is not as safe as it can be, it will come back to bite you.

GM should have taken the high road regarding Nader; of course, this is easy to say now, as GM's actions were not unusual for the times. Management should always look to the downside of their actions.

LESSON: It is good to ask, "What if we get caught?"

8

The Yom Kippur War, October 1973

Surprisingly, the Vietnam War had very little negative effect on the automotive industry. In fact, drafting millions of men and paying them to be soldiers increased the number of potential car buyers. However, there was an upcoming war that would have a profound impact on Detroit.

So in review: the sixties are ending and it is a time of great social and political change. The Big Three are booming and have been able for the most part to avoid being sucked up in the vortex of conflicting social currents. The following challenges facing the American auto industry then were considered irritants rather than huge problems:

- There existed proposed and impending government regulation for safety and emissions.

- The insurance industry was targeting "muscle cars" as a means of generating greater premiums. This was the fastest-growing segment of the automobile industry, and a very profitable one.

- Competition from import cars was still minuscule; the VW Beetle was "getting very long in the tooth," and the initial Japanese imports were considered substandard.

As the American economy continued to boom in the sixties, oil was the energy of choice (regular gasoline sold for twenty to thirty cents a U.S. gallon at this time, or about six cents a litre!). Even though cheap sources of oil were drying up in the U.S., there was a lot of high-quality, low-priced oil in the Middle East—Iran and Saudi Arabia were eager to sell oil to the United States.

By 1970, Syria, Jordan, and Egypt, themselves oil producers of small consequence, were focusing on the military destruction of Israel. The Soviet Union provided armaments to Egypt and Syria, while the U.S. supplied Israel. In June of 1967, Israel had launched a pre-emptive war against Egypt, Syria, and Jordan (pre-emptive, as the Arab states were to attack in a matter of days). It was a stunning success for Israel. They seized the Sinai Desert from Egypt right to the Suez Canal. They captured the Golan Heights, from where Syria had been shelling Israel. They captured the East Bank of the Jordan River and all of Jerusalem from Jordan. Israel controlled the entire West Bank of the Jordan River.

In fact, the victory was so decisive that Israel could have captured the capital cities Damascus, Cairo, and Amman, as there were no opposing military forces left to stop them. Only through pressure from the United Nations and the U.S. did Israel refrain from capturing these cities and countries. It was a humiliating defeat for the Arabs. Since Israel was considered by many Americans as a very close and special friend, the defeat of the Arab states by Israel was seen as just and right. By the end of 1967, the world order—at least in the Middle East—was, as America saw it, as it should be. Soviet influence was diminished, U.S. allies Israel and Iran were the dominant military powers in the Middle East, and the Shah of Iran was supplying all the cheap oil America wanted.

Contrary to Western post-WW II experience and expectations—it was believed that former combatants should and would develop a way to co-exist with the Israelis—Egypt and Syria began a massive rearmament and militarization program to crush Israel, again supported by the Soviet Union. The U.S. was not rearming Israel at the same rate, as they did not want to antagonize the Arab/Islamic petroleum-exporting states. This fed directly into the Syrian-Egyptian military plans: a surprise attack on Israel, with the emphasis on destroying Israeli airpower, which was the key to victory in the 1967 war.

The Soviets provided the latest and best anti-aircraft defences, and in 1973, on Yom Kippur, the holiest day in the Jewish calendar, the Arab states attacked with great ferocity and vengeance.

Initially, Israel was sent reeling by the combined two-front Syrian-Egyptian attacks. The vaunted Israeli air force was suffering huge losses at the hands of the Arabs' excellent Soviet-supplied anti-aircraft defence systems. The war had started on October 6, and by the evening of October 7, Israel had also lost 500 tanks in combat, another area of their former superiority. After a few days, it appeared that the goal of the Arabs to obliterate the Jewish nation from the map was very likely.

The United States government made a rapid decision to not let this happen and began airlifting crucial materiel to the Israelis. (This decision was ostensibly made to prevent a nuclear war. It was believed that Israel possessed nuclear weapons at the time and would use them to prevent the fall of Jerusalem.) Quickly, the Israelis regrouped after the initial setbacks and began to take the upper hand in the ground war. They held the Syrians in place and attacked the Egyptians with a sweeping, encircling move over the Suez Canal. The Israelis had the Egyptian Third Army trapped in the Negev Desert east of the Suez Canal; the Egyptians were cut off from their water, food, and military supplies. In fact, all of Egypt was cut off. The Israeli army had a clear path to Cairo, less than a day's drive, with no military opposition to stop them; alternatively, the Israeli army and air force could massacre the trapped Egyptian army.

The war had turned from a monumental victory for the Arabs to a crushing defeat in a matter of hours. The Arabs immediately accepted a ceasefire.

The Arab world was enveloped in shock and panic. In a matter of days, they had gone from almost crushing Israel to facing yet another terrible humiliation. Of course, the Arabs blamed the United States, and now they had a method of hurting the U.S. directly. On October 16, 1973, they raised the price of crude oil by 70 percent, from $3.58 to $5.11 a barrel, and on October 17, 1973, refused to ship oil to the U.S. and other western countries who were supporters of Israel. Shipments did not commence again until March 1974.

This instantly affected the U.S. auto industry. The price of gasoline went up dramatically. People started hoarding gasoline, which created even greater shortages. Stations started running out of gas. It became media frenzy time. What was the government going to do? What could it do? As it happened, the panic and hoarding really caused the majority of the shortages.

In the U.S., there were 100 million cars on the road, and the average fuel tank held twenty gallons of gas. Under normal circumstances, each driver might have in his car about a quarter of a tank of gas, or five gallons. Back then this was enough for forty to eighty miles of driving. When people started worrying about gasoline shortages, the average driver tried to keep his tank at three-quarters full—an extra ten gallons per car. This translated into one billion gallons of gas taken from U.S. reserves and this produced spot shortages. To compound matters, drivers began to carry an additional five- or ten-gallon container in their cars for emergencies. This took another 100 million gallons of gasoline out of the system and made shortages even worse. A number of cars carrying gas containers were involved in collisions that often became fiery death traps with extra gasoline sloshing around in the cars' trunks.

Besides hoarding gas and driving less, consumers started looking to buy fuel-efficient cars. The Big Three offered the four-cylinder Ford Pinto and the Chevrolet Vega. Unfortunately, both cars were pretty shoddy from a technical point of view.

Toyota, Honda, Subaru, and Nissan/Datsun did have a range of fuel-efficient, comfortable, and durable cars to offer. People who never would have considered a Japanese car were buying them. Consumers were generally very impressed with the Japanese cars, which in most cases exceeded the buyers' expectations. With Ford and GM, small fuel-efficient models were de-contented[2] to keep the price down, while the Japanese offered upscale small cars that were roomy, comfortable, and fuel efficient. This was the thin edge of the wedge that would lead to the collapse of the American car industry. A short war between Arabs and Jews thousands of miles away from Detroit was having huge repercussions. Of course GM's leaders were shocked by the course of events.

---

2   De-contenting is the method by which a vehicle's MSRP can be lowered to reach a lower price point without any loss of profit to the manufacturer. Equipment that was previously standard is removed and either not offered or is made optional at extra cost. Examples of de-contenting at the time would be rubber floor covering instead of carpet, roof drip mouldings and body side mouldings deleted. Radio and heater could be deleted and offered as options. Other examples of de-contenting are lower-grade trim materials, black seat belts, no chrome mouldings, and painted bumpers.

Realizing that fuel economy was going to be of paramount interest to customers in the future, GM committed millions to developing a new line of relatively fuel-efficient full-size and mid-size car lines, which were introduced in 1977. These vehicles were initially very successful until the Iranian Revolution in 1979 created another oil crisis. GM also had the successful Oldsmobile division develop a Diesel V8, which was a disaster.

The two GM future strategic plans were doomed by the continued focus on profitable full- and medium-size cars and to the lack of ability to refine a product before introducing it to the public, as evidenced by the diesel. Curiously, GM had excellent diesel engine-building experience in Europe with Opel and with their own Detroit Diesel Division. It is believed that in order to save the costs in developing a new, purpose-built diesel that both Opel and Detroit Diesel would have advocated, GM decided that they would save by converting the gasoline-powered Oldsmobile Rocket V8 to run on diesel fuel. It was foisted on customers and is said to have set back the cause of diesel fuel efficiency in North America by forty years.

Nineteen seventy-four ended with turmoil, gasoline shortages, the introduction of catalytic convertors, and unleaded gas to meet tighter emission controls. The end of the booming and profitable muscle car era was upon us, and the consumers who were buying domestic were buying low-profit Pintos and Vegas.

There was huge growth for Japanese import sales, and the Japanese makers wanted to expand their dealership numbers.

Many people when faced with a crisis will panic and do the wrong thing. Unfortunately, top management has to fight this urge to panic. When GM was faced with a fuel crisis it should have taken the time to be sure of the diesel's durability and reliability before introducing it to the market.

LESSON: Even if you have the correct plan, if it is not executed properly, you will get bad results.

9

GM Creates the
Japanese Dealer Organization

GM at that time had a policy that an individual could own only one GM franchise. Many GM dealers had been very profitable over the years and had significant capital funds to open additional dealerships. When blocked by GM from acquiring more GM franchises, they acquired Japanese franchises. The Japanese car makers knew their greatest weakness was the lack of a national retail distribution system. When the Japanese began to get franchise applications from well-funded domestic dealers, the future of Japanese car sales in America was assured. What used to be the Chevrolet dealership in many locations became the Chevrolet –Toyota dealership, or Pontiac–Honda.

By the mid-seventies, the Japanese car brands were well established in America. The Big Three were aware of what was happening, but were not sure what to do. They felt things would go back to the way they had been before, and Detroit would assume its rightful dominant role as gasoline prices moderated; and people would switch back to the domestic brands. Of course, the Big Three wanted to stop the Japanese, so they started lobbying Congress (the previous arch-enemy) to restrict imports. The Japanese—ever cunning in international trade matters—blindsided the U.S. government and introduced their own "voluntary import quotas." This mollified Congress but it emaciated the Big Three's political influence and made Japan look like a team player. Because of the artificial shortage, import profitability for both the dealers and the importers surged!

This voluntary quota was a win-win for Japan. Since Japan did not have enough plant capacity at home to supply the future North American demand, they proceeded to build plants in the U.S., and the quotas allowed them to quell the Buy American crusade and increase their profits.

Nineteen seventy-nine arrived, and in Iran, the revolutionaries overthrew the Shah. The Iranian revolution drove oil prices up even more, and as Iran was a very large supplier of oil to the U.S., supplies became short again. The U.S. government froze the price of gasoline, which made shortages even worse.

The American driver reacted the same way he had six years before, hoarding gas and buying more fuel-efficient cars. By this time, Japanese cars were a real option for most Americans, and Japan really benefited from the surge in demand. GM and the others tried to make more fuel-efficient cars but they all seemed to be doomed by technical problems. Many of GM's solutions were not tested properly before being introduced to the market.

The Oldsmobile division was tasked with developing diesels for passenger cars, both in the V8 and V6 configurations. They started with the proven and reliable Rocket V8 gasoline engine block and created an abomination! Diesel engines, though similar in appearance to gasoline engines, have completely different operating parameters. Problems that were of no or minimal concern in a gasoline engine, such as a little moisture in the fuel or freezing temperatures, became significant in diesels. Furthermore, there were problems with engine noise, vibration and harshness, poor acceleration, and even a lack of diesel fuel stations where automobile drivers needed them.

After a few years, Oldsmobile engineers solved all of the technical problems, but by then nobody would buy a GM car with a diesel motor.

As well as offering diesel engines, Cadillac converted their V8, by deactivating a number of cylinders, to provide a Cadillac with the fuel efficiency of a six- or even a four-cylinder car. The result was a mechanical/hydraulic system in the age before automotive computers, and the so-called variable displacement engines never were successful. People bought them, but the cars broke down, and people chose other alternatives. Unfortunately, GM basically destroyed two of their best "brands" with stop-gap and untested technology. By allowing loyal and trusting Oldsmobile and Cadillac customers unknowingly to do the in-field development on these new technologies, GM had started its downfall.

By 1981, there was an oil glut in the world, and GM began to think things would be returning to normal. They had no idea that their best years were already behind them!

For many years, GM had kept a tight leash on their dealers, as there were no alternatives available to them. The arrival of the Japanese was a dream come true for these dealers. To GM, it was treason for a dealer to take on an import brand; to the dealer, it made good economic sense.

LESSON: How you really treat and care for your "independent" distribution system can have a tremendous impact on your core business.

10

The Oldsmobile Rocket

Through all these tumultuous times, it should be noted that one GM brand thrived unbelievably well. Oldsmobile sales began to soar in the early 1970s based on popular designs, positive reviews from critics, and the perceived quality and reliability of the vehicle and the Rocket V8 engine. The Cutlass series had become North America's top selling car by 1976, and the Division set an all-time high sales record of 1,066,122 units in 1985, after reaching a million sales the previous two years. By this time, Oldsmobile had displaced Pontiac and Plymouth as the #3 best-selling brand in the U.S. behind Chevrolet and Ford. Lansing-based Oldsmobile was a winner!

The rapidly soaring popularity of Oldsmobile vehicles resulted in a major issue in 1977. As demand exceeded production capacity for the Oldsmobile 350 cubic-inch V8, Oldsmobile quietly began equipping some very popular Cutlass/Cutlass Supreme and full-size Delta 88 models with the Chevrolet 350 engine instead of the highly regarded Oldsmobile Rocket V8 (each division of GM produced its own distinct 350 V8 engine).

Remember that with the "Division" concept, each brand tried to create the best components to make the best cars. Consumers had learned that in many ways Oldsmobiles were the best cars and had the best V8 engine. But now, people who paid what they believed was a justified premium for an Oldsmobile automobile were ending up with an Oldsmobile powered by a Chevrolet engine!

Of course, from the Finance and Accounting point of view at GM Headquarters this made absolute sense. "We have reached maximum capacity at our Oldsmobile Rocket V8 plant, yet more people want to buy our cars. What to do? Expanding the Oldsmobile engine plant is relatively expensive. Chevrolet Division has surplus engine production capacity. We will probably even make more money if we put Chevrolet engines in Oldsmobile models.

Simple cost-benefit analysis shows it is better for GM to do the engine switch rather than expand the plant."

GM management's total disregard of the brand concept came back to bite GM hard.

Many customers were loyal Oldsmobile buyers who specifically wanted the Rocket V8. They did not discover that their vehicle had the Chevrolet engine until they performed maintenance and discovered that purchased Oldsmobile parts did not fit their Oldsmobile. This led to a class-action lawsuit that became a public relations nightmare for GM. Most important, consumers learned they could no longer trust GM or their favourite brand.

The three classic Cutlass Supremes that led Oldsmobile to a million unit annual sales:

The 1968 Cutlass 442 Convertible, considered one of the best-styled American cars of the time. Oldsmobiles were reliable, durable, and gave excellent performance for the times.
(Photo courtesy of http://www.productioncars.com. Used with permission)

The 1975 Cutlass Supreme. Cutlass sales grew dramatically from the late sixties. In the seventies, the Cutlass became a slightly larger mid-size car with still excellent Oldsmobile quality. Sales grew even more.
(Photo courtesy of http://www.productioncars.com. Used with permission)

The 1985 Cutlass Supreme "Hurst 442" was a performance variation of the great-selling downsized version, with classic styling that still looks good thirty years later. Sales were so strong when this design was introduced in 1978, Oldsmobile ran out of engine production capacity and began substitution with Chevrolet motors—the first crack in the Oldsmobile reputation. *(Photo courtesy of http://www.productioncars.com. Used with permission)*

After the lawsuit started, GM responded by issuing disclaimers stating that "Oldsmobiles are equipped with engines produced by various GM divisions." These legal disclaimers were quickly tacked on to advertisements and sales literature; all other GM divisions followed suit. In addition, GM quickly stopped associating engines with particular divisions, and to this day all GM engines are produced by "GM Powertrain" (GMPT) and are called GM "Corporate" engines instead of GM "Division" engines.

Headquarters missed the whole point. After decades of creating individual brands with millions of loyal customers, GM said "It doesn't matter," and "They are all the same anyway." Wow, what a kick in the teeth for brand loyalty! What a rejection of fifty years of building an identity for each brand!

The consumers responded, slowly at first, by recognizing that all GM cars were the same; if Chevrolet made a poor vehicle, now all brands were seen as losers. By 2001, Oldsmobile ceased to exist; by 2010 Saturn, Pontiac, and Hummer did not exist either!

Do you think the "geniuses" who decided to put Chevrolet engines in Oldsmobiles in the 1970s realized that they were seriously harming the Oldsmobile brand and, as a result, GM as a company?

The term "change" became a business buzzword in the 1980s with phrases such as "Change or Die" and "Change Is Good," often used to justify and cloak questionable decision making.

All life on earth is governed by laws; some are physical and some are natural, but only the man-made laws can change. All others are fixed. However, our knowledge and understanding of these fixed laws can change. The earth was always a round planet even before Columbus proved it so. The earth's shape did not change, but most people's knowledge and understanding regarding the earth's shape changed. Once people embraced this change in their knowledge, it had a multiplier effect by impacting almost every aspect of European civilization.

It is important to realize that Columbus did not change the shape of our planet—he just verified reality. People then responded.

How change relates to GM is crucial to our understanding. Many times in recent history, GM's leaders tried to make dramatic changes to improve the company and in almost every case got negative results. Considered by many a valid natural law is the Law of Unintended Consequences, named and popularized by Robert K. Merton. Simply stated, this law says no matter what you do, there will be results that you did not intend or foresee.

Nobody in 1920 envisioned the pollution problems automobiles would create. Very few prognosticators, if any, envisioned computer hackers, viruses, and identity theft at the beginning of the high-tech revolution.

For us humans, it is extremely hard to change our behaviours; it is exponentially harder for organizations such as GM to do so. With a few exceptions, we humans can only evolve into being better people by making incremental changes that require us to make tough choices. With large organizations, it is much, much more difficult. Always be wary when some organization says it is changing, especially if you are an employee!

General Motors after 1980 seemed to be constantly changing and reorganizing, rather than evolving as it had in the previous seventy years. Maybe there is some merit to the natural resistance to change all humans have, and corporate leaders would be wise to make changes only evolutionary in scope like nature does.

LESSON: If a man destroys his reputation, he destroys himself. Management should care for their brands the same way: When the Oldsmobile reputation was destroyed, so was the brand, and so was the parent.

11

The Management Makes the Difference

Most people became familiar with "Chaos Theory" from the movie *Jurassic Park*.

This phenomenon came to be known as the "butterfly effect." The amount of difference in the starting points of the two curves is so small that it is comparable to a butterfly's flapping its wings.

The flapping of a single butterfly's wing today produces a tiny change in the state of the atmosphere. Over a period of time, what the atmosphere actually does diverges from what it would have done. So, in a month's time, a tornado that would have devastated the Indonesian coast doesn't happen. Or maybe one that wasn't going to happen does![3]

When GM was great (up to 1970), it was based on a relatively small headquarters staff and strong, almost autonomous independent divisions. The divisions had their own design departments, their own manufacturing plants, their own sales department, and their own dealers. This system had been developed and perfected by Alfred Sloan, president and/or chairman of GM from 1923 to 1956.

What these almost independent divisions did was to cause a "creative tension" between themselves. The reward they were vying for was the attention and recognition of headquarters. This divisional competition created many automotive breakthroughs, such as the Chevrolet V8, the Hydramatic transmission, the Pontiac GTO, Oldsmobile Toronado, Buick V6, Turbo Charging, and Cadillac STS, plus thousands of patents and innovations. While each division was trying to outdo its internal competition, it was as well devastating all of the other domestic competitors. By the end of the 1950s, Nash, Packard, Willys, and Studebaker were all

---

3   Ian Stewart, *Does God Play Dice? The Mathematics of Chaos* (Canada: Wiley-Blackwell, 2002), 141.

out of business. Ford, Chrysler, and American Motors were all that remained to fight over 50 percent of the market GM did not control.

The divisions were fiercely independent and their customers were fiercely loyal, and many hours were spent discussing the virtues of their favourite brand.

For all the advantages of the division system, there were some disadvantages. Key was the cost of duplication: At one time, GM produced four different V8 engines with the same 350-cubic-inch displacement, and basically no parts were common to the Chevrolet, Pontiac, Buick, or Oldsmobile motors. Cadillac motors again were different and larger. The engines were made in different plants. For many years, this also was the case for transmissions and rear axles. In fact, wheels that fit Chevrolets would not fit your brother's Pontiac. The number of separate parts that General Motors had to keep track of was mind-boggling. However, these different components were what made the brands different. From the point of view of economy of scale, the divisions were producing more cars than their non-GM competitors, and maintained cost efficiency.

In the late 1960s, two related factors impacted General Motors and created the move from independent divisions; both originated in Washington, D.C. First, with GM approaching and, in some markets exceeding, 50 percent share, the Federal Trade Commission was concerned that GM was turning into a monopoly and was an unfair competitor. The FTC projected that GM could very possibly be the only automaker in the United States by the year 2000. (So much for forecasts!) GM's initial response was to create the GM Assembly Division; this division would take over the actual production of the vehicles and their components.

Two benefits were seen to this change. First, it would be difficult for the FTC to split the divisions up if the divisions became more interrelated and did not produce their own cars. Second, there were cost efficiencies possible from rationalization of the production process. The savings potential was easily calculated by the bean-counters and the financial people and was seen as a win-win.

The second Washington factor was the onset of safety and

emission legislation. To meet this legislation, all of the automakers would have to spend millions of dollars on research and development of new technology that never existed before. Each different make and model would have to be crash-tested numerous times. Each engine and its permutation would have to be modified, tested, and produced with its own specific emission controls. Imagine five different divisions, offering at least three different engines, in three different body styles with two different transmission choices. That is ninety different versions that have to developed, engineered, tested (minimum 50,000-mile durability test), and produced. The bean-counters saw millions in savings by rationalizing the power trains.

Looking back, what is amazing is that the divisions had successfully gone their own way for years. Each division had been able to muster its resources and meet any and all similar challenges in mandated standards or consumer demand that had come forward previously.

There must have been something to the benefits of the divisional concept. The divisions resisted the push for commonality. What the bean-counters could never compute on their calculators were intangibles involved in the car-making process. They could not understand that an identifiable "team" with its own ethos and mission was a very powerful entity. Too bad bean-counters never bothered to ask the U.S. Marines about that concept!

Imagine you are a line worker in Lansing, Michigan, assembling Oldsmobiles where the first Oldsmobile was built by Ransom E. Oldsmobile before the turn of the twentieth century. You are part of the tradition of one of the oldest auto manufacturers in the world. You are proud to be an Oldsmobile man, and the Oldsmobile division manager is your god. You believe you are blessed to be able to build Oldsmobiles and you do the very best job you can because you personally identify with Oldsmobile. Some of your neighbours are friends or relatives of Ransom and knew him personally, as he lived in Lansing until he died in 1950.

One day, you are told after many years of employment that you are going to assemble something else, possibly somewhere else. You are crushed; it was like finding out Rock Hudson was gay and died of AIDS. Your emotional attachment to what you build is now gone; you are just another UAW guy building cars for the man. Your sense of pride and purpose has gone; you have become a grunt!

That's what they did to independent GM divisions!

Automobile companies since their inception seem to have been run by one of two types of managers. The financial types (bean-counters) who believe that every decision can be reduced to a cost-benefit choice; or the product people, who are known as the "car guys." The car guys are not overly concerned with the costs, but want to make the best vehicle possible for a given segment. Both the car guys and the bean-counters, if either faction is in full control alone, will bankrupt any company.

Of course each of these groups has associates. There are the marketers and sales people. They want the best car at the lowest price. They think they know what the consumer wants and have research to prove it. The production people tend to be on the financial side of the court. They want uniform vehicles that can be built efficiently and easily. They believe that reducing the colour choice to black only would be a good idea.

The most famous and legendary names in the automotive industry tended to be car guys: Henry Ford, Ed Cole, Lee Iacocca, and Bob Lutz. In their careers, they hit the home runs! The Model T; the Mustang; the European Capri. Not too many people remember the financial guys. But Wall Street and the investors love the financial guys because they make the money (supposedly).

Now, the car industry has one endemic problem: Overall sales are tied to the economic well-being of the country. If the economy is booming, people buy new cars; if the economy is poor, car sales (and profits) disappear. To be sure, there are economic cycles in North America, so the industry is always in a feast or famine cycle. When it is famine time, the emphasis is on cost reduction—slash and burn is the mantra, and the financial guys do this best. When the economy is good, the emphasis is on producing the next home run. Since the car industry needs huge amounts of capital, the investors have to be placated; dividends and interest have to be paid. During tough times, theoretically this is where the bean-counters shine.

GM had all its departments and divisions headquartered in Detroit and surrounding areas in Michigan, except one. The financial department that deals exclusively with the dollars and cents is located in New York City. The financial guys are interested only in dollars and cents and in keeping the Wall Street money guys happy.

In this book, Wall Street is going to be mentioned many times. It is important to understand that Wall Street is a euphemism for the banks, hedge funds, investors' pension funds, charities, universities, and other individuals and organizations that have pools of cash. These groups with cash have to constantly decide where to invest their funds. They are looking for a safe and secure return on their loans; they are looking for dividends and stock price growth when they buy company shares.

Wall Street is fickle and inconsistent, and share value is affected by thousands of variables. It is also emotionless, unforgiving, and heartless. For many decades, GM was a Wall Street favourite; but that all changed.

We know that the U.S. government lost interest in splitting up GM when other items appeared on the political agenda such as race riots, assassinations, the Vietnam War. Really, GM's centralizing the production facilities of the divisions was an unnecessary decision. Even though there were savings through rationalization of product offerings, this should have been done at the division level, not at corporate. Corporate was choosing the winners and losers, not the customer, to whom the divisions listened and responded.

LESSON: When faced with government pressure or mandates, knee-jerk reactions to stymie the government are not the best action. Overreaction is almost always more harmful than underreaction.

12

The Leaders

GM is run like any big company, with a board of directors that is supposed to represent the owners (shareholders). There is a chairman of the board, who is very powerful. Also on the board are usually members of management who run the day-to-day operations of the company; the top manager is usually called the president. These were the chairmen and CEOs from 1960 to the present:

- Frederic G. Donner, Chairman of the Board, 1958–67
- James M. Roche, Chairman of the Board and CEO, 1967–71
- Richard C. Gerstenberg, Chairman of the Board and CEO, 1972–74
- Thomas A. Murphy, Chairman of the Board, 1974–80
- Elliott M. Estes, President, 1974–81
- Roger B. Smith, Chairman of the Board, 1981–90
- Howard H. Kehrl, Vice-chairman, 1981–86
- Donald J. Atwood, Vice-chairman, 1987–89
- F. James McDonald, President, 1981–87
- Robert C. Stempel, President, 1987–90; Chairman of the Board and CEO, 1990–92
- John G. Smale, Chairman of the Board, 1992–95
- John F. "Jack" Smith, Jr., Chairman of the Board, 1996–2003
- G. Richard Wagoner, Jr., Chairman of the Board, 2003–2009

Frederic G. Donner

Chairman of the Board, September 1, 1958–October 31, 1967. "Benevolent Bean-Counter."

Frederic Garrett Donner was a financial expert who kept out of the limelight, joined GM as an accountant in 1926, and enjoyed a steady rise up the corporate ladder. He was said to have an uncommon ability to absorb facts and figures, and the intricate corporate and financial structure of the giant automobile maker was his forte. In 1948, he was among GM executives to tour Germany's bombed-out industrial plants, and pushed for GM to reclaim its German subsidiary, Adam Opel AG, which had been written off as a loss in the war. In the postwar period, Mr. Donner also helped devise a stock split, the sale of $325 million worth of additional common stock and a $300-million bond issue. He also was largely responsible for revised and expanded pension plans and a stock-purchase plan for salaried employees. He maintained the same organizational structure that had been established before the war and reaped record sales and profits.

James M. Roche

President of General Motors, June 1, 1965–October 31, 1967.

Chairman of the Board and CEO, November 1, 1967– December 31, 1971. "Car Guy."

Roche joined GM in 1927 at the age of twenty-one, as a statistician in the Cadillac Motor Car Division's Chicago sales office. (Due to family financial difficulties, Roche never attended college.) During the next thirty years at Cadillac, he was given responsibilities in business management, personnel, public relations, and sales. He was named Cadillac's general manager and a GM vice-president in January 1957, and the luxury division set sales records during his tenure.

Roche was a humanitarian and worked closely with and showed a genuine concern for the problems of his fellow workers, and how to solve issues for the benefit of everyone involved. He appointed the first black member to GM's board of directors. Roche was known for his commitment to Detroit and to all GM employees, and for tackling tough issues through extensive public service during a tumultuous era in the city's history. As a result of his long experience at Cadillac, Roche had a thorough understanding and appreciation of the important role GM's dealers play, and of the importance of treating customers right. His strong rapport with GM's dealers served him and the company well.

Roche had a long and successful tenure, but there were two questionable actions that had long-term implications. First, to foil U.S. government anti-trust suits, he weakened the Car Division's strength by forming the General Motors Assembly Division. In hindsight, we now know that breaking up GM was not on the government's agenda at this time, and this weakening of the divisions was the "thin edge of the wedge" that would eventually eliminate the divisions. The second action—and a real scar on Roche's record—was the fact he was forced to apologize for General Motors' spying on Ralph Nader. Safety concerns and the Nader issue led to a major switch of the American public's attitude toward the car industry. Based on stories of Roche's character, one wonders if he initiated or was aware of the surveillance of Nader; but he ought to have known.

Richard C. Gerstenberg

Chairman of the Board and CEO, January 1, 1972–November 30, 1974. "Bean-Counter."

Gerstenberg joined GM in 1932 as a timekeeper with Frigidaire Division in Dayton, Ohio, was transferred to the Fisher Body Division, Detroit, in 1934, and to the General Motors Central Office in 1936. He was elected executive vice-president Finance and a member of the board of directors on November 1, 1967. His main rival for the position of chairman was GM president Ed Cole. Cole was a "car guy" with a background in engineering and production and was seen as the logical heir from the traditionalist viewpoint. However, Gerstenberg was chosen by the board because his strengths as a money manager and an articulate defender of the increasingly criticized auto industry were viewed as necessary to handle the problems GM looked to face in the coming years.

Richard Gerstenberg chaired GM for only a couple of years of the turbulent 1970s as the corporation attempted to cope with the changing environmental consciousness of the country and an influx of small, more fuel-efficient imported cars. Gerstenberg was famous for this statement he issued on September 1, 1974, about government involvement in the auto business:

> *The car-buying consumer is burdened today by the cost of a number of governmental requirements that have been placed upon cars and trucks; costs that are in many cases well beyond whatever value these regulations provide.*
>
> *And today still further requirements of questionable value are being proposed both by law and by regulation. The mandated equipment added to our cars and trucks over the four model years (1972 through 1975) to meet regulations for emission control, occupant protection, and bumpers, has added about $270 to the cost of every vehicle we produce for the United States.*

Gerstenberg unfortunately was voicing a narrow and exceedingly unpopular sentiment to the American car buyer. At a time when GM should have taken on the mantle of leadership and proactive co-operation with the government and their customers, GM was "hunkering down" and slowly becoming more insular.

Thomas A. Murphy

Chairman of the Board, December 1, 1974–December 31, 1980. "Bean-Counter."

Murphy is credited with saying, "General Motors is not in the business of making cars. It is in the business of making money." That may be a good mantra for a banker, but not so good for somebody running a consumer products company.

Under his tenure, it was believed that GM was prepared for continued growth. Murphy appeared to have semi-successfully steered the GM ship through the initial Japanese onslaughts, the oil embargos, and numerous domestic political crises. Even though, at the end of his term in recessionary 1980, GM had just suffered a $750 million loss, it still held 46 percent of the U.S. motor vehicle market.

It is difficult to evaluate Murphy's reign during the last half of the seventies. Under his stewardship, in 1977–78, GM introduced a brilliant line of downsized models. However, some of the *planning* for these "winners" occurred before he came to power. Under his guidance, Oldsmobile blossomed as well.

As a chairman, he approved the Chevrolet engines in the Oldsmobile fiasco and the introduction of the disastrous diesel V8; the Citation and Cimarron horror stories all began on his watch. We realize now that Murphy tried to run GM as he had been trained to do for twenty-plus years. With the onslaught of crisis, he acted in a predictable way. Being a financial guy who had started as a controller, his natural tendency would be to look at the numbers. Looking at the numbers led him down the wrong path.

The leader's training background and inclinations will lead him to deal with new and unusual situations by utilizing the same attitudes and techniques that had served him so well in the past.

LESSON: If the only tool you have is a hammer, all your problems will begin to look like nails.

Elliott M. Estes

President of General Motors, October 1, 1974–January 31, 1981. "Car Guy."

Estes was a true "Car Guy" and was an excellent foil for Chairman Murphy. As an engineer at Oldsmobile, he led the company in developing the first high-compression V8 engine, known as the "Rocket V8." He was division manager at Pontiac during the sixties, and his innovation and leadership took Pontiac to #3 in U.S. sales. As GM president, he guided the complete re-engineering of GM's product lines. When he left GM, market share was at 46 percent, not far behind the all-time record of 51.1 percent of 1962.

Roger B. Smith

Chairman of the Board, January 1, 1981–July 31, 1990. "Bean-Counter."

(Rated by CNBC as one of the "Worst American CEOs of All Time.") Not much more to say after CNBC's rating. Roger Smith did many things, not all of them bad. He helped create Michael Moore as an independent filmmaker and gadfly. He brought more attention

upon GM by the media and the public than any other corporate leader, ever.

Rather than being a chairman who would "steer the ship and stay on course," Roger Smith reorganized the company in ways that it would never recover from. Under his leadership, he at one time or another antagonized the customers, the suppliers, the management, the unions, and just about every other segment of America that came into contact with GM. I believe he saw himself as an Idea Man and an Instrument of Change. The real results were that he could not effectively implement even his few good ideas, and the rest of them were ridiculous!

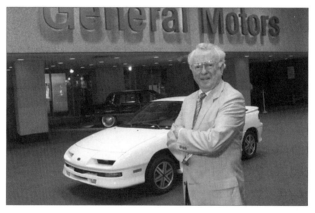

Roger Smith: Called by some a visionary and by CNBC the "worst CEO in American business," standing in front of a Saturn, the brand he created. The Saturn's plastic body was innovative and unique, but was expensive to make, and because of the steel chassis, had to be stronger, resulting in a heavier, less fuel-efficient car than desired. Saturn consistently had the best consumer ratings of any GM brands. The Saturn brand was cancelled in 2009.
(Author's collection.)

A short chronology:

1981. As stated before, Smith acted like a visionary, an instrument for change. He envisioned fully automated factories, paperless offices, and fewer workers (to the chagrin of existing workers).

In 1981, GM formed a new company with Fujitsu Fanuc, a Japanese robotic machine maker. The new company, GMF Robotics, became the world's largest maker of robotics. The biggest problem was that the technology of robotics was not yet fully developed. GM installed painting robots that painted themselves, not the cars, welding robots that welded doors shut. Oftentimes robots were removed from the plant and the old production processes were reintroduced, because of the inadequacy of the robots.

Typical of a non-technocrat, Smith believed machines and technology worked right the minute they were conceived. In actuality, with technology, there is always a steep development curve. The 1986 capital budget for GM was thirty-six billion dollars, mostly for new technology—robots and plants for them. These dollars could have purchased 100 percent of Toyota and Nissan shares that year! With this high-tech push of Smith's, GM became the highest-cost automaker in Detroit.

1982. Smith got directly involved with negotiations with the UAW: He got the union to give concessions, and he cut raises to non-union white collar workers. He then unveiled a more generous bonus package to executives. Workers, unions, and shareholders went berserk, and Smith was forced to backtrack; but the damage to the relationship between the unions and stakeholders was done.

As well in 1982 Smith had the GM10 program initiated. It cost GM seven billion dollars, and it was a plan to produce all of the mid-size cars for all brands except Cadillac. Seven plants were selected to build 1,750,000 of these GM10s—over 20 percent of the total U.S. market! By 1989, GM was losing $2,000 on each GM10 it produced and stopped production in 1990.

1984. Smith eliminates the divisions! Ever since the 1920s, when Alfred Sloan focused on the divisional concept, they had been the core of GM's success. Smith, ever the financial man, could see that the numbers would justify the elimination of the divisions. (A major step leading to the failure of the company was ongoing erosion of the divisional concept.) By 1994, divisions were reintroduced in an emasculated form. Only after a quarter of a century, with billions of dollars of losses and a vaporized market share, did somebody at GM finally realize that the divisional concept had merit. But by 1994 it was too late.

The turmoil created by this change that Smith initiated in 1984 was unbelievable. I believe if the pope in Rome converted to Islam, there would be fewer reverberations in the Catholic Church than this boondoggle caused at GM. This was the tipping point in the downfall of General Motors. Killing the divisions in 1984 was on a par with the German defeat at Stalingrad, or Lee's halt at the Battle of Antietam. Neither GM nor the defeated armies ever again regained ascendency.

Roger Smith also liked to buy things and in 1984 he spent $2.55 billion on buying EDS, a world leader in electronic data systems. It was started by Ross Perot in 1962. Perot was a U.S. Naval Academy graduate and his company was run similarly to a naval ship in wartime: aggressive, cohesive, determined, and successful. EDS had won the contract to computerize the U.S. government's medical records, and Perot became one of the world's richest men. One thing about Ross Perot: He knew how to accomplish things. He took a start-up company from nothing to be a world leader in mere decades.

Ross Perot was very different from Roger Smith, and they did not like each other. First, Ross criticized Roger for spending so much of GM's shareholders' money to buy his company. Second, through the buy-out, Ross became GM's largest shareholder and a member of the GM board of directors. While a member of the board, Ross openly criticized Roger Smith whenever he felt the actions of GM were wrong. Two years later, in 1986, Roger Smith arranged for GM to buy back Ross Perot's GM shares for about $740 million, in a bid to silence Perot. As stated before, Roger had ideas but no skills to implement them. The EDS purchase never did mesh with GM. The cultures, needs, goals, and objectives of both companies were so different, so at odds, without some Messiah to lead them, there was no hope. In 1996, GM spun off EDS as a separate company.

In 1984, Smith also had GM and Toyota reopen GM's shuttered factory in California as a joint venture named New United Motor Manufacturing, Inc. (NUMMI) to manufacture vehicles to be sold under both brands. At the time, it was believed by many that Roger Smith had made a "deal with the Devil." With this agreement, Smith appeared to be telling the world: GM does not know how to build cars; we can learn something from this Japanese upstart; and Toyota will not really benefit anything from the venture.

GM saw the joint venture as an opportunity to learn about lean manufacturing from the Japanese company—truly an excellent goal. Toyota was gaining its first manufacturing base in North America and a chance to implement its production system in an American labour environment. Toyota received a huge benefit that resulted in their establishing more plants in North America.

The divisional concept that I have endorsed could create a closed and insular attitude to new ideas and concepts. The division manager had to be diligent to not allow stagnation to form. It appears that when the divisions felt threatened by headquarters, beginning in the 1970s, there was a tendency to reject any outside influence. It is theorized that all the knowledge gained by GM people when working at NUMMI was lost by the insularity that was becoming entrenched at GM.

The resistance to change at all levels appeared impossible to overcome. Top management and the board, by going on a huge spending program of acquisitions, endorsed this no-change attitude. They did not understand that change must begin from within, and people from the lowest levels on up must be encouraged to learn new ideas, techniques, and procedures—not just change for the sake of change. Neither NUMMI, EDS, nor Hughes ventures were going to be able to make the changes required for long-term company viability.

Another interesting note on what were called "joint venture" cars (Matrix and Vibe; Tracker and Sidekick; Nova and Corolla)—vehicles that were produced by either Suzuki or Toyota, and marketed by GM: In every case, the GM-branded version outsold the Toyota/Suzuki version. When given the proper products, GM dealers could outsell any of the Japanese or other competition.

1985. Roger Smith had GM buy the Hughes Aircraft Company. It cost them $5.2 billion! Smith merged it with Delco Electronics to form Hughes Electronics. Again, a cultural clash with minimal synergy available to GM. By 1999, GM had divested itself of most Hughes assets.

Also in 1985, Smith and GM formed the Saturn Car Corporation. It was believed the initial capital investment by GM was $5 billion, and this was followed by other massive cash investments until the brand was cancelled and written off in 2009. Of all Roger Smith's dreams, Saturn was in many ways the most worthy. I believe its longevity was due to the culture, spirit, and dedication of the Saturn management, staff, dealers, and workers. Just as Smith was crushing any spirit from the various divisions, he gave a little hope to this "different kind of car company." With time, Saturn lost its independence and was brought back to the corporate fold, where it withered and died. (Quick addition: Saturn + Hughes + EDS = \$13.5 billion, in 1985 dollars. If this money had not been spent, what is the probability GM would need government bailouts in 2009?)

1990. Roger was retired by 1990, and the GM market share in the U.S. was down to 36 percent from 46 percent in 1980. Those lost ten points of share were worth about a million vehicle sales per year! Thanks for nothing, Roger.

I must caution the reader to not put all of the blame on Roger Smith for all of GM's disasters in the 1980s. First, the GM organization was so vast that changes of the magnitude Smith tried to make were doomed to failure (assuming that the changes were the right ones). The elimination of divisional structure took all of the flexibility and creativity out of the corporation. Rather than having six or more vibrant and vigorous entities, Smith had created a monolith with so much inertia that it could not move.

Second, change for change's sake is wasteful. We can look at nature and very rarely see a major change take place over a short time span unless it is the result of some cataclysmic event.

Most change in nature is evolutionary, taken in measured steps with a specific goal or objective in mind. In a corporation, change must be evolutionary with measurable goals, checkpoints, and objectives.

By the 1980s, some pundits felt GM needed to change and most until 1990 cheered Roger Smith's so-called visionary actions. But by 1990, the Japanese were becoming stronger and the Big Three were becoming weaker—and GM was leading the fall. GM needed to understand why people were buying Japanese vehicles.

Smith was loved by the media because he always was good for a quote. He believed he was visionary, while others now believe he was delusionary. Ross Perot was one of the few on the board who wanted to stop the madness. Perot was silenced with greenmail, and the board always went along with Smith. How different it would be today if the board had listened to Perot back then! The question one might reasonably ask is: Who were the other guys in authority while Roger Smith was in control?

LESSON: You do not always have to agree with the opponents of an idea, but you should at least always listen to them.

Howard H. Kehrl

Vice-chairman of General Motors, February 1, 1981–December 31, 1986.

Kehrl was an engineering specialist, a "car guy" with an outstanding technical background. He was a spokesman for new research and technology at GM during his time as vice-chairman. One of his pet projects was a coal dust-fuelled turbine engine for Cadillac. Did the American consumer need or want this technology?

Donald J. Atwood

Vice-chairman of General Motors, June 1, 1987–April 19, 1989.

Donald Atwood left GM in 1989 to be George W. Bush's assistant secretary of defence. Atwood was an inventor and development engineer in the areas of electronics and inertial guidance. GM bought his personal company, Dynatrol, in 1959, and Atwood rose quickly up the ladder at GM. At his leaving, Atwood had over 150,000 employees under his supervision from many diverse areas and the acquisitions of Roger Smith.

Both Kehrl and Atwood were scientists and futurists, even though they liked Smith's visions on the whole. It does not appear they had the management skills to carry out Roger Smith's dreams or to temper his recklessness.

F. James McDonald

President of General Motors, February 1, 1981–August 31, 1987.

A genuine "car guy," McDonald succeeded John DeLorean as general manager of Pontiac Division in 1969. In 1972, he became general manager of Chevrolet Division. McDonald was heavily involved in labour-management relations and tried to develop a co-operative relationship with the unions. With Roger Smith as his boss, he had an upward battle. As an ex-divisional manager, he must have been crushed when the divisions were eliminated. McDonald's hands were tied, as he was beholden to Smith for his position and forced to follow the company (Smith's) line.

Robert C. Stempel

President of General Motors, September 1, 1987–July 31, 1990.

Stempel was another "car guy" with a successful background in design and engineering and was highly respected by the GM employees and the "car buffs" in America. There was much optimism in the GM ranks when Stempel came to power, based on his past achievements and successes. Unfortunately, it quickly appeared that Stempel's positive and kind personality was unsuited for the task ahead.

By the time he was made president in 1987, GM was basically in a shambles after six years of Roger Smith's leadership. (For Stempel, the worst was yet to come, as when Smith retired, Stempel became chairman.)

As you can see, the senior people under Roger Smith were all quality individuals with outstanding track records. They were not able either individually, or as a group, to implement the changes Roger Smith initiated or even to correct them.

Robert C. Stempel

Chairman of the Board; Chief Executive Officer, August 1, 1990–November 1, 1992.

Bob Stempel was president of GM under Roger Smith and took over Smith's titles when Smith retired. What Stempel inherited was a disaster, and with Smith gone, it was clear that radical cutbacks in every aspect of the company were required. Plants had to be closed, workers terminated, assets sold off, R&D cut, new product development postponed. When Stempel's humanist personality and background made it difficult to close plants and terminate thousands of workers, the board that had allowed Roger Smith in the previous ten years to wreak havoc far and wide made Bob Stempel the scapegoat for all of GM's problems and had him resign. Bob Stempel was truly one of the good guys who got the shaft for others' sins.

Stempel was just the first of four chairmen who tried, but failed, to save GM from bankruptcy. Stempel was followed by John Smale.

John G. Smale

Chairman of the Board November 2, 1992–December 31, 1995.

Smale was an outside director before he became chairman. His background was with the highly successful Procter and Gamble. He was expected to perform miracles with GM but barely lasted three years. Suffering through the "W" car fiasco, he tried to right the ship, but the problem was getting very large by now.

Smale was always considered an outsider who tried hard but did not have enough time to learn the business. He could not perform miracles as everyone expected he should. The concepts and beliefs that Smale had learned and that worked so effectively at P&G did not seem to fit GM. Of course, P&G runs as a decentralized company, completely the opposite of where GM wanted to go. At P&G, the brand manager and executives of each brand operate relatively autonomously. The creative tension between each brand is very strong and fostered.

There was much optimism when Smale came to power. Smale's personality suited P& G perfectly, a quiet gentleman who did not seek publicity or have the desire to be a "cheerleader." Unfortunately, by this time GM needed a strong executive who would carry the flag and be a visible leader for all of the hundreds of thousands of GM people to follow. He was always looked upon as an outsider by management in GM and was not as successful as expected.

John F. "Jack" Smith, Jr.

Chairman of the Board, January 1, 1996–April 30, 2003.

Jack Smith was a long-term GM financial guy, very good with the "books." Jack was accepted by the GM organization as being "one of the GM guys" and had a relatively long reign. He knew how to appease Wall Street. Under him, GM looked buoyant and had some success, but this was more likely due to the strong world economy, where almost all automakers appeared successful. Under Smith, GM had a period of stability and profitability, but unfortunately market share continued to erode. When he left, GM's market share was 28 percent.

G. Richard Wagoner, Jr.

Chairman of the Board, May 1, 2003–March 30, 2009.

Wagoner's legacy was to be the last leader of GM before bankruptcy. He was always upbeat and confident, but never really did what had to be done. Fired by President Obama on March 29, 2009, he received a twenty-million-dollar severance, retirement and pension package! Wagoner did hire Bob Lutz as vice-chairman, who was responsible for injecting life into several GM brands and car lines. Unfortunately, Lutz could not save GM; that was Wagoner's job.

As a leader becomes more powerful in an organization, his associates lose power. Eventually, there are no longer any checks, balances, or alternatives for the leader.

LESSON: By giving more power to one individual in an organization, the whole organization becomes weaker.

The Death Dive

You Make Vehicles Consumers Do Not Want to Buy

Consumers Buy Other Brands of Cars

Sales and Market Share Fall

Excess Plant Capacity Created

All Costs Increase Dramatically

Corporate Losses Mount

More Loans Required to Finance Operations

Higher Interest Payments/Costs

Losses Grow

Lenders Refuse to Lend Money

Company Must Go Bankrupt

13

Why They Could Not Fix It

The situation that faced the leadership of GM beginning in the last decade of the twentieth century is similar to what a trauma surgeon might face in a disaster scenario: multiple victims, with multiple symptoms and injuries, and many alternative treatment options and numerous diagnostic tools—and medical specialists available to assist and consult with him, which can add to the confusion. Meanwhile, the patients, some of whom have pre-existing conditions like diabetes, heart disease, or obesity are to various degrees bleeding on the table.

The dilemma for the surgeon is what to do first: Which patient is most critical? Who can be deferred? Who has no hope? Trauma surgeons are trained in these scenarios and have specific, proven protocols to follow. Luckily, they do not operate in the glare of the media and do not have to publish their results in the *Wall Street Journal*.

So, let us begin very simply with the symptoms that faced GM at this time. The most obvious is the lack of consistent annual profits from automotive operations.

In any profit-making enterprise, success and profitability are the result of only three factors: costs, gross profit received from sales, and the sales volume. Entwined in the costs/revenue/volume equations are a myriad other factors.

It is a given that costs are always too high, gross profit per unit is always too low, and sales volume should be higher. The objective of top management is to work with the three related variables to maximize long-term profits. How effectively this is accomplished is what differentiates managers.

Note there is a huge difference between short-term profits and long-term profits. Wall Street tends to over-reward short-term profits because by its nature, Wall Street is short-term oriented—the here and now. Every stock market investor and speculator is interested in what tomorrow's share price is, not next year's or five years down the road. If management is in sync with Wall Street's thinking, looking five years down the road is very hard to do. (Note that in Japanese business strategies, five years is usually considered short-term.) Because of lead times involved in the auto industry, where it can take three to five years to get a new vehicle from the drawing board to production, there is an natural conflict between Wall Street's expectations and the car business's reality.

When top managers are in charge of an organization, they must adapt themselves very quickly to the objectives set by the board of directors. The top management of GM and many other American companies in the 1980s–1990s were being compensated through stock options; and "shareholder value" became the mantra for these executives.

Stock options allow the executive to purchase a specific number of corporate shares from the corporate treasury at a set price. The objective of this incentive for the executive is to drive up the share price of the GM stock listed on the New York stock exchange above his set buy price; he can then sell his shares and keep the profits (capital gains), which have a favourable tax rate. The theory is excellent. The executive increases the value of GM as reflected by its share price, and the executive and all the other shareholders benefit. But the problem is, executives can make decisions that will increase share value in the short term but cripple the company in the long term.

For example, an executive team can decide to defer capital spending for new product development (which will have a sales impact three to ten years down the road) but spend the money today on consumer incentives for old product lines that are very profitable (because it is being built on old machinery that is fully depreciated).

During the last twenty years, GM has been notorious for deferring and delaying new product introductions and quality fixes. They also introduced product to the public that was not market ready, unreliable, and of poor quality, all in the effort to reduce costs and improve short-term profitability. With this approach, sales were at times at acceptable levels in the short term, and profits were good, but three or four years down the road, the market share shrank again.

One cannot blame the executive; he has an obligation to himself and his family to maximize his personal earnings. However, short-term share value is a terrible way to compensate an executive, because share values reflect a great deal more than an executive's leadership and skill. After 9/11, all share values plummeted everywhere in the world. It did not mean that the world's corporate executives had some connection with the terrorist attack, or, because of terrorists, the managers became less effective.

In America, it is not usual for CEOs to receive bonuses when the company loses money. The justification given by the board is usually something like, "Under Chairman Johnny Superstar's leadership, we did not lose as much as was expected, and if we do not pay him the big bucks, he will quit and go work for our competitor."

As previously mentioned, there is a great desire by the bean-counters of the world to try and assign values and apply mathematical models and analysis to all business problems. However, as long as companies' customers are emotional human beings, this approach is fraught with danger.

The problem is that over time, GM, especially by the 1990s, became very dependent on Wall Street's blessings. Wall Street lives for quarterly reports, and any GM executive who wanted to stay a GM executive had better be aware of what the "street" was saying.

The most powerful entity at GM is the chairman and the board of directors. The board members represent the shareholders and investors, and in most cases they personally have substantial investments in GM. No member of the board is going to tolerate sub-par financial results for very long, and the board will look to make executive changes quickly if results are not acceptable.

In the American automotive business, timelines have always been short. Daily production and shipment rates, ten-day sales reports, monthly objectives, and quarterly profits were the standard operating reports for management. Executives and supervisors were constantly evaluated on these criteria.

This was the crux of GM's initial dilemma: there were solutions that should have been implemented to ensure the long-term profitability and viability of the company, but all the internal and external pressures, especially from Wall Street, were stressing short-term profitability. The GM leadership had for too many years become focused on short-term profits and calculable objectives (these objectives had in part led to the elimination of the divisional system that had made GM great). The tendency was to look at the "books" to see where the money was being made and lost. Unfortunately, the "books" only tell you what happened, resulting in a tendency to be reactive rather than proactive.

The problems that presented themselves to GM management also kept changing. In the early 1970s, it seemed the government and the divisional concept itself were the main problems; if GM could keep the government out of their business, they would be okay. GM "bean-counters" felt that the divisional concept was costly and was not reaping the economies of scale that were available. After fixing the government and the divisions, it would be clear sailing.

By the 1980s, the Japanese and the recession were the problems, as well as the high production costs. The American auto manufacturers got the Japanese to limit imports, the economy got better, and GM was selling cars. It was thought that the huge capital investments in technology and corporate acquisitions and the elimination of the divisions would control costs well into the future.

By the 1990s, consumers were not buying GM cars. Something had to be done to make them more appealing. GM now decided individual brand identity would be good. This was less than a decade after Roger Smith, with the board's blessing, had decided that great efficiencies—and therefore profits—would result by eliminating divisions and rationalizing product lines, making the company more monolithic. By the 2000s, if it had not been for trucks, vans, and SUVs, the Japanese would have controlled the industry. As hard as GM tried to make their cars better, with some exceptions, they were constantly playing catch-up with the Japanese—and now with some very strong European imports.

Between 1970 and 2009, there were years of excellent profits and sales (albeit short-term profits). At the beginning of each
model year, hope was high that this would be the year that GM
would regain its traditional dominant place in the automotive
world. But even during these bad times, GM did many things
right. However, they could not understand what these things
were, or, more important, never stopped to consider what it was
they were still doing right.

Consumers had an idea what was wrong; Wall Street had an
idea what was wrong; business consultants believed they knew
what was wrong; and business school gurus had an idea what
was wrong. In fact, almost everybody and every group had an
idea what was wrong and what should be done to correct the
problems. With everybody identifying different problems and
proposing different solutions, chaos reigned.

In fact, many of the ideas suggested were completely opposite
to each other. Such as, **"Stick to your core business and get rid of
periphery business assets,"** versus **"Acquire technology-related
and periphery business assets to strengthen the core business."**

The only people GM should have listened to were the customers
who were buying Hondas, Mazdas, Toyotas, and Nissans. Those
people knew exactly why they were not buying GM.

In the last analysis, GM really had only one problem: It failed
to fully grasp and understand why consumers were not buying
their vehicles. In the cases where GM *did* understand that it was
the product that was at fault, they reacted too late and/or inappropriately because of inertia, lack of divisional flexibility and
initiative, and shortage of financial resources.

The simple answer was that the competition was building
better products as perceived by the consumer and consumer mo-
toring media. In 1970, Datsuns and Toyotas were in most cases
superior cars to the Pintos and Vegas of the day. North American
consumers are pretty astute at finding and buying products that
satisfy their needs best. The consumers were saying that non-GM
cars were doing a better job for them. This is, of course, an over-
simplification. GM was still number one in overall sales in North
America up to their bankruptcy. In many segments, they had the

best vehicles and were the market leaders. But in the big-volume segments, GM was losing sales and market share rapidly; mostly, since 1972, to the Japanese.

Segment	Examples	Units sold	Dominated by
Mid-size cars	Honda Accord Toyota Camry Chevrolet Malibu	2386370	
Crossover	Chevrolet Equinox Chrysler Pacifica Honda Pilot	1,810,209	Big Three
Small	Honda Civic Toyota Corolla Chevrolet Cavalier	1,735,488	Imports
Pickup	Chevrolet Silverado Ford F150 Nissan Titan	1,268,697	Ford and GM
Luxury	Lexus BMW Cadillac	756,099	Imports and Cadillac
Minivan	Dodge Caravan	529,936	Chrysler
Mid-size SUV	GMC Acadia Saturn Outlook Ford Explorer	349,425	GM and Ford
Large SUV	Chevrolet Suburban Nissan Armada Toyota Land Cruiser	202,387	Competitive
Small SUV	Honda CRV Toyota RAV Saturn VUE	161,825	Competitive
Luxury SUV	Cadillac Escalade Cadillac SRX Lexus RX 350 &570 Acura MDX	100,178	Competitive
Large	Chevrolet Impala Ford Crown Victoria	81,003	GM

This chart of 2008 U.S. sales by segment shows who dominated the market.
(*Author*)

One confusing factor that prevented GM from understanding the problem was that they were selling lots of profitable pickups and SUVs (basically same chassis), and this segment was growing. In the last decade of the twentieth century, GM really believed they had turned the corner. They were living off good truck and SUV volume and competitive sales volume in the luxury class with Cadillac.

However, they were doing poorly in the large-volume car segments and the imports were constantly introducing new models into the segments the Big Three traditionally dominated. And it appeared that the passenger car segments were shrinking, with trucks, SUVs, minivans, and crossovers appearing to be growth segments.

Category	2003	2004	2005	2006	2007	2008	03-08 Market Share Change
Compact SUV	3.9%	3.8%	4.2%	3.8%	4.1%	6.3%	61.655
Compact Car	14.8%	14.6%	15.7%	17.4%	18.3%	20.0%	35.71%
Large Car	5.0%	5.5%	5.9%	6.3%	6.1%	6.3%	26.75%
Luxury SUV	3.4%	3.7%	3.7%	3.9%	4.3%	4.0%	19.30%
Van	2.0%	2.1%	2.2%	2.2%	2.0%	1.9%	-2.00%
Midsize Car	17.0%	16.0%	16.0%	16.3%	16.1%	16.3%	-3.80%
Midsize SUV	13.2%	12.6%	11.7%	12.8%	13.6%	11.6%	-12.58%
Large Truck	14.1%	14.9%	15.2%	13.9%	13.7%	12.2%	-13.95%
Large SUV	5.2%	5.8%	5.0%	4.0%	4.6%	4.1%	-20.41%
Minivan	6.5%	6.7%	6.6%	6.1%	5.1%	4.9%	-24.47%
Compact Truck	4.9%	4.4%	4.2%	3.6%	3.1%	3.1%	-36.60%

The dramatic shift in five years in the U.S. auto market.
(Edmunds.com)

As you can see from the table, the imports were very strong in the volume segments and were making inroads into segments where they were weak. The other important factor to recognize was that there was a seismic shift in segments as shown by the chart in a very short period of time. Notice all the segments that were shrinking had been the areas of strength for GM sales.

Since GM did not know what the real problem was, it was difficult to find a solution. Under the old organizational layout, I believe the different divisional managers would have gone off in different directions until one of them reported back to head-quarters with the right answer! You can rest assured a traditional Buick or Oldsmobile division manager would never have allowed some of the vehicles produced by GM to have worn Buick or Oldsmobile nameplates and be sold to the public.

If your objective is to lower costs and increase volume (raising prices in the competitive automobile market usually has negative impacts to volume and is counterproductive), you again have a number of alternatives.

You can analyze every process in your company to make sure everything you are doing is the most efficient possible, but that takes too long, is too hard, and not exciting.

What you can do is go after the easy stuff, the low-hanging fruit, as it were. A beginning move would be to reduce value in your product: What was standard make optional; what used to have N years of durability, reduce to N–2 years' durability by using cheaper components.

Blame the union and workers, always handy scapegoats.

Set targets and rewards for so-called productivity and cost reductions.

And the all-time GM favourite was: change the organization. The idea that changing the organization was going to be a panacea for all of its problems was the greatest error GM leaders made.

First of all, before you attempt a change, you must believe the existing system was bad. For example, eliminating the divisional system that had led to the existence of the world's greatest manufacturing company, and had proven itself for over a half century of profits and success, presupposed that it was not a viable operating system.

Second, with employees numbering in the hundreds of thousands, without a dynamic leader and buy-in by the vast majority of those employees, change to corporate culture and processes is going to be fraught with danger and will likely fail, even if the change is justified.

The experience with NUMMI showed that even when GM people returned to their home facilities, their new-found knowledge and expertise was usually rejected at the home plant because the supervisors were not open to change.

Third, change is always implemented best when it is done in an evolutionary pattern and usually in small segments or groups. One man returning from Toyota with new knowledge will not be effective, but a team or group of industrial engineers returning together to a plant will likely be more successful. Divisions are a better setting than whole corporations for these changes to happen.

Even in the face of these challenges, GM had tremendous advantages over the competition.

1. GM had the engineering and technical ability to build world-class vehicles at any price point—if allowed to by top management. Its truck lines, the Corvette, and certain Cadillac models were all examples of this ability.

2. It had the best retail distribution system in North America (its dealers).

3. It had the brands with some of the highest recognition, appeal, customer loyalty, and enthusiast base in the world.

4. It still had a relatively stable, loyal, and determined workforce.

5. GM had millions of loyal customers and millions of their brand vehicles on the road.

6. It was # 1 in North America in sales.

Why They Could Not Fix It

The reason these brilliant and talented leaders of GM failed can be summarized as follows:

Top management focused on short-term profits, calculable objectives, and simple traditional solutions, which in part led to the elimination of the divisional system that had made GM great.

They did not know what the real problem was, which was the fact the consumers preferred the competitors' alternatives.

Top management's tendency was to look at the "books," to identify where money was being made and lost, and react. Unfortunately, the "books" only tell you what has happened, resulting in a further tendency to be reactive rather than proactive.

14

Corporate Culture

When I was a teenager, my behaviour often frustrated and irritated my parents. When I had teenage children, they often frustrated and irritated me as well. Experts tell me those behaviours that I found objectionable are a result of cultural and generational values, many created by peer and media influences. For instance, I think a man should remove his hat in a restaurant; many young men disagree with me. I think removing your hat is a respectful and gentlemanly way of behaving. Many young people think my belief and attitude about hats is irrelevant and ridiculous.

Imagine how much effort would be required by a young man to change my values about dress codes and ball caps, and vice-versa. In our society, many of these cultural rules evolve as a means of organizing society and preventing chaos and confusion. Even the side on which the guests sit at a wedding chapel goes according to an unwritten rule. In the main, most of these cultural rules and values are good.

In an organization such as GM, imagine how many written and unwritten rules, codes, behaviours, and operating procedures were entrenched and followed diligently by each and every employee. Everything from who parked where in the company parking lot to the style of office furniture and where it went was codified (though not necessarily in written form).

This is true for most organizations, because these "rules" prevent chaos. For decades, the GM management dress code was a blue suit and a white shirt with a classic-style tie. GM managers rarely had facial hair.

There were cultural rules and values in the work process as well. Some were formal policies; some were unwritten. Examples are: "We always have two suppliers for Chevrolet interior materials"; or, "We use the lowest bidder on steering systems"; or, "We order in lunch on Fridays"; or, "Senior managers take the first day of deer hunting season off." Most of the codes, policies, and standards evolved over the years and had come to be quite effective in most situations.

When top management would initiate even a seemingly minor change, instantly there were problems. As the Coke experience with New Coke and Classic Coke proved, you had better have a great reason to ask people to change their behaviour, and changes in one procedure often have impact on rules and cultural standards in other procedures or areas.

Imagine you are the GM purchasing agent for widgets at an assembly plant in Ohio. Your fishing buddy and best friend is the owner of Local Widgets Mfg., your supplier. A number of times, his company has bailed you out when you ran out of widgets; it shipped on Sundays; it even ran extra shifts to help you supply another plant in Canada whose regular supplier had a fire. Local Widget Mfg. has always been an excellent, high-quality supplier. Now the directive comes down from the head office that all widgets for all plants will come from Latin Widget Company in Mexico, which underbid everybody by 2 percent. You now have to order six months ahead of time, in three-month quantities.

What will be your reaction to this change? Your buddy is pissed, and his company will likely go under. He feels betrayed after all the outstanding service he has given to GM. He believes that Latin Widget, which is partially owned by a Japanese conglomerate, will jack up GM prices once it has eliminated the competition.

The plant manager gets mad at you when you tell him he has to give you longer-term production forecasts and store more widget inventory in the plant. It would be reasonable on your part to do everything possible to get out of the Latin Widget commitment and give the business back to Local Widget. Imagine the turmoil in your office, especially when the rumours start that your job is being transferred to Detroit, or, even worse—because you have twenty-one years of service—your job is to be eliminated!

When GM headquarters decided to change the way things were, the above scenario was repeated hundreds of thousands of times.

The following tales illustrate the power of corporate culture and its consequences.

A final assembly plant manager was noted for setting and maintaining high levels of production. His skills, for which he was well rewarded, were in maximizing the number of new cars coming off the line every hour. Under his leadership, the plant could really push out the product.

One day, long after the divisions and their oversight were eliminated, somebody in the head office marketing department started looking at the plant's output in terms of defects and warranty claims and discovered that over 30 percent of the new cars coming off the line were not acceptable and should not have been sold to the consumer as produced! For the plant manager, production was all that counted, and he had been richly rewarded for years for his success with this particular culture. Once the plant assembly managers stopped being responsible to division managers, the culture changed.

Because of the cyclical nature of the auto industry, many supervisors made sure that during good times they were 10 to 15 percent overstaffed. The astute manager knew that sometime in the future there was going to be some sort of negative news affecting the company. He also knew Head Office would mandate a 10 percent across-the-board manpower reduction, regardless of the logic in any specific department. The culture was: Pad your staff, because Head Office will demand cuts.

After the GM reorganization in June of 2009, Ed Whitacre, President Obama's pick to be the chairman of the "new" GM, fired CEO Fritz Henderson on December 1, 2009. This was an example of a leader acting decisively, always a perceived important quality at GM. On February 20, 2010, Whitacre hired Fritz Henderson back as a consultant at $3,000 an hour! Whitacre likely realized that without somebody like Henderson who knew the culture, procedures, and operations of GM, there would be more chaos.

Because GM leadership could not understand why people were

buying more and more competitors' cars, and, more important, did not appear to be able to do anything about it, attempted solutions often failed. In 1997, Chevrolet division introduced the new 1998 Malibu (the fifth generation), a nice, solid, reliable car, roomy and comfortable. GM leadership really believed it was best in the class.

At a GM product training session, we retail salespeople were given intensive training on the superior features of the Malibu and the benefits it had over its competition. In fact, GM trainers had acquired a Ford Contour for the salespeople to do a live side-by-side comparison. Of course, after this, we dealer salespeople believed the Malibu was a world-beater.

Here is a comparison ranking of actual vehicle user ratings in 1998 of mid-size automobiles. In reality, the consumers who owned GM mid-size cars have rated them worst in the bunch, while GM was convincing their sales organization at the time that these cars were world class.

1998 Mid-Size	Ratings Out of 10
1998 Honda Accord	8.9
1998 Honda Civic	8.9
1998 Toyota Camry	8.6
1998 Nissan Altima	8.6
1998 Chrysler Cirrus	8.4
*1998 Saturn SL	7.9
1998 Mitsubishi Galant	7.8
1998 Dodge Stratus	7.7
1998 Mazda 626	7.7
1998 Mercury Mystique	7.5
1998 Plymouth Breeze	7.4
1998 Ford Contour	7.2
1998 Hyundai Elantra	7.2
*1998 Oldsmobile Cutlass	7.1
*1998 Pontiac Grand Am	7.1
1998 Hyundai Sonata	6.7
*1998 Chevrolet Malibu	6.6
*GM Brands	

After Five Years of Ownership: Overall Satisfaction with Vehicle.
(Copyright .autos.msn.com; used with permission)

If GM management really believed their cars were the best, you can see the frustration and confusion at the highest levels; the customers were saying with their dollars that GM products were *not* the best. The GM sales trainers were telling the dealer sales staff that the new Malibu was great, and initially, we the salespeople believed them. Back at the showroom floor, the reality was the Malibu was not the customers' first choice by a long shot. Of course, the dealer and his staff lost confidence in GM, and GM blamed the dealers for a lack of support.

At the dealership level, many of the salespeople became frustrated when their long-term customers bought imports. Tragically, we were so loyal to GM that we usually blamed the customer. When my neighbour traded in the Olds 88 I had sold him for a Honda Accord, I felt terribly betrayed. He explained to me that after replacing two transmissions and a couple of steering racks, he had no confidence in GM products. That made me feel worse, as I knew from experience he was justified.

As stated previously, I believe GM really had only one problem: They failed to fully grasp why consumers were not buying their cars! They knew the consumer was buying other brands, and GM Market Research knew what the customers were saying about quality, durability, and reliability. But the key decision makers did not hear or believe what they were being told.

Specifically, Japanese cars were lighter due to unique design features. Lighter cars are more fuel efficient and cheaper to make. In America up until the seventies, adjectives such as big, solid, road-hugging, smooth, secure, and full-framed were positive descriptors of quality automobiles. The Japanese preferred adjectives such as, light, nimble, airy, efficient, economical, simple, and reliable.

In the early 1980s, I was speaking to a GM executive who told me about an experience he'd had while in Detroit. GM R&D people were doing an analysis of a Toyota Corolla's construction. A team of engineers took the car apart piece by piece. They analyzed each nut, bolt, washer, and piece of steel, plastic, and rubber. They compared each component, how it was made, and what it was made of, to the equivalent Chevrolet Cavalier component.

One advantage the Toyota had over the Cavalier was that it was lighter. In 1980, the basic four-door Chevrolet Cavalier weighed 1,072 kilograms or 2,363 pounds. The equivalent Toyota Corolla weighed 855 kilograms or 1884 pounds—an amazing difference of 479 pounds! The Corolla was 20 percent lighter, which resulted in excellent acceleration with a smaller engine, better fuel economy, lower emissions, and potentially longer-lasting components, because with less weight, each part has less work to do.

When looking at the Corolla door, for example, it was significantly lighter than the Cavalier door, yet it was as strong and durable, if not more so. They spent many man-hours trying to figure out how Toyota could build a better door and what industrial process Toyota might have used to accomplish this miracle.

The executive who told me this story ended glumly by saying, "We never did discover the secret." Of course not. The GM technical people were looking through GM eyes and were not open to alternatives. This is where GM corporate culture was a negative. GM people often could not accept that some other company could do something better than GM.

Twenty-five years later, in a comparison test, *Motor Trend* magazine had the following to say about the 2008 Malibu:

> Sit in the Malibu and it feels large, but in fact, at 112.5 cu ft, only the VW Passat has a smaller EPA combined interior and trunk volume. Driving the Malibu LTZ 2.4L heightens the illusion of largeness, though not in a particularly flattering way . . . Countering that expectation, however, is a fairly hefty curb weight of 3503 lbs—that's 165 lbs heavier than the largest-in-class Hyundai Sonata.

The GM executive in the 1980s was right. They never did discover the secret.

The production of an automobile is costly. Under Roger Smith, GM believed that it was the worker that was the problem. Eliminate the worker and costs go down. The Japanese, on the other hand, believed that the worker was the asset, and with the worker, the production process could be improved.

In the auto industry, stamping steel parts like fenders, hoods, doors, and roofs is done on huge presses that cost millions of dollars. The press is most efficient when it is operating. For each part, there is a separate die that is placed in the press, and it takes time to change a die, for example, to switch from stamping the left front fender to the right front fender. Traditionally, in the 1950s, it took one or two shifts or up to sixteen hours to perform a die change. This was the universal average for the Big Three. Toyota realized that as a small automaker it could not afford the press downtime. So it developed ways to reduce the process down to mere hours. Magna, the Canadian company that became the most successful North American parts supplier, supposedly can change dies in about twenty minutes or less now, which is what the best Japanese makers can do.

GM got up to speed some years later. Magna proved it was not something intrinsic with the Japanese that made their production processes more efficient—it was the attitude management took. Even though Japanese culture in many ways is very traditional and appears unchanging, their manufacturing culture expects and demands every worker to develop better processes.

In conclusion, corporate culture, its objectives and goals, its flexibility and malleability, all impact tremendously on business operations. Any leader who does not understand what his business's culture is, and how corporate change can impact culture—and, conversely, how culture can impact corporate change—will not be successful in the long run.

15

Market Segments

I am not sure if Procter and Gamble invented the concept of brands and market segments, but they certainly perfected it. The idea is to divide the market into small pieces or segments based on the different needs of the consumer. At one time, P&G's Tide had the largest market share in the home laundry market, but was faced with new product entries and increasing competition from Colgate–Palmolive, Unilever, and other competitors.

In response, P&G over time introduced a number of new brands: Bold, Cheer, and Oxydol, which had specific attributes for each segment. Cheer was marketed as especially good in cold water, as there was a significant portion of the market that preferred not to use hot water in clothes washing because of the negative effect hot water has on colour brightness. Soon Bold dominated the "heavy-duty" detergent segment, Cheer dominated the cold-water segment, and Oxydol dominated the "bleach-added" segment. Together, each of these brands gave P&G a greater market share in the laundry detergent market than Tide alone had.

Of course, P&G's costs went up due to the additional brands, but overall sales and profits went up much more and stayed that way as separate brand managers sought to make their brand #1 in overall sales. It should be noted that P&G brands always rate #1 or #2 in quality product comparison tests. If they do not, the brand is reformulated to become the #1 quality in the segment.

It is much the same in the auto business. The goal is to dominate a segment. You want to be #1 in a chosen category. If you are really lucky, you can create a new segment and dominate it. The Mustang created a new segment in 1964, and almost fifty years later is still the dominant entry in the "sporty" car category. Corvette dominates its segment but it is a small-volume seller and never brought huge profits to GM. The Cadillac Escalade dominated its segment as well.

It should be noted that automotive segments are very diverse, the needs and desires of one segment being very different than another. Secondly, the segments are always expanding or shrinking. When Chrysler introduced minivans in 1984, it was a new segment, and the volume was phenomenal. Soon competitors entered with various models, and the segment was further compartmentalized into all-wheel drive and rear-wheel drive versions, luxury and sporty versions, then crossovers and SUV versions. Smaller and larger minivan variants also appeared as all the competitors fought to get a piece of the Chrysler pie.

The auto business requires huge capital investment to produce a new model. Even if an old factory building is used, it is not unusual today to spend $100,000,000 to produce and sell a new model. If the factory produces only 50,000 units annually, the car may be a money loser; possibly at 100,000 units it is at break-even; at 150,000 units, things are good; at 250,000 units, a plant's typical maximum production, we have a winner that is making millions for the company.

Imagine there are four brands competing in a segment that will have North American sales of 300,000 units. Each company has budgeted break-even at 20 percent of the segment. (Twenty-five percent of the sales would be profitable.) However, in real life, the segment rarely splits out evenly. For example, Brand A might capture 50 percent of the segment, or 150,000 units; lots of profits and bonuses at Company Brand A.

Brand B and Brand C are very competitive and have the same market share at 20 percent each (60,000 units), or just slightly above the break-even point. The sales and marketing department will be told they must get more sales or heads will roll. They will use their traditional promotional tools, increased advertising, dealer incentives, consumer incentives, special-edition models, and so on.

Poor Brand D has 10 percent market share, and heads are rolling! Likely a new manager will be brought in with the mandate to double sales immediately. The first step is to get the dealers to order cars. An auto company gets paid in full when the car arrives at the dealer's lot. The company will do almost anything to get the dealer to order more cars, so the plant is running closer to break-even to minimize further losses.

One of the biggest challenges for GM with the advent of the information age was the rankings in various magazine comparison tests. *Car and Driver* was one magazine that thrived on pitting various brands of cars against one another and ranking them. *Consumer Reports* had a similar program.

Eventually, it appeared that every media outlet was doing comparison tests, and the results were racing over the information highway. When these comparison tests were done with its foreign competitors, GM rarely won.

In 2008, Malibu was GM's best effort to produce a world-class, mid-size car. Based on a premium German Opel design, this car was to be a world beater. However, in March of 2008 in a seven-vehicle *Car and Driver* comparison test, the Malibu came third behind the Honda Accord and the Nissan Altima. In February 2009, *Car and Driver* compared the Malibu Hybrid, Ford Fusion Hybrid, Nissan Altima Hybrid, and the Toyota Camry Hybrid; the Malibu came in last. If a company was not winning these comparison tests, it would be losing sales and market share.

Even more disheartening for GM, in 2010, *Car and Driver* de facto acknowledged the Accord to be the historical best in the class and did a comparison between the new models of the Hyundai Sonata and Subaru Legacy. No other competitors—such as the Malibu—were even evaluated because they were found lacking when previously compared to the Accord. What was amazing was the Sonata from the upstart Korean manufacturer Hyundai won the comparison test. Some people question the methodology and procedures in rating vehicles in these comparison tests. The winner feels that winning is a real stamp of approval for their brand, and the buying public generally agrees.

The Chevrolet Malibu—the expected volume leader for GM in the huge, mid-size segment, after three years of production—was not even deemed to be a contender for top rank in its class. There is a new Malibu to be introduced as a 2013 model. Hope springs eternal.

The other thing that is noteworthy in this Malibu story is the ability of relatively small companies—Hyundai and Subaru in this case—to develop class-leading vehicles quickly and efficiently. They certainly do not have the resources of GM, Ford, or even Toyota. You cannot blame GM's union workers for Malibu's relatively poor results; unionized workers are not involved in the design, development, or engineering of new products. You cannot blame the Malibu's poor ranking on GM's financial woes, either; the 2008 Malibu project was relatively well-funded from its outset years before the bankruptcy in June 2009.

16

They Got Bad Advice

The leaders at GM were not stupid men; they were well educated and considered to be the best in their field. They, like you and me, when faced with a problem they did not understand, went and searched for advice. One thing about the car business is that everyone has an opinion and everyone feels he/she is an expert. Since the auto business is so high-profile, every one of the millions of stakeholders has an opinion. You cannot believe the urban myths that surround the car business and how many decisions and choices are based on these erroneous facts.

Arthur Hailey wrote a best-selling novel called *Wheels*. There he repeated the old adage, "Never buy a car built on a Monday or a Friday." Sounds reasonable at first, as those are the days when absenteeism is the greatest, so the quality will likely be the lowest. Now, Monday and Friday absenteeism is endemic in most industries, but I never heard anybody say not to buy meat from beef slaughtered on a Monday.

However, anybody who understands auto manufacturing will understand that final assembly of an automobile is only the last step in carmaking. A vast number of components are made in a large number of separate plants and shipped to the final assembly point. So quite reasonably, a car assembled on a Friday could have an exhaust and catalytic convertor system made on Thursday, an engine block cast and assembled on a Wednesday, a transmission built on a Tuesday, tires from a Monday, seats from Tuesday, and on and on. So that car assembled on Friday could have a transmission problem that was the result of a small spacer that was machined undersize a month ago on a Tuesday. Or it could have a side window falling down because the system initially designed was modified to reduce costs and weight, and the strength of the revised assembly became marginal. The problem had nothing to do with the day of assembly, but instead it had to do with a cost/benefit issue at the design stage four years before the car was assembled.

In the past twenty years, most of the advice GM has received was based on reducing costs and becoming more efficient by reducing the number of brands, streamlining the marketing system, and producing low-emission and high-efficiency cars. Some even suggested that GM get out of the car business. Many of the suggestions were either useless, impossible to implement, or impractical.

Some Suggestions

Stop making gas-guzzling trucks and SUVs; people want small, fuel-efficient cars. Based on sales, people were buying GM trucks and SUVs, and these sales were very profitable for GM. In some very profitable segments gas mileage is of secondary importance.

Make electric cars. GM is introducing the GM Volt, the most advanced electric car in the world in terms of range and practicality. It is expensive to produce, and there is much concern about its consumer acceptance. Its long-term durability and operating costs are unknown.

Make hydrogen cars. Okay, where are people going to get hydrogen fuel? Who is going to pay for the fuel infrastructure, Big Oil? Not likely! How is the government going to collect fuel tax on hydrogen to replace gas tax revenues? If you suggest hydrogen not be taxed, then what is the government going to do about the huge shortfall in revenue? The U.S. government is broke already.

When GM went to the government for help, the advice they received was: *You have not been able to stop the loss of market share, let alone recapture any. You have to adjust your company size to the reality of the market.*

In the 2009 reorganization, GM surrendered leadership in the auto industry. They had capacity to produce enough vehicles to supply 40 percent of the market, but were capturing less than 20 percent. Too much production capacity is expensive, so the plan was to cut back production to supply only 20 percent of the market. That is what the 2009 reorganization plan did. In the business world, this is almost unprecedented, where the company with the biggest share in the North American market is giving up.

Now, I admit that by December 2008 it was too late to do much of anything else; and the U.S. banking and financial market collapse in the fall of 2008 ensured the demise of GM. From January 2009, Washington was de facto running GM and making the final decisions, and the mantra was cost cutting above all else. There is an old saying in the retail auto business: "You cannot expense control yourself into a profit." Well, GM did—with $60 billion dollars of taxpayers' cash.

There are many examples of auto companies that have almost been bankrupt, developed recovery strategies, and have come back even stronger. Of course, many received government financial assistance or merged with another automotive entity. BMW, Porsche, Audi, Mazda, Nissan, and Renault are just some examples. In none of these cases did the management who turned the companies around find it necessary to eliminate dealership and car brands on a broad scale.

In summary, this is the advice GM got and followed it into bankruptcy:

- *Eliminate interest and debt costs*. They defaulted on their bondholders and shareholders and they received $60 billion in cash through government handouts.

- *Eliminate brands and dealers*. GM eliminated the Pontiac, Oldsmobile, Saturn, Saab, and Hummer brands. They initially closed nearly 1,500 dealerships in North America, resulting in 75,000 to 150,000 job losses in North America.

- *Reduce union production costs*. With the help of government, GM destroyed the collective bargaining rights of thousands of workers.

- *Reduce pension costs*. GM screamed to anyone who would listen that the retirees were ruining the company; however, if GM had maintained its poor 40 percent market share from the 1980s, their pension costs would be in line.

As noted before, the basic problem with GM was that they failed to fully grasp and understand why consumers were not buying their cars! Notice that none of these "fixes" addressed that problem. Everyone at GM for years deluded themselves by going around saying what great cars GM was building! The customers knew otherwise. Many of the solutions GM and the government implemented were not aimed at the right problem(s), and therefore scarce resources were diverted away from the real needs.

In 2009, the agenda that the government had GM follow most was Wall Street's. The Car Czar appointed by President Obama was Steven Rattner, who was responsible for the reorganization of GM and Chrysler. Previously, before working for the government, Rattner had been deputy CEO of Lazard Freres, a major Wall Street investment bank. Appointing Rattner made some sense when you realize Wall Street controls the money GM needs to operate in the future. The Rattner plan quickly synthesized down to solutions to these perceived problems:

- Your costs are too high.

- You have high money costs.

- You have high labour costs.

- You have high retiree costs.

- You have too many dealers.

Of course, none of these diagnoses dealt with the reality that consumers were choosing to buy other brands of automobiles rather than General Motors products because they felt other brands were better.

17

Bad Advice Leads to Bad Decisions

Back in 2000, GM cancelled the 100-year-old Oldsmobile brand—a brand that just fifteen years before, in 1985, was selling over a million vehicles annually. Let us look a little more carefully at that perceived solution. By 1990, Oldsmobile sales had begun to plummet. The avalanche of lost sales began slowly. In 1978, when Oldsmobile began putting Chevrolet engines in Oldsmobile cars, GM was sued by its customers in a Class Action Suit, and Oldsmobile owners were angry. Then, in the early 1980s, Oldsmobile introduced diesel engines before they were ready and validated for American consumer use. They were totally unreliable and a disaster. Oldsmobile sales were still very strong, but eroding.

The *coup de grâce* came to brand when in 1989 GM discontinued the rear-wheel-drive Cutlass Supreme—a model that had been a top seller since 1968, a car that had great sales, reliability, and consumer confidence—and replaced it with a front-wheel-drive version also called "Cutlass Supreme." GM had already been producing and selling the front-wheel-drive Ciera since 1982; in fact, they morphed its name into Cutlass Ciera, but it was never the volume car the rear-wheel-drive Cutlass was. By 1989, Oldsmobile had two front-wheel-drive cars that were very similar: both had unreliable steering racks and weak transmissions, and the new Cutlass Supreme had rear disc brakes that were a maintenance nightmare.

For the first time ever, the new model Cutlass was a significantly poorer car than the previous rear-wheel-drive model and not significantly different than its stablemate, the Ciera.

In 1986, Oldsmobile also introduced the steadily selling and respected Delta 88 and 98 as new models with front-wheel drive. Between transmission and steering rack failures, these two new versions were unmitigated disasters. In a matter of ten years, Oldsmobile lost 500,000 annual vehicle sales!

In 1966, the Oldsmobile Division introduced the first large front-wheel production car in the world, the Toronado. Oldsmobile had mastered the intricacies of front-wheel technology, and that basic front-wheel platform was used for the next twenty years on models such as the Cadillac Eldorado. The Oldsmobile Division knew how to build front-wheel-drive cars. Unfortunately, by the 1980s, there was no Oldsmobile Division: no Oldsmobile engineering and design staff, no Oldsmobile R&D, no Oldsmobile assembly plants. The front-wheel-drive cars labelled as Oldsmobiles that were being sold to the public were generic, bland, and unreliable vehicles designed and engineered by anonymous committees and "platform teams."

GM decided they would have to save the brand by producing cars worthy of the Oldsmobile name. In 1995, they introduced the Aurora, and in 1998, the Intrigue. Both were excellent designs, but flawed in execution. The Aurora suffered from numerous electronic gremlins, and the Intrigue—which was mechanically reliable thanks to its Buick V6 drive train—had chronic front suspension and steering problems.

After pouring billions of dollars into these new models and not getting the sales results they wanted or expected, GM gave up on Oldsmobile in 2000. At this time, Oldsmobile was selling 300,000 cars a year. GM decided to cancel the brand.

Let us explore the cancelling brands concept further with two mass-market retailers, Walmart and McDonald's.

	General Motors	Wal-Mart	McDonald's
Nature of the retail outlets	Independently owned	Wal-Mart Owned	Independently owned
Customer choices and options offered	GM believed they offered too much consumer choice based on 2009 action of eliminating brands and dealers.	Number of brands and choices offered is in the thousands and now expanding into groceries. Strategy is to offer the consumer more choice, more selection	Menu choices constantly being revised and/or expanded. The consumer options are constantly being refined to suit the needs of the customers. The burger joint becomes a breakfast choice.

Comparison of marketing strategies of three top consumer retail operations in North America.
(Author)

These three enterprises compete in very different market areas, and some would say it is ridiculous to compare them. But in reality, they are competing for the same mass-market dollar. So if Walmart announced it was going to offer the consumer fewer choices in their stores, or McDonald's announced it was going back to its small 1960s menu, would that be a good idea? Simply offering a consumer less choice and fewer options is, with a few exceptions, a bad idea, because the consumer can always shop elsewhere. But that was GM's strategy. What are other automakers doing at the same time? Honda introduced the Acura line; Toyota introduced the Lexus and Scion brands.

When General Motors dropped the Oldsmobile brand, it was believed it was a good thing for GM. In the long run, did it help GM? Initially, in December 2000 when the closing of the Oldsmobile brand was announced, GM share prices shot up (thank you, Wall Street). "Improving shareholder value" was the refrain. Unfortunately, after September 11, 2001, GM shares were trading for less than they were twenty-four months earlier. So there was no positive long-term impact on GM shares.

Did GM save money by closing the Oldsmobile plants and dealerships? It is believed by the time GM had finished closing down Oldsmobile, they had spent an additional $2 billion in borrowed money and had lost over 50 percent of current Oldsmobile owners (millions) to other makers. If GM had spent $1.5 billion on improving the Oldsmobile brand (assuming they did it wisely), they should have turned the corner and still had $500 million left.

At the time of the closure announcement, Oldsmobile was selling about 300,000 cars a year. Poor numbers compared with a million sales achieved previously, but about the same or more than the following brands sold in America at the same time: BMW, Mercedes Benz, Volvo, Jaguar, Acura, Hyundai, Mazda, Mitsubishi, Infiniti, Subaru, Porsche, Suzuki, Lexus, Audi, and VW. I do not think any of those brands could be more successful by closing down in North America.

So why were some experts telling GM to eliminate brands in both 1999 and 2009? I believe that the experts had mistaken impressions about how the automobile franchise system works.

Since all dealerships are independently owned and operated, there were no direct operating costs to GM, which is paid as soon as the vehicle arrives at the dealership; there is no investment cost on GM's part.

And, GM had effectively over the years downloaded many costs to the dealerships. Dealers had to pay for the brochures they gave to the customers; they had to pay for all of the special tools required to repair each vehicle they sold; they even were charged per vehicle to belong to regional marketing associations, which paid for advertising. The dealers paid for computer and satellite hookups to GM. In fact, dealers had to pay to have staff participate in GM sales contests!

The only direct cost to GM of having a dealership was the cost of having a district sales manager and a district service manager assigned to each dealership. These two reps might visit a given dealership once a week or once every month or two, because most communication was through the Internet direct links.

So if a dealership closed, there is no real savings to GM. Note that this contradicts the GM statement made to the U.S. Congress that eliminating dealers saved a company money. To be honest, I never heard a decent explanation of these "savings." A Chrysler expert using what sounded like voodoo economics to me tried to convince some U.S. congressmen that the car companies saved millions by closing dealerships. The main argument was that the corporation lost potential profits due to underperforming dealers, which cost the factory money. I do not understand how having no dealer in a small town is better than when that dealer was open and selling 200 new cars a year. Does Chrysler or GM think the residents will drive to the next county rather than shop at the remaining local dealers?

What I think the bean-counter was saying: If a dealer sold 400 new cars per year, and the factory thought he should sell 600 new cars, the factory was losing the profit on the additional 200 cars. (For the sake of this argument, let us say the factory made $3,000 per car). So, 200 cars times $3,000 equals $6,000,000. Now to me, if you close down a dealer selling 400 cars per year, you will really lose $12,000,000, unless some other dealer gains those sales. The GM Oldsmobile experience shows that GM lost 50 percent of Oldsmobile owners within the first few years to competitive brands, even when GM gave high-value cash vouchers to these owners to buy another GM vehicle.

In small communities where there was only one dealer representing the manufacturer, the loss of customers was even greater than 50 percent.

In closing dealerships, the brand enters a loss-loss scenario. They lose sales and profits, they strengthen the competition, and lose market share. The ex-dealer owner and his employees who sold all of their friends and relatives cars will now push those people to other brands. I believe that closing brands and dealerships is and was the wrong thing to do.

Another bad decision, in my opinion, that GM made in 2005 was the sale of 51 percent GMAC to a consortium led by Cerberus Capital. (Cerberus is the name for the mythical dog that guards the gates of Hell; what there is in Hell that needs guarding, I do not know.)

GM received $10 billion in much-needed cash, and the move was encouraged and applauded by Wall Street. Of course, Cerberus was one of Wall Street's own.

Why this was a bad decision was as follows:

1. GMAC was formed by GM early in the twentieth century to facilitate the sale of GM automobiles. As a captive finance company, GMAC made financing decisions that were in the best interests of GM. If local banking conditions precluded regional banks from financing the purchase of automobiles, GMAC was always available. Having GMAC making decisions based on the best interests of Cerberus shareholders instead of GM was going to have a profound impact on the sale of GM cars. Of course, Cerberus would want a healthy return on their investment of the $10 billion they had paid GM.

2. GMAC made profits every year. In fact, it was not unusual in a year where GM lost money in all operations for GMAC to make so much money that the consolidated financial statements were in the black. (Now that explains why Cerberus paid $10 billion cash for 51 percent of GMAC.)

3. One of the myths GM floated was that because GMAC sold bonds to generate cash for car loans, and because these bonds were backed by GM (which Wall Street began to rate poorly), GMAC was paying excessive interest on these bonds. Being distanced from GM would allow GMAC to fund car loans more cheaply. Unfortunately, since GMAC was now not the cash cow for GM it always was, Wall Street devalued both GM bonds and shares even more.

Since GMAC's lending portfolio was made up of auto and housing loans, GMAC's bond and share value dropped (which was now 50 percent owned by Cerberus). Eventually, GMAC had to be bailed out by the U.S. government in 2008–2009 with the other banks and Wall Street institutions, and the value of their shares and bonds was minimal. The law of unintended consequences strikes again.

4. A related questionable GM decision was in 1995 when the GM board had GMAC enter the residential real estate market. GMAC purchased various real estate agencies. By 1999, it had 1,450 real estate offices, 24,000 real estate agents, and 1,500,000 mortgage customers. This was also the year the Clinton administration relaxed the criteria for home mortgages, which stimulated the real estate housing boom and partly caused the banking collapse of 2008. (There was nothing wrong with Clinton's plan or objective—until Wall Street banks discovered there were billions to be made by selling bundles of sub-prime high-risk mortgages as high-quality assets for investment.)

Under Cerberus management as of October 15, 2008, GMAC had $173 billion of debt against $140 billion of income-producing assets (loans and leases)—some which are almost worthless—in addition to GMAC Bank's $17 billion in deposits (a liability). Even if GMAC liquidated the loans and leases, it could not pay back all of its debt. GMAC received $16.9 billion in aid from the U.S. government by the end of 2009.

In 2007, Cerberus also purchased 80 percent of Chrysler from Daimler Mercedes Benz in 2007 for $ 7.4 billion.

Cerberus gave (lost?) these shares to the U.S. government in 2009 in return for keeping Chrysler Financial. After declaring bankruptcy on April 30, 2009, Chrysler Automotive announced that GMAC was going to be their chief wholesale and retail automotive financing source after that date. In December 2010, Cerberus sold Chrysler Financial to the Toronto Dominion Bank of Canada for $6.3 billion.

Under Cerberus's ownership, both Chrysler and GMAC declared bankruptcy and had to be bailed out by the government. The Cerberus experience says a lot about Wall Street's expertise and knowledge in managing and running businesses.

5. Another ongoing bad decision GM kept making was trying to buy expertise in fields where they thought they were weak, by buying up companies. GM never seemed to grasp that if you want to hear music you do not have to buy the band; just turn on the radio.

Besides EDS and Hughes, GM made investments in auto companies. They had made sizeable investments in Lotus, Saab, Fiat, and Subaru. Each of these companies was and is noted for being quirky and atypical. Lotus was founded by an automotive genius named Colin Chapman; Saab had evolved from the aerospace industry; and Subaru was part of the huge Fuji Industries conglomerate. They all had innovative and advanced technology and with that, a culture that was totally and diametrically opposite to GM's.

As discussed previously, the GM organization had been in constant flux since the 1980s. What was required was internal leadership, stability, and harmony. By trying to assimilate these new firms, it just caused more problems internally.

After spending billions on Saab, GM basically gave it to the Swedish government, which sold it to the Dutch company Stryker. GM paid $1.5 billion for a 20-percent share of Subaru and then sold that same share a few years later to Toyota for $750 million. (The 2011 Subaru Legacy was a top-rated vehicle in the *Car and Driver* comparison test.) GM purchased 20 percent of Fiat and gave Fiat an option to force GM to buy the remaining 80 percent of the Fiat shares. GM paid Fiat $2 billion not to exercise that option out of fear GM would be saddled with weak Fiat.

With that huge amount of money, CEO Sergio Marchionne revitalized Fiat and, in 2009 with the U.S. government's blessing, took control of Chrysler Corporation. GM also wrote off $20 million when they sold Lotus to Bugatti for an undisclosed price. After bankruptcy, Bugatti was acquired by Volkswagen Audi, and Proton, a Malaysian carmaker, acquired Lotus.

Remember, these billions of dollars spent on car company purchases were funded by mostly borrowed money. Ultimately, the inability to finance their debt forced GM to go to the government for help.

GM's management in the twenty years after Roger Smith was still trying to solve their problems by buying other companies. However, their problems could not be solved by external means.

Some advice GM followed worked out well for GM in spite of itself. By 1988, GM was short of money and as usual was told to get rid of the money-losing parts of the company. GM tried to sell Detroit Diesel, but found no buyers.

In the thirties, GM formed the Detroit Diesel Division, which developed and perfected the high-speed diesel engine. This division dominated the North American market. Over the years, new competition arrived, quality deteriorated, and Detroit Diesel engine sales plummeted. This was typical of the malaise that was affecting all GM operations. GM saw no hope or future for Detroit Diesel and in 1988 sold 60 percent of Detroit Diesel to Roger Penske for what was believed to be a token sum of one dollar. Twelve years later, in 2000, Penske, who had retained much of the old management after his purchase, and had increased sales and profits dramatically, sold the company for $723 million to Mercedes Benz.

Detroit Diesel in the eighties had the exact same problems that the parent company had: shrinking market share and sales, unhappy unionized workforce, poor-quality and unreliable products, and record losses. By 1992, after four years away from GM control, DD was profitable again, and by 1993, market share had gone from 5 percent to 26 percent! How did Penske do it?

Roger Penske, who is successful at most endeavours he is involved in, has always emphasized the importance of people in his organizations, and he did the same at Detroit Diesel. Unlike the typical new boss, when Penske took over control of Detroit Diesel, he retained many of the old personnel, continuing to employ engineers and management who had had a long association with GM, but more important, who had had a long association with the diesel engine business. He kept such long-standing Detroit Diesel employees as L.F. Koci, general manager at the time of the takeover—a surprising action to many at the time. By not purging its old brass, he maintained thousands of years of experience and expertise and he simply realigned the corporate goals. The focus became: Build what the consumer wants—reliable and durable engines that work. And he had the managers and the workers who knew how to do it.

Unlike other corporate saviours, he did not lay off workers indiscriminately; however, he eliminated redundant computer costs and consolidated manufacturing operations in an effort to cut the operating budget by more than $70 million. The key was listening to the customers and building the products they wanted.

In 2000, Penske orchestrated a sale of Detroit Diesel to Mercedes Benz. GM, which still owned 40 percent of DD shares, received a $289-million windfall on the sale to Mercedes. Too bad GM did not see the template that Penske laid out for them. There were rumours at the time that Penske was offered the top job at GM but he refused.

So while GM was buying and selling companies, closing divisions, and spending millions in numerous non-productive areas, product development, quality, and vehicle improvement suffered. Customers were being offered better solutions to their transportation needs by other makers.

LESSON: Nobody should know more about your business than your own people. If you find yourself listening to outsiders on what to do, then you have a real problem.

18

They Had Tough, Relentless Competition Whom They Underestimated

One of the biggest mistakes that GM made was continually underestimating the Japanese and other foreign competition. In my experience operating a Mazda dealership, I learned the tenacity, the determination, and the effort the Japanese car companies have to succeed. The Big Three had those traits as well and never realized the Japanese could be so tough.

In fact, the Japanese industry (about which many books have been written) had some excellent advantages over the Americans:

- Top Management in Japan is paid significantly less than American top management. Self-enrichment does not appear to be the primary management goal.

- The Japanese carmakers have a protected home market that generates huge profits for the companies that they use to finance overseas expansion.

- For many years, if a Japanese auto executive was sent to North America, it was considered to be a cross between a demotion, punishment, and a last chance. If the executive was not successful in America, his career in Japan was basically over and the executive would spend the rest of his working life shamefully in a cubicle in an obscure office in Japan. These executives were MOTIVATED!

- The Japanese products were very good.

The Japanese in North America had no traditional way of doing business. They watched and learned what worked (the franchise system, market segments, and price points) and adopted those things. They adapted successful Japanese techniques to North America in both manufacturing and supply.

Sun Tzu states, in his classic book *The Art of War*, **"He who exercises no forethought but makes light of his opponents is sure to be captured by them."**

In my more than thirty years in the GM organization, I never heard a senior GM manager officially acknowledge the quality of the Japanese competition. I did hear a senior zone manager speak before hundreds of retail salespeople and refer to the Hyundai Sonata as a Hyundai "Snot." I did hear GM people say that people who bought imported cars were unpatriotic.

GM senior managers had all the answers when faced with Japanese competitors:

"The Japanese had low labour costs in Japan—wait until they have to build cars in America." Labour costs are now higher in Japan, and many of the large-volume Hondas and Toyotas are made in North America. In reality, labour costs were never a real factor. Even when Japanese cars were more expensive than domestic makes, consumers still bought them.

"Japanese cars cannot stand up to our driving conditions." This was initially true, but when Hondas rusted, they gave the owners free fenders and repairs. When Mazdas broke, they flew parts in from Japan.

"They cannot afford to establish a national dealer organization." The Japanese concentrated on the coastal states and expanded; often new stores were owned and operated by Big Three dealers.

"They can only build little cars." Lexus, Honda Odyssey, Nissan 350Z, and Toyota Tacoma trucks are examples of Detroit's naiveté. Toyota regularly races and wins in NASCAR; Honda motors have powered the last six winners of the Indy 500. Subaru has a plant in Indiana, and BMW makes vehicles in South Carolina.

By underestimating the Japanese, GM did not make a number of decisive moves that could have helped them, such as:

- Encouraging successful GM dealers to invest in GM franchises rather than discouraging them, with the result that many import stores are owned and operated by successful GM dealers.

- Lobbying the U.S. government to limit the number of imported cars shipped into the United States, much the same way European countries do. (However, GM believed it could get into Asian markets by their link-ups with Isuzu, Suzuki, and Subaru and did not want to be perceived as anti-Japanese. The American people will never forget the War.) Just as there is a NAFTA trade pact on automobile trade between Mexico, the U.S., and Canada, GM should have insisted for the same with Japan. For each Japanese-produced car sold in North America, there must be one North American car produced or equivalent dollar value sold in Japan.

- Setting minimum quality and durability standards for GM cars higher than Japanese cars; the whole of GM's emphasis had to be on making the best product—and the product that the consumer wanted.

The focus of GM toward the competition should have been a long-term war, not a skirmish until the next quarterly financial statement.

The Japanese Were Not Fair Traders

GM had little experience with the Japanese way of doing business. The concept of fairness and a level playing field are not comprehended in the Japanese business mind quite the same way as in ours. Many of the cultural traits that were seen in the Japanese war effort during the Second World War did not evaporate with the signing of peace treaties. Some of these were:

- *No obstacle is too great to be overcome.* Only Japan, which was in a full-scale war with China in 1941 (the most populous nation on earth then), would attack the U.S. and the British Empire.

- *Do what is unexpected, for your opponent will not be ready.* The Japanese motorcycle industry lulled the American industry into believing that they could not produce large-displacement machines. Honda introduced the 750 in 1969, and today Japan dominates the industry. The Big Three felt the Japanese could not build anything but small cars, and today they offer a full line of trucks, vans, SUVs, and luxury vehicles. The Big Three did not believe the Japanese could build vehicles in America, yet today they all do.

- *Protect the homeland at all costs and fight the battle on the enemy's terrain.* Today it is almost impossible to buy an American-made GM car in Japan; it is prevented by various tactics and strategies on the part of the Japanese government and auto industry. By having a huge, closed domestic market, the Japanese make big profits at home that allow them to fund international expansion.

- *Exploit the enemy resources for the sole benefit of Japan.* Japan's war aims were economic domination of Asia. With few resources of their own, Japan wanted rubber, oil, food, and other necessities from their opponents. Today, the strategy is to make money in foreign lands and buy whatever the homeland needs on the open market. For example, the money Toyota makes in America is repatriated to Japan and used to support Japanese industry, infrastructure, universities, hospitals, and government.

- *Do not be concerned with what happens until you have reached your goals.* Just like in war, the Japanese operate on a scorched-earth policy. Destroy the enemy! Here is a list of some famous American companies that faced the Japanese and lost:

Xerox—photocopiers
Zenith—televisions
Kodak—cameras
IBM—personal computers
NCR—cash registers

The sad fact is that the Koreans and the Chinese have copied the Japanese techniques and are dominating even more segments of the market.

GM consistently either underestimated their Asian competition or foolishly tried to coexist with them.

LESSON: Competition is a zero sum game; somebody will lose; make sure it is not you!

GM Had Bad Luck

There are all kinds of expressions about luck.

"I'd rather be lucky than good"; "The harder I work, the luckier I get."

There is no denying that luck can have a huge impact on individuals and companies.

GM again made many structural changes to their balance sheet in the summer of 2008; however, when the U.S. financial markets in the United States collapsed in the fall of 2008, there was no way that GM could issue bonds to pay off the bonds coming due. New vehicle sales also collapsed with the economic crash, with the result that cash revenues fell dramatically. For all intents, GM was bankrupt already when it went to Washington in December 2008 asking for help.

GM might have survived this national banking collapse if they had not spent borrowed money on billion-dollar acquisitions, many of which were failures. They might have survived if they had been financially astute and had not used so much debt to finance operations (Ford was fiscally much more conservative).

They might have survived if GMAC had not had huge exposure in the real estate mortgage market. They might have survived if GMAC could have made car loans when the bank financing of retail purchases stopped in fall of 2008. Or maybe it was poor luck that GM did not have the right leadership to protect itself from the economic downturn of 2008.

In December 2008, when GM went to Washington, I was reminded of the story of the man who murders both his parents and asks for mercy at the sentencing because he is an orphan!

GM could not have it both ways. By divesting themselves of non-automotive assets, GM became vulnerable to the cyclical economic nature of the automotive business. By taking advantage of cheap money and financing the company's operations with debt, they became vulnerable to the credit markets. By investing corporate funds in pipedreams such as On Star; FIAT's technology; the front-wheel-drive-only mandate; and residential real estate sales, they ensured they would be cash poor when the crunch came.

By allowing their market share to drop by more than half in thirty years, they could not fund commitments they had previously made to employees, retirees, bondholders, and shareholders.

If you make bad decisions, you tend to have a lot of bad luck.

19

Corporate Delusions and Myths

One question I keep getting from people is: "The top management of GM was supposed to be the best and brightest in the corporate world. How could they let it go so wrong?"

The only answers I can give are:

- The car business is very tough; sometimes the difference between making $100,000,000 and losing $100,000,000 is trying to save ninety-five cents in cost per car.

- GM had extremely tough competition.

- GM forgot that customers want the best for their dollar, and too often built "good enough." Some GM products were outstanding, but too many were mediocre or less.

- By eliminating the divisional concept, they became more centralized, more massive in terms of corporate inertia, and more unmanageable. The huge company became less agile, less responsive, and more monolithic, exactly the opposite of what was needed in the dynamic and competitive automotive industry.

- GM's management was blinded by the fact they were #1 in sales in North America, and if you ignored the protected Japanese home market, they were #1 in the world. It is very difficult to say to any leader that he has to make adjustments to his plans after so much success!

Your name is Captain Edward John Smith. You are the captain of the finest ship in the world—the *Titanic*. You are setting record time across the Atlantic and the weather is wonderful. Your boss and the ship's designer are on board as you make this historic voyage. Everybody is happy, and you are confident. Every other seafaring captain in the world envies you. Are you going to worry about a million-to-one chance an iceberg will show up in your path? In the twelve years since the turn of the century, there had been only forty-nine reported collisions (eighty confirmed deaths) with icebergs out of thousands of ocean crossings Even if you hit an iceberg, you have been told the ship is unsinkable, so why worry?

As Captain Smith learned: the chaos theory exists. A unique amalgamation of ocean winds and temperatures, the speed *Titanic* was travelling at, and her three-propeller design with a relatively small rudder would not allow quick enough manoeuvres to avoid the iceberg.

I believe GM management also spent too much in reinventing the organization, rather than perfecting an existing organization that was quick and responsive to the rapidly changing market and business environment they were competing in. Often these very crises were brought about by the constant reorganizations and realignments that were supposedly going to improve things. All of the employees became anxious about their jobs and careers; everything seemed constantly in flux. Everybody was waiting for the next shoe to drop. What if they close this plant? Where would I be working? What would I do . . . should I buy a house or continue to rent? Would I be forced to retire? What if they cancel this brand? What about those GM shares and bonds I bought? Thousands of life decisions were unnecessarily introduced into the GM workers' lives since 1980. That affected morale!

Finally, in the managerial ranks, there was a basic requirement for an employee to be a team player. As an employee, you learned that if you wanted to rise up the corporate ladder, the only attitude acceptable was one that was fully supportive of the GM leadership's company stance.

Unfortunately, the company stance became one of arrogance, false confidence, and delusions.

Let me give you a poignant example. As a used car manager, one of my duties was to buy used vehicles at the wholesale auctions, recondition them, and retail them. I was aware that GM had a serious intake manifold gasket leaking problem on their U vans (Montana, Venture Silhouette, etc.). As the engine warmed and cooled, the gaskets would fray under the movement of the intake manifold, the cylinder head, and the engine block, all of which expanded at slightly different rates, due to their structural makeup. With the fraying of the gasket, material coolant would escape. If the coolant leaked outside the engine, the only harm was the loss of coolant, and some drips on your driveway; but it was still a significant issue. However, the majority of the time, the coolant leaked internally and contaminated the lubricating oil. If left unrepaired, the engine would seize and have to be replaced. Even if the engine was not damaged, the gasket replacement was usually a $1,000 repair. I do not have the exact failure rate statistics, but I would estimate that it was at least 70 percent and could be in excess of 90 percent.

Before I bid on any vehicle with the suspect engine series, I always checked the coolant to look for signs of oil contamination. On one particular day, I checked ten vans, all three years old with thirty- to forty-thousand miles on them, and six had contaminated oil! (The models were Chevrolet Ventures and Pontiac Trans-Sports.) The specific vans I was considering that day were lease returns being auctioned off by GMAC. Knowing which vehicles had contaminated oil allowed me to adjust my bidding to take repair costs into account.

That afternoon, I returned to the dealership and I bumped into the GM district service manager. I asked him directly, "When is GM going to do something about the gasket leak problems on the U vans?"

His response was: "We do not have a gasket leak problem on U vans."

I then told him I had just checked ten three-year-old vans at the auction and six had contaminated oil!

His response was: "I guess the other four had been repaired already."

GM knew they had a problem; the official response was to deny it existed. This was so typical. Of course if word ever got back to head office that this district manager had admitted GM had a quality problem, he would be in big trouble. GM stopped selling minivans in North America after the 2006 model year due to poor consumer demand.

(At one time alone in Canada, there were 12,000 gasket replacement sets on back order by GM dealers alone. That means there were at least 12,000 vans tied up waiting for repairs. How many of these owners ever bought another GM vehicle?)

GM had another huge problem early in 2000 with fuel sending units in gas tanks. The sending units that gave input to the gas gauge would become corroded and would give false gas gauge readings. Imagine you are on the expressway, and your gas gauge reads half full—but your engine dies because you are out of gas! Thrilling! The official GM response was that the cause of the corrosion was the fault of the oil companies, which were selling contaminated gas. It is interesting that only certain makes and models of GM cars were affected with this problem. The so-called "bad gas" went into everybody's car and did not cause a problem in the majority of vehicles, just certain GM models—yet GM insisted it was not a vehicle defect.

If these examples of arrogance, false confidence, and delusions were obvious at the dealership level when dealing with the lower levels of GM management, imagine how clouded the decision making was at the higher levels of the corporation. Even today, after declaring bankruptcy and having to grovel to the government for financial support, those attitudes still exist.

Another example of arrogance was GM's declaration that they paid back the government.

GM PAYS BACK GOVERNMENT LOANS IN FULL

April 21, 2010 11:57 AM PDT
By Suzanne Ashe

General Motors today announced the company has made its final payment of $5.8 billion to the U.S. Treasury and Export Development Canada, paying back its government loans in full, ahead of schedule.

Company Chairman and CEO Ed Whitacre made the announcement at GM's Fairfax, Kansas, facility.

"GM is able to repay the taxpayers in full, with interest, ahead of schedule, because more customers are buying vehicles like the Chevrolet Malibu and Buick LaCrosse we build here in Fairfax," said Whitacre. "We are now build-

*ing some of the best cars, trucks, and crossovers we have
ever built, and customers are taking note. Our dealers are
increasing their sales, we are investing in our plants, and
we are restoring and creating jobs.* "[4]

This was a typical media article based on a GM press release.
Most people reading it would believe that GM has paid back all
the money they had received in government bailouts. I have had
several knowledgeable people tell me that as a fact.

However, in fact General Motors received $52 billion from
the Canadian and American government in aid. This was divided
into $5.8 billion in loans and $46.2 billion in share purchases.
GM does not feel it has any obligation to buy back these shares.
They paid all the loans back, but kept the $46.2 billion that were
not loans.

GM is still acting as if they believe they have corrected their
problems by crippling the unions, destroying the dealer organization, and stiffing the investors. GM acted, based on their press releases, as though their problems were gone after June 2009; even
though retail sales had shrunk further, employee morale was col-
lapsing, and the executive offices appeared to be in turmoil. The
board believed the worst was behind them.

Over the previous forty years, GM did not realize that the
light at the end of the tunnel was a train coming at them.

What is a billion dollars?

The problem when talking about vast sums of money is that
we lose track of the magnitude involved.

Let us say an individual makes $33,000 a year; if he/she works
for thirty years, he/she will have earned $1 million, a pretty im-
pressive number for many of us. How many people would have
to work thirty years to earn *$1 billion*, you may ask?

The simple answer is 1,000 people. One thousand people
would have to work for thirty years to earn $1 billion; or, stated
another way, 30,000 work-years are required to earn that amount.
Another interesting calculation is, since the government gave GM
our tax dollars, how many workers would have to pay taxes for

---

4   Susanne Ashe, *GM Pays Back Government Loans in Full*, CARTECH Blog,
CNET Reviews (April 21, 2010).

thirty years to generate $1 billion? Assuming a tax rate of 20 percent, 5,000 individuals would have to work and pay taxes for thirty years to generate $1 billion for the government.

When you realize that GM received $46 billion to keep, that would be the taxes paid by 230,000 workers for thirty years! Or, putting it another way, all the personal income tax revenue collected from the residents of Rochester, New York, for the next thirty years is already committed to the General Motors bailout. I wonder what the people of Rochester think about that.

The car-buying process has evolved in North America since 1990 with the widespread use of the Internet. Information about vehicles is easily available. Prior to the Internet, if you bought a new car and it was troublesome and unreliable, you could possibly tell 200 different people about your experience. Now you can tell thousands on various Internet forums. There are hundreds of sites with people saying what cars to buy and what cars to avoid. Unfortunately, GM was getting a lot of "avoid" comments. The consumer magazines and the buff magazines also became more critical of the cars they tested. In fact, everybody was doing comparison tests, ranking various makes side by side. GM rarely scored in the top half of these comparisons.

What was truly alarming was the fact that the editorial writers were being very specific in their criticism. These reviews had a definite impact on the GM purchaser's ownership experience even if he or she had already bought the car before reading the review.

Imagine that a consumer has just bought a new Grand Prix, and is really happy with it. A few months later, he reads a comparison test where it does not do so well. The article mentions that the brakes are spongy and do not have the stopping power of the top-rated brands and also have a history of rapid wear. The next time he is out driving he pays attention to the brakes—and as a matter of fact, they *are* spongy. His happiness with the purchase just dropped. When he has to get a brake job at 20,000 kilometres, the consumer is even less happy.

Here are some of the major expensive defects I can remember from 1980 on that affected millions of vehicles.

- Citation family: steering racks, engine leaks

- Celebrity family: steering racks

- Olds 88/98 front wheel drive family: steering racks and transmissions

- Cutlass front wheel drive family: steering racks, transmissions and rear calipers, ABS

- Early 1990s Cadillac STS: rear suspension

- Blazer: oil cooler line leaks

- All models: power windows, brake rotors and pads, fuel gauges, strut bearings, electronic dashboards, ABS sending units, wheel bearings, water pumps, interior fan motors

I am mentioning these weaknesses because they were chronic, serious, and expensive to repair in these models. As a used car manager, I factored these deficiencies into appraisal values, so in reality, the consumer lost monetary value because he/she owned these brands.

In fact, a major factor in the purchase price of a new vehicle is the trade-in value of the used vehicle.

Prior to the 1970s, GM brands consistently had the highest used-car values in the industry. The number one determinant of used vehicle value, after mileage and condition, is brand reputation. One way to kill a brand's used vehicle value is to have a poor durability and reliability history; the other is to discontinue the brand so the vehicle is now an "orphan." The last thing a consumer wants to hear at appraisal time: "They don't make that car anymore."

When GM discontinued Oldsmobile, Pontiac, Saturn, and the other brands, they decreased the value of millions of car owners' equity. At trade-in time, it was not unusual for these brands to be worth much less than the outstanding loan amount. The owner did worse over the ownership period because he/she had bought a brand that GM later discontinued.

20

What the Consumer Really Wants

The North American auto market is very diverse and has many segments; there is not a homogeneous consumer, and there is not one vehicle that can satisfy everybody.

One of the common themes that has come through loud and clear from every politician, expert, academic, guru, and blogger in the GM crisis is: "They built the wrong vehicles!"

This is absolute BULLSHIT!

GM built the cars people wanted to buy; otherwise, at bankruptcy time, GM would not have been #1 in sales in North America!

GM built the right products, just not very well! It was the quality, durability, and reliability that GM fell behind on for thirty years. Millions of people voted for GM with their dollars. Unfortunately, over the years their experience with the vehicle was unsatisfactory, and they drifted to other brands that offered them what they wanted.

All of the non-automotive people were weighing in on what GM should build, such as:

More fuel-efficient cars. The American driver has the cheapest retail gasoline price in the developed world. In Canada, the price of gasoline is close to the world average. Canadians buy more fuel-efficient cars on a percentage basis than Americans. In 2009, GM was #1 in sales in Canada as well. If the U.S. government were to increase, on a phased basis, the gas tax by two dollars per gallon, Americans would buy more fuel-efficient cars, and the government would solve many of its deficit and economic problems. That's how other countries do it!

Safer cars. GM has been a pioneer and leader in safety research, far ahead of the Japanese. To really appreciate the automobile in the safety context, it is important to realize that the driver is the number one determinant. The vast majority of accidents that result in injury and death are "speeds too fast for conditions" and "impaired driving" (DUI). The manufacturers have no control over these two items. Historically, the vast segment of car buyers will not pay extra for safety options. (Remember, almost as many American people died in motor vehicle collisions annually as died in the ten years of the Vietnam War.)

There have been two historic precedents about safety and vehicles that most people have forgotten.

The first involves seat belts. By the 1970s, safety research by the automakers, the governments, and independent researchers identified that seat belt usage was the most effective safety device and the most cost-effective means of dramatically reducing injuries and deaths in motor vehicle collisions. As a result of these findings, the National Highway Traffic Safety Administration (NHTSA) determined that increasing seat belt use would have a dramatic positive impact on safety. On January 1, 1972, NHTSA required that passenger vehicles for sale in the United States be equipped with passive restraints to protect vehicle occupants in frontal barrier crashes up to and including thirty miles per hour, or, alternatively, with a buzzer/light reminder system.

With few exceptions, most cars were sold without inflatable front cushions (airbags) because cost-efficient technology had not been perfected as yet. The automobile manufacturers opted for the reminder system. The system consisted of a flashing light and buzzer, which activated continuously for at least one minute if the vehicle was placed in gear and the driver or front outboard passenger was not belted. The simple sensor system used to activate the reminder system, however, could be bypassed, removed, or ignored by the vehicle operator. Moreover, once the belt was left in an extended position or buckled, the reminder system would not be activated again. So, many vehicle operators would simply buckle up the seat belts and sit on them.

When it became evident that most drivers were not buckling up, and the manufacturers were not installing the very expensive passive restraint systems, the NHTSA moved to require ignition interlock systems on all cars. Understand the NHTSA was mandated by the United States Congress to reduce injuries and deaths in motor vehicle collisions.

Effective August 15, 1973, NHTSA required that all model year 1974 passenger vehicles be equipped with an ignition interlock that allowed the vehicle to start only if the driver was seated and the belts were extended more than four inches from their normally stowed position or the belts were latched. This meant the car would not start unless the driver had his seat belt properly attached around his or her body. In addition, an audible warning was activated if seat belts were unfastened while the vehicle was running.

It was hypothesized that the ignition interlock would increase seat belt use by eliminating two of the most popular ways of defeating the early belt reminder systems: leaving the belt fastened and tucking it behind the seat, or tying a knot in the belt so that it was held out of the retractor. The NHTSA felt that this would result in significant seat belt usage and a dramatic reduction in injuries and deaths.

The American new car buyers went berserk with the introduction of the 1974 models. In an unprecedented reaction due to the public hue and cry, Congress quickly passed legislation prohibiting NHTSA from requiring either the ignition interlock or continuous buzzer systems.

NHTSA changed Federal Motor Vehicle Safety Standard (FMVSS) 208 to a less aggressive requirement. Passenger vehicles manufactured after February 1975 were required to have a warning light of four to eight seconds in duration that is activated when the ignition is turned on regardless of whether the seat belt is fastened, and a chime of similar duration that sounds unless the driver's belt is buckled.

The American people spoke loud and clear to their elected representatives; they did not want to and were not going to wear seat belts regardless of the safety benefits. The watered-down legislation stayed in effect until April 1989, when the NHTSA mandated all passenger vehicles to be equipped with a passive restraint for the driver. An air bag or an automatic seat belt would meet the requirements of the standard.

Note that an air bag is properly called a "supplemental restraint system," or SRS. It is vitally important that drivers and passengers be aware of this. In the majority of cases of death caused by air bags, seat belts were not worn. Manufacturers emphasize that air bags are not, and cannot, be an alternative to seat belts. A supplemental restraint system, all manufacturers emphasize, is only supplemental to a seat belt.

So, as much as the media and certain segments of the public criticize GM and the other automakers for not making safety their number one priority, time and again the American consumer has deliberately obstructed and foiled the availability of cheaper and safer automobiles.

The second involves brakes. In 1991, GM developed ABS IV, the first low-cost anti-lock braking system in the world. GM decided it had a marketing coup and in 1992 began offering no-charge ABS on all North American-produced vehicles. Even the low-priced Cavalier came standard with it.

GM's ad campaign that year stated, "Safety Is Not an Option." The Japanese imports either did not offer ABS or charged an additional $1,000 for the feature. As a dealer and aware of the huge benefit that ABS offers in accident avoidance, I was positively excited. In fact, in 1992, the Cavalier was the best-selling car in Canada and continued to be for several more years. However, when the Cobalt was introduced in 2005 to replace the Cavalier, ABS brakes became an option. What happened? The competition started bad-mouthing ABS and, to bolster their negative attitude, used news stories about Impala police cars that were crashing in the U.S. This created a huge amount of negative publicity initially, and GM was forced to delete ABS on police vehicles. The problem was, if you were not trained and had never driven an ABS-equipped vehicle, the feedback the car gave you could be disconcerting or confusing. The press and consumers created such an uproar that GM made this valuable safety device an option on many vehicles. The American public spoke again.

Greener cars. Now that the belief of Americans wanting safer cars is debunked, let us look at the myth that Americans want greener cars, such as electric cars, hybrids, and alternative fuel cars.

A mother once said, everybody wants to clean up the environment but nobody wants to do the dishes. That just about explains consumers' affection toward alternative energy vehicles. First of all, everybody wants one, but nobody wants to pay the real cost of these energy alternatives. Most people do not understand how incredibly complex the modern automobile is. The spacecraft that landed on the moon had less computing power than any new car today. Cars have to operate in a range of weather conditions today that no other consumer good is expected operate in. When you add these new technology factors, the complexity goes up exponentially. Second, consumers do not want any more involvement than they already have with today's cars. Extra maintenance and additional charging or fuelling systems at home will not be acceptable if extra consumer effort or costs are involved. Most consumers want the government to pay, but since the government will be collecting less gas tax, they will not have the money.

The fact is that today's vehicles are amazingly "green," and consumer driving behaviour will have a greater impact on the reduction in fossil fuel emissions than any new technology. (If existing mass transit, carpooling, and ride-sharing systems were truly utilized, alternative energy vehicles would be a non-issue.)

One afterthought: can you imagine the effect on our power grid of fifty million electric cars needing to be plugged in each day?

21

Traditions of GM

With the divisional system GM had established and optimized up to the 1960s, an ethos had developed within General Motors. It was a culture of Leadership, Pride, Achievement, and Confidence. There was no goal that GM could not achieve, no obstacle GM could not overcome.

This culture also developed some questionable aspects, however, as typified by these kinds of statements:

- As your boss at GM, I am right, always.
- If it came from outside GM, it cannot be any good.
- Do not argue or question; this is the GM way.
- Do you want to be a team player or not?
- We know what the customers want; we do not have to ask them.

All junior management employees who wanted to enjoy the benefits of a management career quickly learned to follow the program. They became narrow in outlook, insular, and with a few exceptions, restrained their creativity and independent thinking. As American society was changing at light speed in the 1960s and 1970s, GM was still reluctant to adjust to the societal and cultural changes. Corporate politics became very important. By shifting away from the divisional concept with their independent division managers and creative tension between divisions, uniformity and sameness became the philosophy.

GM's number one source of university graduates was its own university, GMI. Student applicants were almost always referred (vetted) by a GM employee, and the seventeen-year-old student spent the next four years learning business and life the GM way. When there was campus recruiting, the recruiters were looking for young men who fit the GM mould.

The problem was, the leaders of GM in the 1980s and 1990s were poor clones of the GM leaders of the previous decades: they were more insular, less creative, and less understanding of the human factors in the organizational environment. When the "great leaps" in reorganization were initiated, there was no understanding of the impacts of this on the people within the organization. These inbred and insular leaders believed and behaved as if they had supreme wisdom.

For example, when an interviewer asked Roger Smith what new GM car a consumer could buy for under $10,000, Roger replied insouciantly, "a two-year-old Buick." In a sense Roger was probably right—a two-year-old Buick was better value than any new car that GM could sell for $10,000; but his response completely missed the point, when the imports were selling perfectly fine new automobiles for less than $10,000 at the time.

As business and competitive challenges grew in the last two decades of the twentieth century, the company developed an even more bunker-like mentality. For example, any dealer who questioned GM policies was accused of disloyalty, not being a team player, and being part of the problem. Dealers were told that if they did not support GM policies 100 percent of the way, they should consider resigning their franchise. Absolutely no constructive input was accepted or desired from the dealer organization.

Of course, GM had dealer communication teams, where dealers were supposed to share their concerns with GM management and resolve any difficulties that might arise. In reality, these dealer communications sessions resulted in GM's publishing and distributing to all dealers a summary of the discussions, with reasons why GM had to continue things the way GM desired.

As with most organisms in nature that do not evolve, GM stagnated and fought to maintain the status quo in the environment they were living in. Consider this: Commercial fishermen, when discovering that a preferred fish species has disappeared, have two options. They can fish for other less desirable species, or they can start fish farming. Currently, 98 percent of Atlantic salmon consumed in the world is raised on farms. But the fishing industry had to be open to making this transition. GM tended not to be really open.

GM faced the last two decades of the century with a highly inbred and closed culture. Even when there were some initiatives to open up the culture with new leaders, the ability to internally innovate and adapt had gone from the company.

This ability to innovate and adapt was destroyed by years of corporate mandates to downsize, change, and rationalize, which always resulted in indiscriminate layoffs, buyouts, selloffs, and consolidations. With each and every "change," individual employees went into survival mode: "I will do my job, not cause waves, and wait my time for either retirement or a good buyout package. I will keep my eyes open for options outside the company with some other firm, or I will work for myself after quitting time to provide financial or mental independence."

The long-time dynamic employees of the strong and powerful divisions of GM were now bureaucrats of the worst kind.

In the late eighties, I attended a luncheon with three mid-level GM zone sales managers. The bulk of the conversation was focused on a small housing development that one of the older managers was developing in Florida. He had six weeks' annual vacation, which had allowed him to start the project. This project was directly in sync with his GM career, as he felt that when the next crisis hit GM, he would be offered a buyout to retire early, and he then would move to Florida to complete the project. His goals and GM's goals were literally miles apart!

Here is a more publicized account of the deterioration of the GM management mystique. Daniel Bealko was GM's Global Commodity Manager from 1996 to 2003. One of his assignments at that time was to divest GM of its extensive bulk aluminum holdings, which were estimated to be worth about $1 billion. Bealko conspired with a metals broker to skim millions of dollars in profits from the sales. Both Bealko and the metals broker were convicted and sentenced to jail. Estimated loss to GM was $83 million. A similar incident happened in Canada, where GM transportation employees were receiving large kickbacks from trucking companies shipping GM parts.

These were not junior low-level clerks or line workers, but managers who had power.

There are other examples of the deterioration in the character of GM's people.

In 1994, Ron Zarrella was hired to be a GM vice-president; he was promoted to president in 1998 and left GM in 2001. He was supposed to be the wellspring of change for GM. A marketing brand guru with an MBA from New York University's Stern School of Business, Zarrella was recruited from Bausch & Lomb. He attempted to revolutionize how GM designed automobiles, trying to introduce a strong "brand focus" to GM. Since Zarrella had no automobile experience, he was on a very steep learning curve.

His reign had little positive impact on GM. He returned to Bausch & Lomb, and it was later discovered that he had falsely claimed his MBA from the Stern School of Business. He attended the program from 1972 to 1976, but he never earned his MBA. His claim was never checked by GM or Bausch & Lomb. When Bausch & Lomb finally discovered the truth, he was forced to forfeit $1.1 million from a bonus that could have potentially reached $1.65 million at Bausch & Lomb.

It is hard to believe that GM would hire and promote to the position of president a man who had lied on his resumé. Imagine how all the other GM employees who were passed over felt.

By the mid-1980s, the deterioration in the traditional culture and ethos for what GM once stood for had begun. The higher one was on the hierarchal ladder, the less likely that one could see the problem. There began a major shift in view. Top executives were interested in share values, which impacted their pocketbooks through stock options. Share value was most impacted by current earnings reports and analysis by Wall Street and investment gurus.

The emphasis became one of maximizing short-term profits. Market share, sales volume, and customer appeal became secondary. By the year 2000, the emphasis of GM's marketing had switched from extolling the virtues of the product to "selling the deal." Rebates, cash-back plans, and special interest rates became the emphasis. Leasing grew exponentially, as GM discovered that this was a great way to keep the plants going. The virtues of the product became secondary to the "deal," and GM was going to have the best deals.

So GM stopped selling cars and started selling deals. But deals are expensive over the long term, and with a shrinking market share, GM had a lot of fixed costs that were not shrinking. Something had to be done.

The most insidious of the "deals" the Big Three offered customers were the lease deals. Leasing is a great concept for everybody. The consumer gets a new car every few years and pays less per month than if he bought and financed the car. The manufacturer loves it because traditional buyer/owners tend to keep their cars five to seven years, while four years is a long term when leasing. So a consumer who leases will have more new cars in a lifetime than one who buys.

Leasing involves a very simple calculation; you need to know only four things:

- What is the car worth today?

- What is the term of the lease?

- What will the car be worth at the end of the lease?

- What is the money cost (interest) for the lease term?

Example

Car costs $30,000.

Term is 36 months.

Car is worth $15,000 at end of lease (also known as the residual value); therefore, depreciation is $15,000 (50 percent).

Interest cost is $3,000 for three years.

Dealer wants $2,000 profit.

Monthly Lease payment is: Depreciation + Interest Cost + Profit divided by Term

($15,000 + $3,000 + $2,000)/36 = $555.55 per month.

There is one key variable, and that is the predicted value of a vehicle three or four years down the road. In our example, we used $15,000 or 50 percent, but what would the monthly payment be if the value were 45 percent or $13,500? The depreciation is now $16,500. And the monthly payment has shot up to $597.22. Customers will walk to another brand to save $5.00 a month. A $45.00 monthly increase will send customers away in droves.

As you can see, the residual value (what the vehicle is worth at the end of the lease) has a major impact on the monthly lease rates a manufacturer can offer (given that all things such as mileage and vehicle condition are equal).

So how does GM or GMAC determine what a vehicle is worth three years down the road? First, they study auction reports to see what similar three-year-old vehicles are worth as a percentage of their MSRP. What factors affect used car values? Consumer appeal is made up of a vehicle's reputation for quality, reliability, prestige, and value. One car that sold three years ago for the same MSRP as another could now easily be worth $5,000 less. The lease company that owns that vehicle could be faced with a big loss on disposal.

How this impacted GM and GMAC is dramatic. Because over the past twenty years the consumer appeal of GM vehicles was declining, GMAC, who set the residuals, always wanted to set conservative residuals. GM, which knew that low residuals meant high, uncompetitive lease rates, always wanted GMAC to set high residuals.

There were many cases where GMAC had thousands of three- and four-year leases returned, with losses on disposition in the millions of dollars.

In the mid-seventies, a local Toronto Ford dealer leased several hundred brand-new Ford Torinos to a local rental company for one year. Between the time the vehicles went on the road and twelve months later when they were returned, there was a lot of publicity about Torinos rusting. Instantly, the demand for Ford Torinos in Canada evaporated, and the value of one-year-old Torinos dropped by $1,500. The dealer lost so much money on the transaction he had to declare bankruptcy.

If your brand is booming with the resultant increase in, or maintenance of, strong residuals, your monthly lease rates will be very attractive as compared to your competition. If, on the other hand, your brands values are declining to keep your monthly lease rates attractive, you will have to subsidize the residuals or incentivize the selling price. Both options are very costly for the manufacturer.

Since the lease portion of the retail automobile business was approaching and exceeding 50 percent of sales, GM was trapped by its short-term focus. Residual values were dropping in the long term due to poor reputation, and GM could offer only short-term incentives, which is a very costly way to keep sales acceptable. Still, market share dropped.

22

More Myths and Delusions

Most successful organizations have positive myths and legends that anecdotally tell what the company stands for. The key myths GM perpetrated were as follows.

Myth #1:
"It is the fault of the unions and the workers."

"If it were not for those bastards, we would be okay. The retirees are living longer than we ever expected; and in fact, for each active worker, we have two and three retirees. Health-care costs are ridiculous, and active employees and seniors now want us to buy them Viagra! The Jap plants are not unionized. Why doesn't the UAW go after them?"

In reality, GM got the union they wanted.

If GM or any volume car company could eliminate all the labour costs from a new vehicle, the maximum the manufacturer could reduce the price would be about 10 percent. On a $30,000 car, that would be $3000. Manufacturers have been known to give $5,000–$9,000 rebates to spur sales (they are cutting into their margin), so the labour costs are in reality not a huge factor. But GM likes to make it sound like a big factor for public consumption. (A UAW study that has never been refuted by General Motors stated in 2006 that the actual labour costs per vehicle were 8.4 percent.)

Second, GM negotiates with the UAW, historically the most ethical, reasonable, democratic, and progressive labour union in America. There are many unions that would not be as accommodating to the employers as the UAW has been over the past fifty years. (I do not want to disparage any unions, but one only has to look at the past history of the Teamsters, East Coast Longshoremen unions, and New York, Montreal, and New Jersey construction unions for examples of corruption that the UAW has avoided.)

Third, unions began and continue to exist in companies where the management has failed their workers in some areas, and the workers sought redress by joining the union. This is an American tradition. Pro baseball players belong to the Major League Players Association, to ensure that the millionaire players are not abused by the owners. There are firefighters' unions and teachers' unions; even lawyers and physicians have professional associations that set wage and fee guidelines. What is the American Medical Association if not an advocate for physicians, their incomes, and working conditions? It is amazing, really, that some of the highest-income earners in our society belong to unions and associations that set working conditions, minimum pay scales, and benefits, just like auto workers and miners. The only difference is that nobody is blaming the decline of the economy on these millionaires, while auto workers and other unionized workers are often blamed for America's downfall.

In their relationship with the UAW, GM knew they gave as good as they got, and the UAW served many beneficial purposes for GM.

GM used the union as a tool against Ford and Chrysler.

Traditionally, at contract time, the UAW followed the concept of "pattern bargaining." The union would pick a strike target—the company they saw as the weakest, which was usually Ford or Chrysler. The union negotiated with them and would then have the other two companies match the deal the UAW got with the target company. This allowed GM to work without a threat of a strike, and the GM workers' union dues would support their union brothers if there was a strike at Ford or Chrysler. This had two benefits for GM. They usually picked up sales when one of the two weaker sisters was on strike, and because they were the largest, most efficient carmaker, they could match wages and still have lower average wage costs per unit than their competitors. For decades, GM in fact used the UAW as a tool to maintain a competitive advantage over their competitors.

The union, on the other hand, wanted to keep all three carmakers healthy and prosperous to ensure there were lots of union jobs.

The Union performed lobbying and "politicking" on behalf of GM.

The UAW was up front and centre in 2009, lobbying politicians so GM could get bailout money. The Union was always at the forefront condemning Japanese unfair trade activity, which GM, having at times financial investments in Japanese companies, would not do. Over the years, GM owned substantial shares of Subaru, Suzuki, and Isuzu, as well as Chinese and Korean auto companies, and could not readily complain about unfair trade practices to the U.S. government when they had their hand in the import cookie jar. The UAW served this purpose perfectly. When GM was trying to extract state government financial assistance for plants and renovations, the UAW was there in lockstep pleading their case.

When you consider how much union-bashing (much of it unofficial until Roger Smith's term) emanated from GM over the years, the UAW was in reality GM's staunchest ally.

The UAW was the most sensible union.

For all the blame GM heaped on the UAW, GM was dealing with one of the best unions in America. Neither corrupt nor mob-controlled, the UAW was progressive in many ways.

- As early as the 1960s, union leadership went to GM management and suggested a joint effort to convince Washington to institute a national health-care policy. This would have saved General Motors billions of dollars and this alone could have helped GM avoid bankruptcy in 2009.

- As said before, the UAW wanted to slow imports, while GM had interests in the imports.

- The UAW instituted all types of job sharing, retraining, and creative employment practices to save all of the companies millions.

- The Job-Banks system that was negotiated by GM and the Union had its start back in the sixties as well, where the workers and company contributed pennies an hour into a fund so that when sales slumped (the natural order in the auto industry), the employees would still be paid a high proportion of their salaries (up to 95 percent). The benefit to GM was that the workers would not quit and drift to other jobs during layoffs.

The company could close a plant to let inventories adjust, call back the workers after two months, and have 99 percent of the trained, experienced workers ready to work on a day's notice. This was a huge benefit to GM and all of the companies. It allowed the employer flexibility while maintaining a stable workforce.

One also has to remember that closing plants is not the big money saver the public is led to believe. Shuttered plants are full of million-dollar machinery that GM often borrowed money to pay for, so the payments continued, along with property taxes, security, heat, and power bills.

- The UAW represented workers in hundreds of companies throughout the U.S., including the agriculture industry, the aerospace industry, and even in car dealerships. As exemplified by the flexible contract the Union had negotiated with Saturn when that brand started, the UAW was always ready and willing to work with a co-operative employer. When there was friction with the UAW, it was usually initiated with management intractability.

They paid Union what they wanted, raised prices, and then blamed Union.

One of the favourite tricks of the automakers was to raise prices after a contract settlement with the workers. "We just gave the workers a 6 percent increase and we are only raising prices 4.5 percent; we are the good guys." Voodoo accounting at its best.

Let us consider a $20,000 car, with 10 percent labour content, or $2,000. The workers get 6 percent more, so the labour content cost is now $2120. (.06 x $2000 = $120.) GM raises prices 4.5 percent, or an extra $900, to $20,900. They give $120 to the workers and keep $780 for themselves and then tell everybody how bad the unions are!

I honestly believe if GM did not have a union, it would be cost-effective and beneficial for them to insist the workers form one—because of its value to GM.

They expected the UAW to be docile and complacent while the executives received millions!

One characteristic of the Big Three was their executive compensation plans. The top men made huge million-dollar incomes, often many hundred times what the so-called "greedy" UAW worker was earning. They even received bonuses and incentives when the company lost money; and they were never subject to layoffs! The Japanese executives were never in these pay categories. Just two examples:

Robert Eaton, the Chrysler CEO who sold Chrysler to Daimler Benz, earned $70 million on his stock options at the time of the sale.

GM's head man going into bankruptcy was Richard Wagoner, the company's chairman and chief executive. He received a 33 percent raise for 2008 and equity compensation of at least $1.68 million for his performance in 2007, a year for which the automaker reported a loss of $38.7 billion! The salary increase puts Mr. Wagoner's salary for 2008 at $2.2 million, compared with $1.65 million in 2007. In addition to his base pay, Mr. Wagoner was awarded 75,000 restricted stock units valued at $1.68 million, based on GM's closing stock price in March. He was also given stock options representing 500,000 shares. After President Obama fired him in 2009, the *Los Angeles Times* reported that Mr. Wagoner had worked out a deal with his ex-employer that will "only" pay out $8.2 million, plus $74,030 per year for life, along with health and life insurance plans. Wagoner's retirement became official on August 1, 2010, at which time he began reaping the benefits of his golden parachute.

Alan Mulally, when hired by Ford in 2006, received $28.2 million to become president and CEO. That is a pretty good signing bonus. At least he did not lead Ford into bankruptcy three years later.

Myth # 2: "It is the fault of the dealers."

In the early days of the automobile business, the manufacturers developed and refined the franchise system. It is an excellent way to distribute and market automobiles on the North American continent.

Why does the franchise system work so well for GM, you may ask?

- *It eliminates capital expenditure by GM for dealership facilities.* As hard as it may be to believe, the North American General Motors dealers had more money invested in real estate assets than GM had in plants, warehouses, offices, test tracks, and facilities. The dealer organization had more employees than the parent company and paid significantly higher taxes to various governments. To replace its dealer organization, GM would have to spend an estimated $100 billion, which is twice what the governments gave to bail them out. GM could not replace its dealers.

- *It ensures a positive cash flow for GM.* The biggest cost for many companies in the consumer business is the cost of wholesale receivables. GM has structured its franchise agreements so the dealer has to have sufficient capital available to pay GM the instant the vehicle arrives on the dealer's lot. Let us assume GM is going to sell three million vehicles this year, and the dealers carry sixty days' inventory, and the average wholesale cost is $15,000. That works out to be $7.5 billion that GM dealers have paid for. That is a lot of money GM does not have to worry about borrowing.

- *It allows GM to build inventory for cyclical sales seasons at no additional cost.* The sixty-day inventory target is ideal, but in slow months or in months prior to seasonal sales boosts, the dealers will often have ninety days' or more in inventory, resulting in bigger savings for GM. Plus with the dealers absorbing the valleys and peaks in cyclical car sales, GM can run its plants much more efficiently, with fewer shutdowns and less overtime.

- *It allows the dealer to do GM's dirty work in dealing with the customer.* The most burdensome task for any GM manager is to deal with a customer. Even the GM consumer help lines are staffed with non-GM employees. For a million different reasons, they do not want to deal with the actual operator of the car. By giving this role to the dealer, GM has saved itself and its employees much grief. And since they do not deal with the customer, they can set policies that will be distasteful to the consumer and not have to face the flack.

Many GMC Jimmys and Chevy Blazers of the mid-1990s were equipped with engine and transmission cooler lines that ran from the engine and transmission to the front of the radiator. At that time, the warranty was three years or 36,000 miles or the equivalent in kilometres. If the lines began leaking during the warranty period, they were replaced at no charge to the customer. After warranty, the customer paid around $300–$400. These vehicles were especially popular on our used car lot, and as I knew the failure rate on these oil lines approached 100 percent, we sold/included GMPP (General Motors Protection Plan) or Optimum extended warranties on every Jimmy and Blazer we sold.

In almost every case, the oil lines would leak; the customer paid the deductable and was happy with new lines. Before long, all GM dealers got a memo from GM and their extended warranty division that oil cooler lines were not "lines" but rather "hoses." Since lines were covered by warranty, but hoses were not (hoses being a maintenance item like light bulbs and brake pads), effective immediately they would *not* be covered by GMPP or Optimum warranty.

We had sold customers extended warranty to protect them against oil line failures, and now we had to tell the customers that the extended warranty we had provided them would not cover the failure that was anticipated.

GM saved thousands of dollars by changing the definition of what was a line and what was a hose. Of course, our customers were royally pissed. They took it out on the dealer. When some customers contacted GM (really an independent call centre), they were told that it was a dealer decision to charge the customer to replace the hoses, and had nothing to do with GM! "Those damn dealers screwing the customer again."

Another example of dealers being the fall guys: Dealers were not to solicit warranty work. If a customer driving a Pontiac Montana comes in for an oil change at 34,000 miles (he has 2,000 miles left on his warranty) and he does not mention a little seepage beginning around his intake manifold gaskets (our tech would have noticed it when he was checking the air filter), we could not tell him that the intake gasket was beginning to fail, and he should have it repaired now. No, the dealer service department was not to say anything.

The customer comes back in with 41,000 miles for his next oil change, and now the little seepage has become a leak that he noticed on his garage floor. He asks us to check it out. We tell him what it is, what it will cost, and that it is not covered by warranty. GM saves millions. "Those damn dealers screwing the customer again."

Over the years, we have heard the expression, "The dealer does not want to do warranty work." Why is that? GM pays the same to the dealer for warranty work as the customer would pay. Why would a dealer not want to do warranty work? The answer is surprisingly simple. Once into the 1980s, and dealer cost control became the mantra, the bean-counters really got into warranty expense analysis. Warranty expense was a huge item for GM by this time, and since they could not believe or accept that GM was building some crap cars, it must be the dealers stealing from GM.

The tool GM developed, and used more effectively than any Spanish Inquisitor, to elicit the proper response was: "warranty costs per new vehicle sold."

This way, GM could compare any GM dealership by dividing the amount of money they gave a particular GM dealer in warranty payments divided by the number of cars that dealer sold. This was in theory a very simple and consistent way to compare dealers as to who were efficient with GM's warranty money and those who squandered it.

The good dealers had lower warranty costs per new unit sold and the bad dealers had higher costs. The bad dealers would have

GM auditors sweep down on them to find out a) where the dealer was squandering the money, and b) where the dealer was improperly taking GM's money (stealing). All moneys deemed by the auditors improperly taken by the dealer were then charged back against the dealership. It was highly unusual if an audit did not recover some serious money back from the dealership. Usually the dealer fired the service manager for a bad audit result. So, career-wise, it was in the best interests of the service manager to avoid an audit. This was done by keeping his warranty costs down.

Did not well-run, honest dealerships avoid audit chargebacks? Of course not, because GM has very detailed sales and service agreements that are extremely specific. Many years ago, we had one excellent mechanic do our pre-delivery inspections at an off-site location. The new vehicles were delivered to this location and Cor (his name) would prepare the car for delivery. Now Cor was a very conscientious employee, and at this time in the late seventies there was a lot of crap coming in from GM disguised as new vehicles. He would align hoods, adjust doors so they would close, reattach headliners, connect loose electrical wires, and so on. Now, GM paid the dealership for two to three hours to prepare the vehicle, but Cor often found that water leaks and electrical problems could take much longer to repair, so these additional hours spent on the repairs were charged to GM. (Remember the plant producing 30 percent defects story.)

Now, like all good flat-rate mechanics, Cor kept excellent records on timecards with time punches. When the auditors arrived, they discovered that each additional time punch was not initialled by the service manager. The auditor did not deny the work had to be done and he agreed the work was probably done. It did not matter that Cor worked off-site, all that mattered was that every minute of additional work had to be signed off by the service manager, even if it was a ten-minute job. They charged back the dealership $6,000, and we had to fire Cor because as far as GM was concerned, he was stealing.

The warranty cost per new vehicle sold was a beautiful tool for GM. They could compare a dealer to anyone they wanted to get the results. The way for a dealer to circumvent the system was to sell a lot of cars to customers who would not come back for service. Fleet sales are an excellent way to lower the cost ratio. Let's say, two competing dealers are Central Chevrolet and Country Chevrolet. A large pharmaceutical company is located next to Central Chevrolet but purchases 100 minivans from Country Chevrolet. All maintenance, service repairs, and warranty work is done at nearby Central Chevrolet. In that year, both Central and Country have sold 400 new cars (not counting the minivans), and both are spending about seventy dollars on warranty per vehicle sold.

At the end of the year, their warranty reports would look like this:

Country Chevrolet: $56 per unit; Central Chevrolet: $87.50 per unit.

How would you like to explain to GM why your warranty costs are 55 percent higher than the neighbouring dealer? Here is how they got those numbers.

Country Chevrolet

Total warranty costs $70 times 400 cars serviced= $28,000.

Divided by the 500 cars sold = $56 (the extra 100 units they sold to the pharmaceutical company).

Central Chevrolet

Total warranty costs $70 times 500 cars serviced = $35,000. (They serviced the pharmaceutical company's cars, even though they did not sell them.)

Divided by the 400 cars sold = $87.50.

Of course, Central Chevrolet was on the watch list, and the service manager knew it. If you came in for warranty and it was a "grey area," forget about it.

If you were a dealer, and because of your sales mix (lots of trucks), you were a "low-cost" warranty dealer, this gave you a lot of leeway to keep your customer happy.

A true story: We sold a Hi-Cube van to a local business. The vehicle had 48,000 kilometres (about 30,000 miles) on it, and the motor was seized. We took the oil pan off, and found that the oil had turned to tar. The vehicle was used in commercial service and had never had an oil change. We refused to install a new engine under warranty, as the failure was due to lack of maintenance. The customer called us all kinds of names and called a small out-of-town dealership that had a very favourable warranty cost ratio because they sold many cars into the big city that never returned for warranty. Their shop, like ours, was slow, so they did the job under warranty! A case where our dealership did the right thing, took the abuse, and lost a customer.

Dealerships provided GM with a ready scapegoat. GM really wanted satisfied customers, and really believed that owners of GM cars should be completely satisfied. If the customer was not completely satisfied, they blamed it on the dealer.

GM told the dealers that if we did the proper job explaining GM policy and procedures, there should be no customer complaints. If there was a complaint it must be the dealers' faulty explanation. Let me give you an example.

Customer buys a used Venture van with 48,000 kilometres; the three-year warranty time period has expired. The intake manifold gaskets are leaking and the customer is faced as a second owner with a $900 bill. The customer is not happy. GM expects that a good dealer will explain to the customer that the vehicle is out of warranty and GM has no obligation or responsibility. Plus, as the second owner you bought the vehicle for less than a new vehicle, so you have no right to expect the same consideration as the first owner in terms of warranty. And, you should have bought an extended warranty when you bought a used vehicle. Now, according to GM's thinking, a good dealer would explain these facts to the customer in such a way that the customer would be happy and satisfied after paying the bill. In fact, GM encouraged the dealers to hire service advisors who had such good people skills that no customer would ever be unhappy with GM.

The corollary was that if GM got a customer complaint, it was obvious the dealer had been weak in dealing with the customer!

Just a side note: Over the years when administering GM policy and procedures, angry customers would threaten to call GM and tell them how we at the dealership were treating GM customers. I always chuckled to myself because I really knew that GM was not going to support the consumer beyond saying (a) try talking to the dealership again, or (b) try another dealership. As I said, GM hated dealing with consumers; that's why they have dealers.

Often, a customer would come in for a check on some vibration or noise that the dealership could not correct. A mechanic would spend hours trying to diagnose the problem he could not replicate; or, after diagnosis, finds that a simple bushing needed replacement. Mechanics are paid on a flat rate system. GM decides that a job is supposed to take an hour to do. If the mechanic can do it in ten minutes, he still gets paid for an hour; if it takes three hours, he still gets paid for the one hour. This supposedly protects both GM and the consumers from lazy or incompetent mechanics. Unfortunately, diagnosis takes time and is not paid for by GM. The good mechanics, if they are busy, do not want to do any warranty work that involves diagnostics, as it costs the mechanic money. So customers wonder why their car was tied up in the shop for so long. The mechanics were busy on more lucrative jobs.

The dealers expend thousands of dollars and man-hours in community service and activity that GM could never ever replace. Sure, GM ran ads on the Super Bowl—but who sponsors the Little League team your son plays on, who is the chairman of the local United Way, who provides the van for the local food drive? Chances are it is your local GM dealer. Throughout the nation, local dealerships and their owners have been the lifeblood of their communities. This goodwill built up over decades by individual dealers has been a positive boon for GM.

Myth #3:
GM can say anything, and people will believe it.

GM seemed to think that if they gave a good explanation for every vehicle problem, the public would accept that and not hold GM responsible. So the key, in GM's eyes, was to have a good story. It almost seemed that whenever there was a crisis with a vehicle, they followed the following template that I call:

The Six Stages of Corporate Denial.

- Stage 1: Deny there is a problem.
  "We do not have a gas gauge problem, we do not have a brake problem and we do not have a steering rack problem."

- Stage 2: Blame the victim.
  "Obviously the customer has been using bad gas or improper maintenance; or it is due to driver abuse."

- Stage 3: Hide the truth.
  Even though GM was aware of the problem with gas gauges for over a year and introduced a fix on the production line, they waited until the media made it an issue before they publicly acknowledged a problem could exist—"in a few instances."

- Stage 4: Blame somebody or something else.
  "There is no problem with GM gas gauges; it is the dirty fuel the refining companies are selling, or it is an environmental problem."

- Stage 5: Minimize the scope of the problem.
  "Only some customers were affected, a few hundred, max." In reality, thousands were.

- Stage 6: Implement a superficial solution.
  After a customer had run out of gas twice, GM would replace the sending unit for free, maybe, if the DSM said it would be okay and if the dealer could not convince the customer to pay first.

Over and over, the official GM position on most issues followed this template. In light of this behaviour, it is not surprising that General Motors, at the time of its bankruptcy, faced over 300 consumer lawsuits, several being class actions seeking over $1.25 billion in damages. As one observer remarked: "That is a lot of pissed-off ex-customers!"

There is an organization in the United States called the Josephson Institute that promotes ethics in young people. They teach the Six Pillars of Character, which are:

Trustworthiness

- Be honest • Do not deceive, cheat, or steal • Be reliable—do what you say you'll do • Have the courage to do the right thing • Build a good reputation • Be loyal—stand by your family, friends, and country.

Respect

- Treat others with respect; follow the Golden Rule • Be tolerant of differences • Use good manners, not bad language • Be considerate of the feelings of others • Don't threaten, hit, or hurt anyone • Deal peacefully with anger, insults, and disagreements.

Responsibility

- Do what you are supposed to do • Persevere: keep on trying! • Always do your best • Use self-control • Be self-disciplined • Think before you act—consider the consequences • Be accountable for your choices.

Fairness

- Play by the rules • Take turns and share • Be open-minded; listen to others • Don't take advantage of others • Don't blame others carelessly.

Caring

- Be kind • Be compassionate and show you care • Express gratitude • Forgive others • Help people in need.

Citizenship

- Do your share to make your school and community better • Co-operate • Get involved in community affairs • Stay informed; vote • Be a good neighbour • Obey laws and rules • Respect authority • Protect the environment.

Awesome stuff! Too bad GM leadership for the past thirty years was not exposed to this knowledge and training—it might have saved taxpayers billions of dollars and thousands of jobs.

23

The Customer Satisfaction Index

The Customer Satisfaction Index Surveys were used as a tool to intimidate the dealers, not to improve the customer experience.

*In 1864, the French poet Baudelaire wrote a short story titled, "Le Joueur généreux." In the story a preacher speaking from the pulpit terrifies the devil when he speaks these words: **"My dear brothers, never forget, when you hear the progress of enlightenment vaunted, that the devil's best trick is to persuade you that he doesn't exist!"***

One of the biggest challenges of any consumer products company is to convince the consumer you care about them. One way is to genuinely care about the customers by offering them the best product or service at the best possible price.

That is a very expensive proposition, especially in the age of maximizing short-term profits. The other way you can convince the customer you care is to institute procedures and tools that give the appearance of caring.

Two of the tools and procedures that can be effective are call centres and help lines; and customer surveys. Call centres are very cheap, especially if they are subcontracted to a separate company or to an offshore agency, and the staff at the call centre is not empowered to really do anything. The customer survey is a more serious proposition.

In-house Customer Surveys

These surveys give appearance that you care, but they sometimes are not even read by senior management. Plus you can word the questions to solicit the answers you want. You score them how you want and can release them to the media when they serve your purpose.

These surveys can be used legitimately by a company that is actually interested in their customers, or they can be window dressing. In the automotive industry, J.D. Power basically invented the concept of customer satisfaction ratings. There are other companies that also do similar work. Unfortunately for GM, their cars tended to do poorly on these third-party ratings, and these ratings were getting huge media attention. Somebody at GM decided that there was a solution that would solve three problems at once. The solution was to do an in-house satisfaction survey.

The problems it solved were: better scores; some scientific validity; and controlled media access. Plus, the customer would think GM cared.

It would show that GM vehicles scored better than the independent surveys, and that results could be justified by the fact that every GM buyer got a survey—not just random buyers, as in the third-party surveys. In fact, GM could tout the fact that their survey, since it was so inclusive, had more scientific validity.

If the scores were not good, GM could keep them under wraps away from the media. And GM discovered that they could use a survey as a tool to impact the dealers.

Let me expand on this last point. Tons of research and consumer studies had shown that people tended to prefer import dealers over domestic dealers. I also had anecdotal evidence of this fact, based on working in domestic and import dealerships. The consumers believe since the car is better, the dealer is better. GM took it to heart that import dealers were perceived as better and decided they had to upgrade their dealers. What better way than a customer survey to show how their dealers were failing?

As you know if you have watched any courtroom TV show, what and how a question is asked determines to a great extent what the answer will be. Are you still beating your wife? Have you ever looked at a woman lustfully? GM decided that with the right survey, they could achieve all their goals.

GM sent out surveys to customers to complete six weeks after delivery of their vehicle. Upon receiving the survey, almost all customers felt GM really cared about them just because GM asked for their opinion.

These surveys were statistically invalid, mathematically unsound, and scientifically worthless. Proof: Saturn division consistently had the highest General Motors CSI scores, and both the brand and the dealers are now defunct. More proof: GM's CSI scores went up annually from the time the surveys were introduced until GM went bankrupt. Scores went up, sales tanked. So whatever these surveys were measuring, and how GM was using them, was neither valid nor effective.

Customer satisfaction surveys were a constant battle between the dealers and GM. GM asked the questions and had an outside company calculate the scores based on a formula GM had developed (remember, GM people did not want to get too close to the customers); then the factory rep reviewed the results monthly with the dealer.

The results were never good enough because the silly consumers thought they were evaluating the vehicle they had just spent $30,000 on when in fact they were evaluating the dealership . . . what hours it was open, and if the people were nice. What GM was saying to the customer was, "You liked ABC Chevrolet enough to spend $30,000. What do you think of them?" Also, the surveys were scored and weighted in such a way that one "Not at all satisfied" customer could ruin your score for months. As well, different questions had different weights; and there were no specific questions about the vehicle. Especially ironic was the fact the customer was asked for comments and recommendations about his/her vehicle. GM was not concerned with these comments. I doubt if many senior GM managers saw surveys after the outside survey company was done with them!

Since these surveys were such powerful tools in the hands of GM, dealers resorted to numerous and creative means to influence the survey results.

Examples of these, both ethical and unethical, were:

- Total commitments by the dealer and his staff to ensure all customers were completely satisfied with their experience at the dealership
- Intensive dealership employee training programs, often using outside consultants and trainers
- Special new vehicle delivery protocols and procedures for staff to follow

- Incentivizing employees and managers based on their CSI scores

- Assigning management staff to follow up and monitor CSI reporting

These were all good programs endorsed by GM but were minimally effective at improving scores, because the dealer could not fix the problems with the product before it broke.

More effective dealer-level policies were as follows.

At the time of delivery, the salesperson would review a sample CSI survey and explain that the survey was his/her report card. The salesperson would explain that if the customer was not happy, tell him/her; if the customer was happy, tell GM that on the survey. Most salespeople would call the customer prior to the new owner's receiving the survey and remind him/her how to complete the survey.

Some dealers provided extra encouragement to the customers for good scores. Dealers would provide free oil changes, or a dinner for two, and other incentives for every unfilled survey brought in to the dealership. The dealer would then complete them for a perfect score.

Some dealers knew right at the time of delivery that the customer was especially cantankerous, and the dealership would have the customer's address changed so he would not receive a survey at all.

For example, Joe Buyer needs a new truck for his business right away. He is renting a truck until he takes delivery of the new one. Unfortunately, Joe has a bad credit rating, and insurance on a new commercial vehicle is very high. Joe is initially turned down for financing, and it took four days for Joe to be approved with an alternate lender. Joe wanted a blue truck, but the only one available with the options he needed was black. Joe is not very happy at the time of delivery: He feels he is being ripped off for the rental, the insurance, the interest rate, and the financing (he is high-risk); and he did not get the truck he wanted. What scores do you think he would give the dealership?

Here are some actual survey questions with my comments.

Remember that a score of very satisfied or less was deemed unacceptable by GM.

ABOUT YOUR DEALERSHIP FACILITIES

Thinking about your dealership, how satisfied were you with:

The convenience of your dealership's showroom hours?
The cleanliness and attractiveness of the facilities?
Variety of vehicle/options available for your inspection?

The first question that GM asks the customer is about dealership facilities—very revealing. Why did GM want to know about the showroom hours, the cleanliness and attractiveness of the facilities? How many evaluate these criteria prior to buying a new GM vehicle? What about the Internet buyers who never set foot in the dealership? Maybe you were not really interested in the dealership facilities when you bought your work truck, and marked Satisfied. Too bad for the dealer! I am not at all satisfied my dealer never closes because he has a lot of part-time staff? What does GM really want to know, or is it just asking questions to have a survey?

Dealers maintain the same hours as their competition and, in some communities, are open twenty-four hours per day; how would you score those dealerships? I am satisfied my dealer never closes? Ontario legislation prohibited car dealers from opening on Sundays, which most dealers supported. But we had customers complain about the dealership's being closed on Sundays.

Regarding the variety and options available for your inspection: At our dealership, we strived to inventory popular colours only, which usually were two or three of the ten or so colours the factory offered. One customer who bought a diamond-white Cadillac STS, the most popular colour, put "somewhat satisfied" on her survey.

I asked, "What was the problem?"

She said that we did not have a lot of colour choice.

"But Mrs. Jones," I replied, "you told me you only wanted a diamond-white Cadillac."

"Oh, that's true, but it would have been nice to see the other colours Cadillac offers."

Yes, I guess it would be nice to stock dozens of $70,000 Cadillacs in all the colours available so people could look at them—but not very practical. Now the factory would like to carry a lot of inventory, so probably that is why they selected that question.

ABOUT THE SALES CONSULTANT

1. How satisfied were you that you were treated in a courteous and professional manner?

2. How satisfied were you with the sales consultant's
   - Willingness to take the time necessary to thoroughly understand your vehicle needs?
   - Knowledge of his division's vehicles?
   - Knowledge of other vehicles in the market?
   - Assistance in selecting an appropriate vehicle?

3. Were you offered a demonstration ride/drive in the vehicle of your choice?

4. When you picked up your new vehicle, were you greeted with friendliness and enthusiasm?

5. At the time of delivery, were you offered
   - An orientation tour of the dealership, including the service department?
   - An orientation drive to become familiar with your new vehicle before taking it home?

6. How satisfied were you with the explanation of
   - Your vehicle's features and operations?
   - The warranty, owner's manual, and maintenance schedule?
   - General Motors Roadside Assistance?

7. At the time of delivery, how satisfied were you with
   - The appearance of your new vehicle?
   - The operation of your new vehicle?

8. Since taking delivery of your new vehicle, has your sales consultant contacted you to thank you for your purchase and resolve any concerns?

9. Overall, how satisfied were you with the assistance you received from your sales consultant?

These questions also give little useful information, because most people will not buy a vehicle from an unacceptable salesperson. The fact the consumer bought a GM car says a lot of positive things about the salesman and the dealership in the first place. (A side note: I operated a Mazda dealership for a few years and I staffed the showroom with salespeople who had sold GM previously. I cannot believe the number of Mazda buyers who told me how impressed they were with my salesmen compared with those at a domestic store.) As mentioned previously, the imports had a "halo effect" that even covered the salespeople. The first and second questions seem especially gratuitous; why the heck would you buy a car from somebody who did not satisfy you on these issues? What relevance is question 3 if you have already bought the car? Most people will not buy a vehicle without driving it.

A sales skill we imparted to our sales staff: Most people when they come to a dealership are in some way dissatisfied with their current vehicle. Having them drive a nice, new vehicle is the best way to reinforce that dissatisfaction and get a sale. In fact, we as policy would not accept an offer to purchase from the customer until they test drove the new vehicle. Of course you were greeted with friendliness in question 4—the salesman only gets paid after you take delivery.

When a repeat customer picked up a car, why would I offer him a thirty-to-sixty-minute tour of the dealership that he has been to numerous times? Only because it is a CSI question! With questions 6 and 7, if you were not completely satisfied, logic says, (a) you would have asked for further explanation, or (b) you would not have accepted the vehicle. The fact that you purchased and accepted the vehicle leads one to believe you were happy to that point.

Question 8 addresses concerns the customer might have. Most customers I dealt with over thirty years called immediately when they had a concern; they never waited for the salesman to call. As well, concerns occur usually in the first few days of ownership, prior to the salesman's calling. Finally, Question 9 assumes that the salesman exists to provide assistance to the customer. The reality is that most car concerns consumers have deal with the mechanical operation of the vehicle, which usually means referring the customer to the service department. If your air conditioner stops working the day after you picked up the car, how much assistance can the salesperson really give?

ABOUT THE FINANCIAL PROCESS

10. How satisfied were you that the vehicle price and/or payments were discussed in a thorough and straightforward manner?
    • Were you given a thorough explanation of financing options?

11. How satisfied were you with the review and explanation of all the paperwork?

12. Overall, how satisfied were you with how the financial process was handled by your dealership?

Why would GM be concerned about the financial process? They had very little or no impact on it. Again, the customer has already bought the car. I would hope any consumer before buying a vehicle would be happy with the financial process; otherwise, why would he/she buy it? We had one customer complain that the price of the car was too high, the interest rate was too high, and the term was too short; plus we wanted too much for a down payment and too much documentation. In reality, the down payment, the term, the pricing, and the interest rate were all set by GMAC or the bank. The dealership had no influence on these matters; but the customer still rated the dealer poorly.

SUMMING UP YOUR EXPERIENCE

13. Based on your overall purchase/lease and delivery experience, how satisfied were you with your dealership?

14. Based on your overall purchase and delivery experience, would you recommend this dealership?

15. Based on your experience to date, how satisfied are you with your new vehicle?

16. Do you have any recommendations about your dealership?

If you have a concern requiring immediate attention, we encourage you to first contact your dealer directly by calling Customer Assistance. If further assistance is required, you may contact GMCL at their Customer Assistance Centre [phone number].

Now question 13 was the key question used by GM to evaluate dealers.

This question was extremely crucial to the dealer, as every customer I ever spoke with rated the dealership poorly if they had a problem with the vehicle. Their reasoning was, "You sold me the car—you should have checked it out better before you gave it to me." This makes complete sense, and it is hard to disagree with. I remember driving my own Olds 98, which was only a few weeks old, and the alternator failed and left me stranded in the country. Who was responsible? Of course, the dealer, who ought to have known that the alternator was defective on this premium luxury car. I certainly was not satisfied. Here was a case where I looked at myself, because I was the dealer as well as the customer, and asked what could I as the dealer have done better or differently to prevent this problem that cost me half of my Sunday.

The problem was an internal failure of the circuitry in the alternator. I know at the Delco factory, the unit had been tested and passed; I know the alternator worked perfectly when the car was being prepared for delivery; but it failed. As a customer, I was not satisfied. Even though my lack of satisfaction had nothing to do with the dealership, rating the dealer was the only way a customer was able to express his opinion.

With question 15, finally, in this whole CSI questionnaire, GM is asking about the vehicle that the customer purchased. Six weeks into a purchase period that will likely last three years or more, GM is asking the customer how satisfied he/she is with the vehicle. What are they hoping to learn? That most GM customers were not happy with their purchase after the warranty ran out? That the Japanese were building better and more reliable cars? Or did GM want to know that Tony Soprano of New Jersey was completely satisfied with his 6,000-pound Cadillac Escalade?

GM for decades harped on CSI. In fact, the implication was that the loss of sales and market share by GM was the result of dealers' poor CSI scores. If a dealer dared comment about the product being produced by GM, the conversation quickly was turned to the dealer. "We are making the best cars we ever built. When your CSI scores are in the nineties and higher, you can question GM's competency; but your scores show you have much work to do at the dealership level."

CSI became such a hot issue at almost all dealerships, that compensation plans for most of the sales management, salesmen, service management, and service advisors had significant linkage with CSI scores. In our dealership, the difference between high and low CSI scores meant thousands of dollars per year in income to these individuals. It was the ultimate goal to earn and retain high CSI scores.

Surprisingly, many smaller-sized and rural dealerships, which tended to have the highest CSI scores, were terminated by GM in May of 2009. Saturn dealers who also tended to have even higher scores than the other GM brands — and highest in the industry at times on independent surveys — were all terminated, as well as the brand.

Even though the dealerships put real money and effort on the line to maintain high CSI scores, this concern may not have been matched by GM. In fact, there appears to be a real discontinuity between the brands and dealers terminated by GM and their CSI scores, leading one to believe that GM really did not put much importance on their customers' satisfaction.

The subjective ratings that the consumers gave on the CSI survey were converted to numeric values as follows:

Completely Satisfied=100
Very Satisfied=75
Satisfied=50
Somewhat Satisfied=25
Not at All Satisfied=0

This again shows the danger of applying numeric values to emotional responses and then using those numeric values as grades. For example, an individual's personality or mood may preclude them from being "completely satisfied" with anything. Alternatively, from a semantics point of view, being "satisfied" with an explanation of the vehicle's warranty could be the highest rating conceivable for many people. Not many of us go into raptures over explanations of maintenance schedules.

Just one example of the trouble with this sort of grading system: The dealer has ten surveys completed and returned in a given month. Five are Completely Satisfied, two are Very Satisfied, two are Somewhat Satisfied and one is Not Satisfied. The numerical raw score is 750, giving an average score of 75. During my years in the dealership, this was not considered a very good score. The problem was with the weighting: a Somewhat Satisfied score and a Not Satisfied score were killers.

Let me give an example. As a student in high school, I did poorly in French, and usually scraped by with a 50 percent. And I was usually one of the poorest in the class. Using the GM scoring system, I would have received a zero.

The injustice to the dealership was as follows. Say our dealership has done everything perfectly, but when it comes time for the customer to drive away, the service engine light comes on. We ask the customer to leave the car and come back tomorrow. The next morning, the mechanic discovers that for some reason the computer in the car triggered a "false positive." It could have been a loose gas cap, or any of a number of glitches that trigger a warning light. The customer is not at all satisfied when he has to make a second trip to pick up his car and on his survey, he marks Not at All Satisfied. But is it the dealer's responsibility? Is it the dealer who must be chastised? The customer has no place else to express his displeasure, so the dealer becomes the bad guy.

GM's explanation to the dealers was: "The questions are the same for all dealers' customers, and the raw scores are not nearly as important as your relative ranking against other dealers. Dealers should spend less time complaining about the survey methodology, and focus on satisfying their customers."

This statement has little validity and makes about as much

sense as comparing the health-care systems in various states or provinces by asking every adult: **How satisfied are you with your health?**

States with a higher composition of elderly residents would tend to have poorer scores. Does that mean those states are doing a poor job in the area of health care? Can you imagine someone in Florida complaining about that state's health care because the residents are not satisfied with their health?

24

The American Way of Doing Business: Reward with Money

In the 1980s, a profound change appeared in the way Americans thought about business. It led thirty years later to the greatest financial separation between the rich and everybody else and to the financial crisis of 2008. It was characterized by Michael Milliken, and fictional Gordon Gecko, junk bonds, and leveraged buyouts. Enron, Global Crossing, Bernie Madoff, Fannie Mae, AIG, and hundreds of other scams, swindles, and rip-offs seemed to emerge from the glorious eighties.

YEAR	Worker Average	CEO Average
1970	100	2,800
1980	100	4,200
1990	100	8,500
2010	100	34,300

This simple chart shows CEO compensation versus average worker pay. After doubling every decade as compared to workers' salaries, by 2010, the CEOs' earnings were astronomical as compared to those of the average worker.
(U.S. Bureau of Labor Statistics)

New concepts were brought forward on how a business should be run. The emphasis became profits, record profits, and more profits. Profits drove up share prices, which made investors richer. Then somebody decided to link executive pay to share value through stock options, giving top people the right to buy shares from the company treasury at some low price and then sell them on the open market at a later date. That way, if the share price goes up, the executive can exercise his/her option and get a windfall bonus. What better way to maximize shareholder value! Welcome to multi-million-dollar paydays for executives.

Company executives learned that short-term profitability was the key because it impacted share prices. No need to worry about the company five or ten years down the road, they will be rich and gone. Weird things started happening never before seen in American business, such as oil companies buying other oil companies because it was cheaper than drilling for oil. Companies were earning more profits through currency exchanges and commodities hedging than by making products for consumers to buy; high-risk loans were being "bundled" together and being sold as "asset-backed securities." Consumer electronic retailers were making more money selling warranties on the products they sold rather than on the actual products.

Wall Street prospered. When the business culture begins to view everything in terms of short-term earnings and tomorrow's stock values, important long-term issues are ignored.

For an automotive company, there is a requirement for huge capital investment, long lead times for new products, and a requirement for future research and development; these factors are completely alien to the "make a lot of money, fast" concept.

So when this emphasis began to permeate to GM management, it sounded like this:

- You have too many brands, and it costs a lot of money (in the short term) to have them bringing out new products.

- You must spend less on R&D; it does not pay off in the short term, and you will never catch the imports.

- Subcontract all you can. You will save on labour costs in the short term. (You will not have a pool of quality employees down the road, but by then you will be retired.)

- Analyze every decision from a cost point of view down to every penny — it impacts the bottom line.

The customer is fickle; who knows what he or she will do in five or ten years.

Remember, you are here for a good time, not for a long time.

The new philosophy was diametrically opposite to the Sloan philosophy. In fact, here are some of his quotes that tell much about how he built GM.

"Technological progress — and it is a pity more do not appreciate it — is the one sound approach to increased employment and higher wages. There is no other way"

"General Motors was becoming large through a process of evolution, but only because it was rendering a service to community. As its volume of business expanded it became able to do more for workers, stockholders, and customers."

"Scientific management means a constant search for the facts, the true actualities, and their intelligent, unprejudiced analysis. Thus, and in no other way, policies and their administration are determined. I keep saying to the General Motors organization that we are prepared to spend any proper amount of money to get the facts. Only by increased knowledge can we progress, perhaps I had better say survive."

"The greatest real thrill that life offers is to create, to construct, to develop something useful. Too often we fail to recognize and pay tribute to the creative spirit. It is that spirit that creates our jobs."

"There has to be this pioneer, the individual who has the courage, the ambition to overcome the obstacles that always develop when one tries to do something worthwhile, especially when it is new and different."

"Competition is the final price determinant, and competitive prices may result in profits which force you to accept a rate of return less than you hoped for, or for that matter to accept temporary losses."[5]

These are not the words of a corporate leader concerned with stock options, short-term returns, or leverage buyouts.

American auto executives are paid substantially more than anywhere else in the world. When Jurgen Schremp, the head of Daimler Benz, purchased Chrysler Corporation and formed Daimler Chrysler, he was amazed to learn that Bob Eaton, the

---

5   Alfred P. Sloan, quotations courtesy of SearchQuotes http://www.search-quotes.com/.

boss of Chrysler (the company that Benz was buying), was making millions of dollars more annually than he was. But he quickly learned, when nine years later, he was replaced by Daimler Benz and received a $134 million severance package!

Whole industries in North America are now sourced from China and the third world. Many business leaders believe they can make more money making goods overseas and selling them to the American consumer, than actually making the products in North America. Forget about plants, pensions, insurance, property taxes, workers, the EPA, OSHA, state and local municipal laws, and bureaucracy. Make it cheap overseas, sell it here, and keep the profit.

This is extremely short-sighted, and already we see in 2011 the fiscal crisis in America that this thinking has created. It is incumbent on the citizens and their political representatives to enact legislation and tax policies that guarantee the industrial health of society.

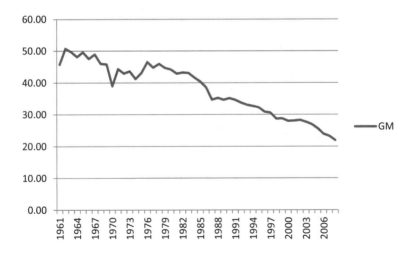

This is a year-by-year plot of GM's U.S. market shares. Notice that after 1978, GM's market share loss was almost always consistently downward. It did not seem to make a difference who was running the company or what plans and strategies they had, things were tending down all the time. The share number for 2010 was 18.81 percent. But because GM has so little debt and so much cash in the bank via the bailout, GM has the potential to earn profits of about a billion dollars per month.

25

Car Guys versus Bean-Counters

The constant dilemma for the auto industry is that of controlling costs, because there are so many diverse inputs into making automobiles: labour, commodities such as energy and metals, taxes, marketing, research and design . . . there is constant cost pressure on the automaker. Unfortunately, competitive pressures impact on pricing, and consumers are very value conscious.

Ford Motor Company was controlled by Henry Ford II, the grandson of his namesake and founder of the company. Henry the Deuce (as he was known with affection) was a creative car guy but always ensured the company had numbers guys or "bean-counters" to balance the car guys. For example, Lee Iacocca, a car guy, learned the importance of financial controls while at Ford and went on to greater management success, saving Chrysler in the eighties.

In the late seventies, Bob Lutz was president of Ford of Europe, and Red Poling was his boss. Poling had been a navy pilot, and Lutz was a marine pilot, and even though they had an amicable personal relationship, they were constantly at loggerheads over business decisions. Lutz understood the human aspect of the car business, while Poling tended to see only the numbers.

Bob Lutz

One of their classic battles was over vehicle pricing in Germany. Poling had an analysis done that showed that the Ford line was underpriced vis-à-vis the competition in Germany, Ford's largest European market. Poling wanted Lutz to raise prices immediately.

The German unions were at that time in contract negotiations with all the German automakers, and Lutz did not want to raise prices until after they had settled. He believed that the German government, media, and consumers would react negatively to the price increase by Ford. The tradition in Germany had been for

Even in his seventies, Bob Lutz was a charismatic and brilliant "car guy" who was responsible for most of GM's vehicle successes prior to its bankruptcy in 2009. He loved the media attention and always had a great quote, such as: "Foreign companies aren't smarter, and their people don't work harder—it's just their senior management didn't go to business school"; or, "There used to be a view expressed: 'Hey, let's just make these cars. Nobody cares about them. Nobody cares whether they are bad or good. It's for the people who can't afford anything better, and price is the only thing that counts.'" Or this gem: "Imminent GM bankruptcy was always fiction, created by Wall Street and the media." *(Photo courtesy of Joe Polimeni Photography. Used with permission)*

all automakers not to raise prices until union negotiations were completed and contracts were signed.

But Poling had numbers that showed how many millions Ford was losing in revenues. He challenged Lutz to quantify his rationale to not raise prices. Lutz could not, and Poling ordered him to raise prices immediately. The reaction in the German Parliament and in the media was immediate and completely negative. Ford was characterized as a greedy, insensitive, multi-national that was not cognizant of German culture, values, and traditions. By the end of the year, Ford of Germany was estimated to have lost two points in market share, which cost them millions in revenues and profits.

Buying decisions and consumer behaviour are often driven by emotional factors. In the auto business, it is not possible to quantify every input, action, and reaction of the consumer—so traditional tools and analysis can fail. It is believed "car guys" have an intuitive feeling and nature for the business that works on an emotional/social basis.

Traditionally, window regulators, the device by which a side window can be raised and lowered, were made out of steel. When GM was designing 1986 full-size cars, weight and cost reductions were of primary concern. The engineers came up with an ingenious cable system that saved both weight and money. The original material for the cable was a toothed, plastic/nylon belt. The power window electric motor would engage the teeth on the belt and raise or lower the window as required.

Testing in cold climate conditions, engineering discovered that the belt could become less pliable in the cold, and since the glass window could stick to the rubber moulding in freezing conditions, more force would be applied to the cable to move the window. The electric motor had sufficient power and overrides to prevent it from damaging itself in these conditions, but the nylon belt would break, and the window would fall down. The engineers recommended that a more expensive cable material be used that would not break, and if the window was stuck, its internal override would prevent any damage. When the window freed itself up (when the car was warmed up), everything worked normally again. The more expensive cable cost an extra fifty cents per car and annual sales numbers for vehicles that used this design of regulator were expected to be in the 300,000 range; so we are talking about $150,000. The bean-counters insisted that the lower-cost cable be used.

At our dealership, we had a customer who had driven Ford luxury cars for years. He was a skier and in fact he belonged to an exclusive ski club. He ordered a beautiful Oldsmobile 98 two-door. (The model with biggest front doors and windows made.) He picked up the car on Friday and drove two hours north to his chalet in a blizzard. Near his destination, he tried to roll down the window, the nylon belt broke, the window fell, and he arrived at his chalet with a new car and no driver's window. He used green garbage bags and duct tape to seal the opening up and drove back to the dealership on Monday, and we replaced the belt. He never bought another GM vehicle. And he told many members at the club about his experience.

GM financial analysts could justify the cost savings and say this was a fluke incident. Unfortunately, the nylon belt breakage was an epidemic, and within two years, GM re-engineered the regulators to use the stronger cables that were initially recommended.

When you use short-term quantifiable financial returns as the ultimate arbitrator for decisions, often the customer suffers, and you pay the price. When one reviews General Motors and its leadership in the last quarter of the twentieth century, one almost begins to wonder how they survived until 2009. They had several close calls, and often the national economy would come around to save them. Luckily, GM had many competent leaders who did their utmost to fight the trends and keep the company viable.

Unfortunately, the credit and economic crisis of 2008 was too much for both GM and Chrysler to survive. The final straw for both was that their access to cheap money dried up and they could not finance existing debt that was due and for ongoing operations. Their only recourse was to go to the government, hat in hand, in December 2008. The rest, as they say, is history.

Two more stories from the annals of Ford Motor Company illustrate the eternal struggle between car guys and bean-counters.

Prior to introducing the Ford Pinto in 1970, Ford engineers discovered that the fuel system was susceptible to rupture in rear-end collisions. These ruptures and resultant gasoline spills could cause fires. To reduce the fire hazard would require significant money and time to redesign the rear structure and change the assembly line. Since the public was craving fuel-efficient cars, a cost analysis study was designed to help make the decision as to what to do. The study estimated there would be 180 deaths and 180 serious injuries due to the risky design. Costs were allocated to each death and each injury, and Ford decided it was cheaper to produce the Pinto as designed because deaths and injury payments would be less than making the design and plant changes.

Of course, this was the right decision on economic grounds and would be applauded by all the financial stakeholders in the Ford Motor Company. In 1981, when a Pinto accident killed Lilly Gray and severely burned thirteen-year-old Richard Grimshaw and led to a court settlement of $6 million against Ford, it far exceeded the analyst's forecasts in terms of costs and negative publicity. Business leaders should take this as a warning about quantifying people's lives.

Some studies have shown that the Pinto had a lower incidence of fires as a result of rear-end collisions than many other brands. In fact, the fuel filler design Ford initially used was no less safe than what all the automakers were using. However, indelibly etched in the mind of the American public was that Pintos were firetraps and that the Big Three did not care about safety.

Our next example shows the danger of focus groups and how market research can potentially stifle leadership. Donald Petersen became president and COO of Ford in 1980 and became chairman and CEO in 1985. Under his leadership, the revolutionary Taurus was designed. Petersen approved of the radical aerodynamic styling, and the car's Euro-tuned handling. The steering feel was heavier and the suspension firmer than the typical American car. In other words, both in appearance and in driving, the Taurus was distinct and different than competitive cars on the market.

Prior to actual public introduction, Ford held a number of focus groups where potential customers were able to drive and evaluate the Taurus. The reports came back glowing—except almost unanimously, everybody either remarked or complained about the heavy steering! Marketing wanted Engineering to reduce the steering effort in the power steering system. The bean-counters believed that if money was being spent on market research, it should be followed up with action.

Petersen said NO! Yes, the steering was heavy—the focus group members were not used to it—but to lighten the steering would negatively affect the excellent stability, handling, and feel engineered into the car and would result in the same old, same old American design.

Petersen put his name on the line. By 1989, over a million Tauruses had been sold. It was a winner, praised especially for its firm suspension and steering. In 2010, the latest version of the Taurus is still a top seller for Ford.

This is a cautionary note to all business and political leaders: if you blindly follow the views and opinions of the public, you fail at being a leader and instead will be led down the wrong path.

26

Whack the Dealers

Neither Chrysler nor General Motors has published exact lists of the names of dealerships terminated and retained. As accurately as possible, I have ascertained the following numbers.

Chrysler

In the U.S., Chrysler terminated 789 dealers out of a total of 3,181. Approximately 25 percent of Chrysler dealers were terminated. In Canada, Chrysler did not appear to terminate any dealers as a result of the reorganization.

General Motors

In the U.S., General Motors terminated 1,100 dealers out of a total of 5,969. Initially, approximately 18 percent of the U.S. GM dealers were terminated. Later, GM in the U.S. reinstated 600 dealers, so the net culling was approximately 8 percent, not much more than the typical annual dealer attrition rate.

In Canada, General Motors terminated 240 dealers out of a total of 785. Approximately 30 percent of the Canadian dealers were terminated. Later, after being forced by court actions, GMCL reinstated ten dealers, so the net culling was 29 percent. Some publications have reported that GMCL claimed they would terminate 42 percent of their dealer body; I cannot substantiate that.

As well, nobody at General Motors has ever explained the difference in Canadian and U.S. termination rates.

Everybody but top management paid for thirty years of mismanagement at GM. I may be biased but I believe that the dealers received the worst blow. The dealers were the only stakeholders (the others being shareholders, bondholders, creditors, unions, and governments) who were not involved in any negotiations in GM's restructuring. Over the months after GM's bankruptcy, I was asked by friends and strangers why GM had closed our dealership. We had just spent four million dollars on expansion and renovations. Of the two local competitive dealerships that were allowed to continue, neither was up to current GM facilities standards. We were located at the busiest intersection in Durham Region, a community of 500,000 people. The more I studied the so-called parameters for choosing dealerships for wind-down, the more I realized the decisions were politically based.

So I went back to GM's plan for restructuring and looked at the statements they made to the U.S. government. General Motors explained that normal attrition in the U.S. had reduced the dealer body by 15 percent between 2004 and 2008.

GM claimed it had long recognized this issue and, since 1970, has reduced the U.S. dealer body by over 6,000 dealerships. Key drivers have been natural attrition, consolidation of franchises in smaller markets, and, more recently, actions to phase out 2,800 U.S. Oldsmobile franchises and realign Buick, Pontiac, and GMC into a single channel.

Three thousand, two hundred GM franchises have been eliminated since 1970, if you do not include the 2,800 Oldsmobile dealerships. That means, on average, GM dealer numbers were reduced by about 300 a year in the United States. (When the Saturn brand was introduced in 1990, GM added, over time, in excess of 400 dealers in North America.) That works out to about 5 percent a year if GM does not add more franchises. Because of the continuing sales decay of GM products, dealers would voluntarily divest themselves of GM franchises, in most cases acquiring other brands or developing their real estate assets for other commercial purposes. Contrary to what GM was telling Congress, there was no master plan to shrink the dealership count. "Wait and see" was the only planning activity that was going on.

With the exception of Oldsmobile, most dealer consolidation had utilized private capital rather than relying on GM funds. Since closing Oldsmobile cost GM an estimated $2 billion, it is nice to know the dealers paid for the other consolidations out of their own pockets. Certainly GM did not have the money. Even if they did have the money, dealer consolidation was not a specific GM policy.

Here is a statement GM made in its restructuring proposal to justify the elimination of dealerships. In February 17, 2009, GM states: "Improving the profitability of GM's independent dealers helps the Company by increasing sales, attracting private investment, and driving greater customer loyalty."

This statement is completely false, based on the year 2000 closing of 2,800 Oldsmobile dealers in the U.S. When Oldsmobile dealerships closed, GM sales at other dealerships did not increase; private investment steered away from GM dealerships, as the company displayed an inability to stop their sales losses; and Oldsmobile customers went to other brands. These are the realities, and it appears that even when GM was asking Washington for help, they were still delusional. As to improving profitability, this is doublespeak at its finest, as for many GM dealers in North America in recent years there were only losses in their new car sales departments. Improving profitability in reality meant getting dealers to a break-even point first!

I am not aware of a case where a franchisor like GM has reduced 18 percent of their retail franchises in North America and was able to maintain—let alone regain—market share and profitability. Usually when franchisees close, it is the death knell of the franchisor. If, in Walmart stores, McDonald's closed their outlets (which are small and generate less revenue than their free-standing stores), would that help McDonald's be more successful? I think not, and I do not think it will happen.

Even if those 18 percent who were whacked provided only 10 percent of GM's sales volume, this could easily be 200,000 units annually in North America, all contributing to cover GM's high fixed costs. It is volume that makes the carmakers money!

Second, by eliminating 18 percent of the dealer body, it is harder for customers to find GM's brands; if there is no GM dealership nearby, it is harder for a potential customer to shop GM.

If each of these approximately 1,100 dealers in the U.S. who were eliminated had approximately twenty dealership-owned GM demonstrators at any given time, about $100,000 in parts inventory, and about sixty new vehicles in inventory, then just directly by closing these 1,100 dealerships, GM lost 2,000 new vehicle demonstrator sales; $1,100,000,000 in parts sales; and new dealer inventories (a source of cash for GM) of 60,000 units.

The most loyal supporters of General Motors were dealership employees who made their living daily by selling and servicing GM vehicles. Approximately 110,000 dealership employees lost their jobs in North America during the worst economic times since the Depression. Now a great proportion of these ex-GM dealership employees are recommending to their friends and family, "any vehicle but GM."

One justification that GM used to justify whacking dealers was what is called throughput—the number of new vehicle sales per dealer. They said they had to get the throughput up, and the best way to do that was to eliminate dealers. Do you know what brand of GM's had the highest throughput per dealer? Saturn. As well, in Canada, both GM and Chrysler, which needed bailouts, had higher sales per dealer than Ford, which is doing just fine, thank you. The amazing fact is that Saturn dealers enjoyed one of the highest sales rates of all brands in the U.S.—and was cancelled. It is hard to understand GM's logic when they say sales per franchise are very important, but not in Saturn's case.

Another one of the justifications GM gave for eliminating both the brands and the dealers for Saab, Hummer, and Saturn was that these brands had a $1.1 billion average annual loss before interest and taxes. Of course, based on previous examples of GM's voodoo accounting, these numbers do not have any real validity. Bearing in mind that GM started Saturn and bought both the Saab and Hummer brands from others, it reinforces that there has been misguided leadership at the top of GM.

The logic of these accounting losses is further convoluted when comparing to overall GM results. In 2007, General Motors lost $38.7 billion; $2.0 billion in 2006; and $10.6 billion in 2005. By using profit and loss comparisons, GM should have kept Saturn, Saab, and Hummer and gotten rid of everything else. GM said these three brands were losing $1.1 billion a year, which was less than the other brands combined.

If reducing sales outlets (dealerships) was not going to benefit GM, why did they do it? This is going to be a stretch for most people to believe, but for GM, it was a great way to crush the dealer organization. With the help of government, GM was able to roll back years

of collective bargaining agreements with the unions. They eliminated and financially crippled the "pesky" bondholders and shareholders who constantly stirred up trouble at GM Annual meetings.

By crushing the dealer organization, GM reduced the power of
national, state/provincial, and local dealer organizations and individual dealers. It also made sense to GM management, who believed the myths that the dealers were the problem. By eliminating up to 50 percent of the dealers in any given area, GM had a
"club" they could use to intimidate any of the remaining dealers.
No more was GM going to have a co-operative and collegial attitude with their dealers; now everybody knows who is in charge.

It happened almost instantly when the remaining dealers began receiving GM Home Office letters stating that for the future
myriad of transactions and relationships dealers would have with
GM, they now were going to cost the dealer more money. Un-
stated was the threat: "We cancelled thousands; what will one
less dealer mean to us?"

Just like organized crime often orders a "hit" to send a message to others, GM whacked dealers because they could, and it
sent a very clear message to the remaining dealers. Initially, these
remaining dealers were pretty pumped in June and July 2009
when they realized they had been spared; but then, as time went
by and sales went down and costs from GM went up, they wondered if it would have been better to be whacked.

To make it perfectly clear, we know, based on the Oldsmobile experience, that cancelling brands and closing dealerships
cannot generate more revenue or profits. We know that GM was
very aware of the financial size and power of the dealer organization. They were especially concerned with certain companies
that owned multiple dealerships becoming too powerful—such
as the AutoNation (250 dealerships); Group 1 (143 dealerships);
Penske Auto Group (325 dealerships); and Hendrick (59 dealerships and sold 120,000 cars in 2005).

For years, GM had fought the right of anybody but a single individual from owning a single dealership. The groups won in court.

Many of these dealer groups were very concerned with the
decline of GM's fortunes in the marketplace, as many of their
costly real estate assets and their investment capital was tied up

in slumping GM franchises and they were exerting pressure on GM directly or indirectly to get their act together. With the closure of 18 percent of its dealer body, no doubt GM expected that pressure to subside for the time being.

In the U.S., as a result of being terminated by GM, the dealers went to Congress and the government, who told GM it had set up an arbitration program whereby dealers could appeal their terminations. As of January 2010, approximately 50 percent of the terminated dealers had applied for arbitration for reinstatement. (The Canadian dealers had a different situation that we shall discuss later.)

To put the U.S. situation in context, over half the GM dealers in the U.S. believed GM was wrong in how and whom GM terminated. These dealers were ready to incur significant legal costs at these arbitration hearings because they believed they were in the right. It again brings into question GM's leadership and their view of reality, when a company determines that certain dealers are not viable—and those dealers actually can prove they are! On January 7, 2010, the new chairman of GM, Ed Whitacre, told a group of reporters that he expects many dealers to be reinstated, guessing the final number would be somewhere "in the hundreds."

GM quickly became aware that independent arbitrators would recognize the foolishness of their actions and apply some reason. On March 5, 2010, GM reinstated 661 of its previously terminated U.S. dealerships. On June 9, 2010, GM reinstated 900 more previously terminated dealerships. In the end, GM simply skipped the whole arbitration process and reinstated all the dealers who asked to be.

The statements given by GM to the governments and the media to justify closure of dealerships in 2009 made no sense and make even less sense in hindsight. It is ironical that after reinstating these dealers in 2010, GM publicized the fact that they had to ramp up production to meet demand from reinstated dealers!

Now, over the years, both Ford and GM specifically have been dissatisfied with the traditional franchise system and have tried different alternatives to "improve the system."

By the turn of the century, the single-brand dealer/owner/operator was disappearing. Now there are many dealer groups, owned privately or publicly, some with over a thousand separate retail outlets in the U.S.

Some alternatives considered by the factories were:

Factory stores, where the manufacturer actually owned and operated the dealership. Mercedes Benz has numerous factory stores. The advantage is that retail profits flow through directly to the manufacturer; the manufacturer is assured that its policies are carried out at the retail level, and there is a consistent retail experience for the customer at all their retail outlets.

There are disadvantages. One reason factory stores are so rare is the huge capital investment the manufacturer has to make for each retail outlet ($20 million is not uncommon). Since all the employees of the dealership are employees of the Corporation, they tend to be better paid and have better benefits than the independent owner operator would pay, so operating costs are higher. Finally, retail is a specific type of enterprise and the factories have had difficulty recruiting and managing the right people to operate the store. In almost every case, the domestic manufacturers avoid factory stores now.

Enhanced territorial rights. One of the problems for most dealers was the fact that their territorial rights in most communities were very limited, a small geographical area sometimes only with a radius of five miles. For example, you open a Ford dealership in Anytown, USA. Business is good; very good, in fact. The town grows, and Ford decides that the town can support another Ford franchise at the other end of town. You cannot do anything about it, but you now have a new direct competitor. Saturn (a cancelled GM brand), to encourage a greater level of co-operation between the dealers and Saturn, gave a dealer a large geographic area of responsibility. So after building your Saturn store in Anytown, if you (and GM) felt there was a need for a second Saturn dealership, you would be the dealer. You became your own competition, and Saturn got another outlet. Good for everybody—until Saturn got whacked by GM.

Consolidation. GM specifically would from time to time financially assist in merging two or more competing dealers in a community. Because GM sales were shrinking, often a dealer would become unprofitable and would want to leave the business; GM would help to put a package together in which one strong dealer would remain where two or three existed before. This unofficial program was very popular and cost-effective, as compared to the alternatives. However, GM financial people did not like it because it cost cash money; philosophically, it was hard for GM to accept (we are paying dealers to get out of the business?). It meant negotiating with dealers, and could involve making some dealers even wealthier.

The bean-counters felt it was cheaper to let the weakest go bankrupt, or find a justification for termination (bankruptcy). Unfortunately, when the weakest dealer(s) in an area eventually closed, the other remaining dealer was usually too financially weak to capitalize on the opportunity.

It is interesting to consider that the Japanese never seemed to have a great problem with the North American franchise system, and never tried to reinvent the wheel. Their most stringent demand over the years was a separate showroom and sales staff for their product line. The Japanese were always ready to adapt to the distribution systems already existing in a particular market. In fact, in the early years, the Japanese sold their vehicles through independent regional distributors until they themselves were able to take over national distribution of their vehicles in America. Today, Subaru of New England still is the independent distributor of Subaru cars in New England.

Chrysler's Justification for Closing Dealers

Like GM, Chrysler attempted to publicly justify the closing of 25 percent of its dealerships in the U.S. They did not close any Canadian dealerships, unlike GM, which terminated 30 percent of their Canadian dealer organization. In the U.S., compared to GM, which has reinstated all dealers who have asked for reinstatement, Chrysler is taking the long process through the courts and reinstating the dealers they are ordered to. Fiat of Italy now controls Chrysler and to date has not been effective in stopping the Chrysler sale slide. Jim Press, the president of Chrysler in June

2009, is no longer with the company.

In June 2009, Jim Press appeared before the U.S. Senate Committee on Commerce, defending Chrysler's actions and attacking "dealer" myths.[6] Press showed this table to the committee:

Examples of Lost Revenue and Cost Associated with Discontinued Dealers

Product engineering and development for "sister vehicles"[1]	$1.4 billion over 4 years
Lost sales due to dealer underperformance	$1.5 billion revenue annually
Administrative cost to maintain the 789 discontinued dealers	$33 million annually
Marketing and advertising	$150 million annually

Let us examine each of these points individually to see if Chrysler could really save almost two billion dollars per year by closing dealers. The company was convinced that discontinuing 789 underperforming dealers will strengthen the remaining 2,393 dealers. In support of its decision, Chrysler points out that its average dealer retailed 405 vehicles during 2008, while other brands' dealers averaged 525. First of all, the fact that Toyota or Audi sells more cars per dealer on average is because more consumers choose to buy Toyotas or Audis, not because of the number of dealerships in existence. For many years, GM outsold Toyota worldwide, yet Toyota had more dealerships.

The number of Toyotas or Hondas or Ferraris sold per dealer has no impact on the number of cars sold at a given Chevrolet or Chrysler dealership.

There are many GM and Chrysler dealerships that outsell some Toyota dealerships; should Toyota close those dealerships?

The argument that when a dealership closes, the customer migrates to another dealer offering a similar brand is shown to be faulty by the Oldsmobile experience. By closing dealerships, overall sales for both GM and Chrysler have gone down. That will cost both companies millions.

---

6   The complete transcript of the hearings is available at: http://frwebgate.
     access.gpo.gov/cgi bin/getdoc.cgi?dbname=111_senate_
     hearings&docid=f:52752.wais.

Market Share Comparison—2007 vs. 2010, United States and Canada

	2007	2010	CHANGE[1]
GM USA	23.24	18.81	Down 4.43
GM CDN	24.20	15.80	Down 8.40
TOYOTA USA	15.96	15.01	Down 0.86
TOYOTA CDN	12.20	11.00	Down 1.20
FORD USA	14.59	16.44	Up 1.85
FORD CDN	13.50	17.50	Up 4.00
CHRYSLER USA	12.62	9.22	Down 3.40
CHRYSLER CDN	14.10	13.10	Down 1.00
HONDA USA	9.43	10.45	Up 1.02
HONDA CDN	10.30	9.10	Down 0.80
NISSAN USA	6.49	7.72	Up 1.23
NISSAN CDN	4.60	5.30	Up 0.70
HYUNDAI USA	2.84	4.57	Up 1.73
HYUNDAI CDN	4.50	11.10	Up 6.60

Notice that the three entities that cancelled dealerships—GM USA, GM Canada, and Chrysler USA—had the greatest loss of market share. GM of Canada, which terminated the most dealerships, had the greatest loss by a dramatic amount. Notice that Chrysler Canada, which did not terminate dealerships, did relatively well during this period, even gaining share on Toyota, and suffering one-third the share loss of their parent in the U.S. Depending on total sales, one point in market share in the U.S. is about 100,000 to 150,000 units. In Canada, one point of share is about 10,000 to 15,000 units.

Any time you have a one-point share change, it is considered a dramatic and significant event. A loss of 8.4 share points in three years is unfathomable and anxiety-provoking.

(Courtesy of Wards Automotive Group)

Product Engineering and Development for "Sister Vehicles"

In his prepared statement to Congress, Jim Press states: "As an example, we have to build and market two similar minivans: the Chrysler Town and Country and the Dodge Caravan, to satisfy multiple dealer networks. Any separate Dodge and Chrysler franchise in close proximity competes with each other—not other makes—in order to sell and later service what is basically the same vehicle. As a result, the company spends more while the dealer network is, as a whole, not viable and not profitable." He then goes on to say, "Product complexity is increased because of the need to provide products in the same segment to different networks. For example, Chrysler currently supplies dealers with two similar minivans, Chrysler Town and Country and Dodge Grand Caravan; two similar full-size sport-utilities, Chrysler Aspen and Dodge Durango; two similar mid-size SUVs, Dodge Nitro and Jeep Liberty; and two similar sedans, the Chrysler Sebring and Dodge Avenger. Based on six major vehicle launches between 2005 and 2008, Chrysler incurred approximately $1.4 billion in incremental costs to develop these multiple pairs of "sister vehicles."

If the company built, say, a Grand Caravan minivan just for Dodge, it would leave the Chrysler/Jeep dealers without a minivan to sell. This could be acceptable, but the Chrysler "brand" needs a minivan entrant. There are consumers who want a Chrysler Town and Country and will pay for it. High-end buyers wanted equipment, options, and trim not available on the basic Dodge minivan. It is not, contrary to what Jim Press stated, the dealers who drive product planning and development, but corporate head office in trying to meet the needs of the consumer and the market. Honda created the Acura dealer network to sell the Acura line of cars; it was not the Acura dealers (who did not exist) that went to Honda and said, build us a new line of products. Press is blaming dealers for factory decisions.

These additional costs were far less than the additional sales volume generated by this dual distribution. Notice that GM has kept the GMC and Chevrolet truck, van, and SUV lines; they are both built on the same assembly lines. The variations on the minivan were introduced by Chrysler to appeal to a wider segment of buyers. If Chrysler is going to save $1.4 billion over four years in this process, just think what they could save by producing just one version of the basic Plymouth K-car and dropping all other models; imagine the economies of scale! Henry Ford did it for years, offering just the Model T in black, until GM outsold him.

This is just another example of "voodoo accounting." If in 1960 Chrysler had never added more brands and dealerships, would they be $1.4 billion richer now, forty years later? The problem is not sister vehicles, it is a problem of building vehicles people are not buying; this $1.4 billion savings is in reality zero savings.

Lost Sales Due to Dealer Underperformance

Press went on to say, "Finally, poor performing dealers cost us customers. It's true that dealers are our customers, but it works both ways. If they don't sell cars, we don't, either. Poor performing dealerships cannot afford to keep facilities up-to-date or hire and train the best people, resulting in poor customer experience and lower sales. In fact, in 2008 the 789 discontinued dealers achieved sales of only 73 percent of the minimum sales responsibility, representing 55,000 lost unit sales and $1.5 billion in lost revenue in 2008."

Since this area makes up the majority of the two billion dollars in savings, a careful analysis is required. Press is saying that *if* these dealers had sold 100 percent of their sales target, Chrysler would have received an additional $1.5 billion in revenue. Will closing those 789 dealerships not put you further away from your target? You had 73 percent of your target; now those closed stores will give you 0 percent of that target. If 27 percent lost sales cost $1.5 billion in sales, logic tells you that losing the remaining 73 percent that you actually had, means you will lose an additional $5.5 billion in sales that these 789 stores produced. Restated, these stores produced $5.5 billion in revenue, but they wanted $7 billion, so Chrysler closed them, and now they get zero revenue. To make these sorts of decisions and present these explanations, Jim Press was paid $2.4 million a year and received a $3-million signing bonus when he joined Chrysler in 2007.

Finally, we know that for years Chrysler has not hit its corporate sales and profit targets. We also know that Chrysler set the dealer sales targets with the same accuracy they set the corporate targets, so what validity do any of these target numbers have in the first place? Why use "if" statements about what could be or might be? If you won the lottery, you would be rich . . . if bookstores sold enough copies of this book, it would be a best seller . . . if I ate less and exercised more, I would be healthier . . .

The reason the dealers did not sell 100 percent of their target was because people thought certain Chrysler products were not worth buying. That is the reality.

Administrative Costs to Maintain 789 Discontinued Dealers

Later, Jim Press goes on to speak about how expensive these 789 dealers were to maintain from an administrative point of view—$33 million annually. But $33 million in the auto business is chicken feed, small potatoes, a mere bag of shells. It might just get you five minutes of Super Bowl ad time, not including ad production costs. The fact that he uses this savings to justify terminating dealers and thousands of jobs is offensive. (By the way, on June 1, 2009, the 789 dealers had about 42,000 Chrysler vehicles in inventory. That is about $800 million in Chrysler sales that will not be replaced next year.)

Marketing and Advertising

Chrysler estimates an annual savings of $150 million in advertising costs, claiming they often help defray a dealer's cost of advertising, and fewer dealers means less money paid out. Chrysler spent a little over $1 billion on total advertising in 2008, and based on the $150 million savings cited, they are claiming that

$600 million of their billion-dollar ad budget went to dealers. That does not make sense. (Total budget $1 billion; Chrysler says 25 percent reduction in dealers saves them $150 million; therefore, total spent on dealers was $600 million.)

Advertising support is usually given to dealers based on the number of vehicles sold. If Chrysler sells the same number of cars through 2,000 dealers or 3,000 dealers, the cost per car to Chrysler is the same. If they expect to pay out less, then they expect to sell less. I do not believe any of their numbers are valid. First, if these numbers were valid, why didn't the companies make these changes years ago and reap the benefit of the so-called savings? Because there are no savings! Again, I refer to the Oldsmobile closing. In their statement, GM did not believe there would be any saving in advertising costs accrued by closing dealers.

Advertising budgets are generated on budgeted costs, usually a function of the expected or desired sales volume of the brand. The number of dealers selling the brand has no impact on the budget. Do you think Coca Cola changes its advertising budget based on the number of stores selling their brand? Not likely. Neither GM nor Chrysler set their advertising budget that way.

In summary, there was no economic justification for the mass closure of dealerships by either Chrysler or GM.

27

Convoluted Thinking

Many GM apologists have defended GM's management decisions in 2008 and 2009 as having been carefully planned, studied, and analyzed. I beg to differ and I have three examples that show there was little difference between the old GM and the new GM thinking, basically because the same cabal of managers is making the decisions, and the same operating structures and values exist.

Example 1

The Buick LaCrosse was introduced in the U.S. in 2005. However, the brand gurus in either Detroit or GM's Canadian headquarters in Oshawa had discovered that in slang French, spoken by some in the province of Quebec, "lacrosse" was a euphemism for "self-love." So the alarm bells went off, and a new name, the Allure, was chosen for this car. Now here is where the stupidity comes in. The official national game of Canada is lacrosse. In Quebec, there are two province-wide leagues—the Quebec Senior Lacrosse League and the Quebec Junior Lacrosse League—and hundreds of community teams in local leagues. The Quebec population does not have a problem with the name lacrosse. Rest assured GM did not consult any of its francophone dealers in Quebec for their input.

What is the big deal, you say? Well, GM spent thousands of dollars designing and producing different sales literature, service literature, vehicle nameplates, and signage for the cars shipped to Canada. They had to develop and produce different television, radio, and print ads for Canada. They also introduced complexity to the production line—always a bad thing. Finally, there would be no spillover of American media ads seen in Canada for the Buick Allure. Now, get this: in 2010, five years after its introduction, General Motors discontinued the Allure name in Canada and replaced it with LaCrosse!

By the way, GM never had a problem with the name "Hummer," which has an interesting slang definition of its own.

Example 2

J.D. Power ranks the various vehicle brands in several categories. On February 25, 2010, they issued a ranking of the brands based on customer service at the brand's dealerships. Here is a customer-based independent survey to prove that your dealers are pleasing the customers; but if you cancel the top two brands, you are losing 42 percent of the dealers who got you the high scores! Further to show GM's incompetence, GM could not even sell at fire-sale prices the Hummer or the Saturn brands, factories, and facilities. In the end, they recouped nothing for the billions of dollars they had invested in Pontiac, Saturn, and Hummer. Nothing.

	Rating out of 1000 points	Brand Killed	Dealers Whacked?
Cadillac	922	No	Some
Buick	919	No	Some
Saturn	897	Yes	Yes, All
Chevrolet	896	No	Some
GMC	896	No	Some
SAAB	896	Yes	Yes, All
Pontiac	895	Yes	Some
Hummer	892	Yes	Yes
Industry Average	882		
Chrysler	882		
Ford	875		

Based on J.D. Power 2008 Customer Service Index Study rankings: General Motors dealers were ranked higher by customers than their domestic competition, and higher than the industry average. Arguably the differences may not be statistically valid, but one wonders how GM could terminate the dealers and brands that were above average in Customer Service ratings.

(Data courtesy of J.D. Power and Associates, The McGraw-Hill Companies, Inc. Used with permission)

Example 3

To make money in the auto business, you have to sell cars. Let us look at the brands that GM cancelled and their sales volume for the year to date, November 30, 2008, which was just prior to when GM went to Washington asking for help; and it should be remembered that both Saab and Hummer had significant overseas sales. How do Pontiac and Saturn numbers relate to the competition, you might ask? Here are some comparisons. These are U.S. volumes.

	Units	Comments
Pontiac	250,902	Looking at this chart, can you
Mazda	245,984	see why GM cancelled Pontiac
Lexus	236,725	and Saturn and kept Buick?
BMW	231,053	
Mercedes	206,494	In 2000, when GM cut
Volkswagen	205,551	Oldsmobile, that brand was
Saturn	176,434	selling 265,000 units annually.
Subaru	170,412	How did that work out for GM?
Cadillac	147,924	
Buick	128,288	
Mercury	111,375	
Lincoln	98,242	
Audi	80,046	
Volvo	68,149	

Year-to-date U.S. sales as of November 30, 2008. *(Author)*

Hummer sold 25,315 units and Saab 20,180 units.

GM's justification for keeping Buick in America was somehow linked with the popularity of Buick in China. Since most of Buick models sold in China are made in China, how does this justify keeping Buick plants open in North America and closing Pontiac plants?

Is their thinking convoluted or what?

28

GM Reorganization Strategy

Q) Why was GM in crisis?

A) It did not have any cash to finance its continued operations.

Q) Why didn't it have the cash?

A) Because nobody would lend it to GM.

Q) Why did GM have to borrow the money in the first place?

A) Because GM was not selling enough cars or making money and generating the cash it needed for continued operations.

Q) If GM had had 45 percent market share in North America like it had in 1978, would it have been in financial trouble?

A) No way.

Q) How about 40 percent, like they had in 1985?

A) No way.

Q) How about 30 percent in 1996?

A) Not likely, but with less than 22 percent market share in 2008, which was half what they had had less than thirty years earlier, they could not exist.

So the problem was thirty years of almost non-stop sales and market share loss. And the people who ran the company then and trained the people who were going to run the new GM were all the same in continuing to blame the lenders, the unions/workers, and the dealers.

The stakeholders were:

- Customers
- Secured lenders
- Bondholders
- Shareholders
- Unions
- Dealers

The key question was:

Q) What was GM trying to accomplish in the reorganization?

I believe these were the goals:

A1) To eliminate debt and other financial obligations. What was crippling GM in 2008 was its inability to borrow cheap money to meet its cash obligations, most of which were repayment of previous debts.

A2) To reduce the fixed operating costs that were not sustainable at GM's current rate of sales. The new GM was going to try to be profitable with a North American market share of 15 to 20 percent. With essentially very little debt and huge cash reserves of government money, this would be feasible. In fact it is believed that with the estimated $30 billion+ in cash reserves earning 2 percent interest annually, that alone would generate $600,000,000 in profits! Since dividend payouts to shareholders were eliminated, it was very easy for the new GM to be profitable.

It is important to understand if the 2008 credit crisis had not occurred in the U.S., GM would probably have carried on as if nothing had happened. The fact that GM could not borrow money to continue operating was what sent them to Washington, hat in hand. Once the government got involved, it was a new ball game for GM. First, GM needed cash; the government (read taxpayers) has lots, so that problem was quickly solved. Second, GM had to do something with the bondholders, whom they owed $27 billion.

GM and the government forced the bondholders to accept $9 billion—and swoosh! $18 billion in debt disappeared. The interest payments alone at 4 percent per annum were $60,000,000 per month! Third, GM owed various union pension funds $13.5 billion, and additional billions in unfunded health-care liabilities. The union was forced to accept shares in the new GM as payment instead of the money they were owed. This information is contained in the appendices of the restructuring plan submitted by GM to the U.S. government.

Now that GM had eliminated the financial liabilities that were draining the company, they really did not have to do anything else. (If most of my debts and payments were eliminated, and I had a multimillion-dollar nest egg given to me, I would have a nice life, too.) However, the U.S. government believed it had a mandate to fix the way GM operated and told GM to come up with a plan. As the reader probably has ascertained by now, GM is really good at coming up with plans and organization strategies. What they are absolutely atrocious at is coming up with good plans and strategies that can be implemented and be successful.

For example, by 2008, GM realized that the great Saturn plan of Roger Smith was not a money-maker and they decided to cancel the brand, shut down the plants, and eliminate the dealers. Initially, nobody at GM realized that the Saturn brand had value! It had a strong North American distribution network; it had a great reputation in the public's eyes; and there were over a million Saturn vehicles on the road needing parts and service. Saturn also absorbed some of GM of Europe's Opel brand's production. Finally, somebody got through to GM that Saturn was an asset, and GM negotiated for Roger Penske to buy the brand. Foolishly, to my mind, GM refused to sign an agreement to source cars for Penske. When Roger was unable to find another manufacturer to supply him with cars that met U.S. mandated standards and were not currently sold in the U.S., he called off the deal. Of course, GM was the loser.

GM of Europe was another example of ineptitude on GM's part during the reorganization. They announced they were going to sell Opel and the other GM of Europe brands. They spent months negotiating with potential buyers, and when it was believed a deal had been made with Magna Corporation, GM decided it was going to keep GM of Europe. How much thought can have gone into this plan if it was to be reversed only months later?

It goes on and on: The reversal on dealer terminations; the cancelling of the high-volume Pontiac brand and keeping the low-volume Buick; firing Fritz Henderson and then hiring him back as a consultant; a reorganization of the top management ranks within ten months after the previous reorganization and the formation of the new GM; the proposed closing of 42 percent of the retail outlets in North America. Most important, the continued free fall in new vehicle sales after GM's best attempts to "reinvent" the company points to continued failure of the New GM's plans.

GM is going to have to maintain that 20 percent market share, or it will come crashing down. Even this will be difficult to do. If you eliminate 42 percent of your dealers, and chop the Pontiac, Saturn, Saab, and Hummer brands, which had contributed 2 or 3 percent market share themselves, alienate potentially over a million former bondholders, shareholders, and associated ex-employees, your chances of holding even 20 percent market share are slim to non-existent. As of July 2011, GM had 20.3 percent of the flat U.S. market; in Canada, they had only a 14.4 percent share and trailed Ford at 19.3 percent.

The real question is: How was the new GM going to bring back customers to buy GM cars? Unfortunately, GM told the public what they have been telling them for the past thirty years: "Our cars are the best." The consumers have not believed GM for thirty years and are not likely to start believing GM now.

As I said previously, after General Motors went to Washington in December 2008 asking for money, they were sent away to come up with a plan. General Motors already had a plan on how the company was going to operate for the next several years but they did not believe Congress would accept the standard auto company forecast and projections. You must understand that GM and all automakers have very specific targets and budgets that are set out in writing for the years ahead. GM was not initially interested in changing their corporate planning, as in management's eyes, they already had a good plan for the future. The only problem was that due to the economic and banking crisis of 2008, GM could not access funds to finance operations. Nobody would lend them any money. This liquidity crisis struck thousands of American companies, resulting in thousands of business bankruptcies. Most of these smaller businesses did not have access to government funding as GM did.

The initial plan GM presented to Congress and the U.S. Treasury in February 2009 was rejected by the Obama administration at the end of March. GM was told to go back and get greater concessions from the stakeholders. The rejection of the GM plan was not surprising, considering the political considerations that came into play. Depending on the elected representatives' particular agenda, GM was going to be made to conform. One of the key reasons for the rejection of the February plan was the fact that GM forecast continued excellent sales of their profitable trucks and SUVs. This was totally unacceptable to the congressional eco-greens, who saw these vehicles as gas-guzzling, resource-wasting abominations.

Regardless of the fact that the American consumer continued to need and want these vehicles, the forecast that reflected this was unacceptable. Anti-union right-wingers felt the UAW was the cause of all GM's problems; therefore, the unionized worker would be made to bear the burden. The left-wingers really believed that Wall Street and financiers were the cause of the problem so *they* would have to suffer, not realizing that many of GM's shares and bonds were held by pension plans, universities, and private pensioners. The Obama administration and Congress wanted to appear tough and astute to the taxpayer before showering GM with billions of dollars in free money. There was a real desire to avoid the backlash that occurred when the Wall Street banks were bailed out with over $700 billion, with few or no conditions.

In Summary

- GM wanted money only to finance operations to maintain the status quo. They wanted this money from the government because it was not available anywhere else.

- The U.S. Treasury Department wanted to eliminate GM's ongoing and long-term liabilities to ensure that the company could be profitable at much lower sales levels and there would be no requirement for future bailouts.

- The Democrats wanted the top management and the financiers to bear a significant burden of the calamity and make GM more "socially responsible."

- The Republicans, several of whom were against any bailout at all, wanted the unions to bear a significant burden in the reorganization.

- GM was faced with a real dilemma. First they had to get the money, which meant pleasing everybody in Washington (an impossible task). They had to come up with a business plan that looked innovative and acceptable to Washington.

Closing plants, terminating more workers, paying the remaining employees less, reneging on previously negotiated benefits and pensions, and not honouring commitments to investors and lenders was what was needed; but how to make this politically palatable was the challenge. Here, GM got help from their government overseers. The U.S. and Canadian governments basically told the unions and the lenders, "This is what you are going to get or you will get even less if we do not bail out GM."

Once GM's liabilities to lenders and the union were dramatically reduced, GM was home free. However, the public and the politicians demanded GM do something different, so GM came up with the "Whack the dealers and Whack the brands" strategy.

GM should have known in the spring of 2009 that whacking the dealers was a stupid idea. Proof is by July 2010, they have reinstated all terminated dealers in the U.S. who asked for reinstatement. They should have known that cancelling brands was a no-win strategy based on the $2.0 billion disaster when they cancelled Oldsmobile and even lost more market share. Of course, initiative and creativity had been sapped out of GM top management for years, and they could think of nothing else. The explanation given when confronted with the short-sightedness of these two strategies was a) "We were forced by government," which is blatantly untrue; and b) "There was nothing else we could have done," which also is untrue.

GM could have recreated the divisional organization system. This was exactly what they did when they offered Saab, Opel, Hummer, and Saturn up for sale. These divisions were offered for sale as basically intact, independent, self-contained units. With the exception of Saturn, each of these divisions is doing quite nicely, either operated by GM or some other corporation. Saturn would have continued to be very viable under Roger Penske, the proposed buyer, if GM had allocated Penske manufacturing facilities. Of course, if GM continued to manufacture Saturns for Penske to sell through the Saturn retail organization, the public would really see how incompetent GM was with the brand. GM felt it was better not to produce 170,000 additional vehicles a year, close plants, and terminate workers than have Saturn be a success.

If in 2000 GM had instead reorganized into the divisional system, kept all the brands, started focusing on producing durable, reliable versions of their existing product line, which in most cases were quite acceptable, GM recovery would have been even faster. They would not have faced the sales and market share losses they endured into 2010, nor the negative publicity associated with cancelling dealers and brands. They would not have had to spend up to $15,000 in per-vehicle incentives in the summer of 2010 to slow the market share loss.

In December of 2008, GM was analogous to a family that is made up of a father and a mother and five kids. They have a big mortgage to pay on their 6,000-square-foot luxury home, and Dad gets laid off. The government comes in and tells the mortgage company, we the government are going to pay you off at thirty cents on a dollar. They then tell the utilities company that the family will pay only half of the monthly charges. The government also gives the family $750,000 to tide them over.

In appreciation of the government's help, the parents kick three of the five children out of the house, because this will reduce grocery bills. They also cancel their holiday cruise this year. Father, being astute, realizes he can live quite nicely on the $750,000 nest egg, which he has invested. He is making more money than when he was working and pays less income tax. Both the government and the family declare the government intervention a success and an example of government working with families. Nowhere is it mentioned that the three kids evicted are on social assistance; the mortgage company applied for and received TARP funds; and the utility company had to be bailed out by the State.

Somebody should put a billboard up across from GM headquarters in Detroit that looks like this:

IT'S THE PRODUCT, STUPID

The leaders at GM should recognize that many of the vehicles they build are *not* the most reliable, durable, or appealing in their sales category, and if you are not best in a category, you are equal to all the other losers. Until the vast majority of GM-produced vehicles are number one in their respective categories, as they once were, the government will have trouble recouping the taxpayers' investments.

Government Track Record in Running Companies

Many people believe that what with the U.S. government being the largest shareholder, and Ed Whitacre chosen to be chairman of the board of directors, GM will be a better-managed company.

History has shown that often governments use companies they control as implements of government policy. Unfortunately, once a company becomes a major shareholding of the government, there is a great tendency for the managers to act as if they are not subject to market forces; and in many ways, they are not. There will be great pressure for GM to launch an IPO so that the government's shareholdings can be reduced.

In the initial General Motors restructuring plan, GM had presented the government with some forecasts, one of which was that trucks and SUVs would continue to be significant contributors to the new GM's bottom line. This forecast was rejected by the government oversight committee because politically it was believed that a government-controlled carmaker should not be so dependent on these gas guzzlers. By actually budgeting to sell fewer profitable trucks and SUVs, politics already had usurped normal and logical business decisions.

Here is a current example of how the good intentions of the government can backfire because our elected representatives have goals and agendas that may not be compatible with running a business.

The Federal National Mortgage Association (Fannie Mae) was established in 1938 as a mechanism to make mortgages more available to low-income families. In 1968, the government converted Fannie Mae into a private, shareholder-owned corporation in order to remove its activity from the annual balance sheet of the U.S. budget. Consequently, Fannie Mae ceased to be the guarantor of government-issued mortgages, and that responsibility was transferred to the new Government National Mortgage Association (Ginnie Mae). In 1970, the government created the Federal Home Loan Mortgage Corporation (FHLMC), commonly known as Freddie Mac, to compete with Fannie Mae and thus facilitate a more robust and efficient secondary mortgage market. Since the creation of the government-sponsored enterprises, there has been debate surrounding their role in the mortgage market, their relationship with the government, and whether or not they are indeed necessary. This debate gained relevance due to the collapse of the U.S. housing market and the sub-prime mortgage crisis that began in 2007. Despite this debate, Fannie Mae, as well as Ginnie Mae, and later, Freddie Mac, have played an integral role in increasing home ownership rates in the U.S. to among the highest in the world.

Fannie and Freddie were originally created to help ensure that financing for homes would be available and affordable to more consumers. The two firms buy mortgages from banks and other lenders and bundle them together into securities. They then either hold those securities or sell them to investors with a guarantee that they will be paid the money owed by homeowners.

The first big government bailout of the 2008 financial crisis was the takeover of mortgage finance giants Fannie Mae and Freddie Mac. Since Congress essentially wrote a blank check to the Treasury Department in July 2008 to do what needed to be done to inject capital into the two firms, Fannie (FNM, Fortune 500) has received $34.2 billion of direct government support, while Freddie (FRE, Fortune 500) has received $51.7 billion. As more homeowners defaulted on their mortgages, the two firms will likely book additional losses well into the future. Experts now believe that the bailout funds now required will exceed $200 billion.

Both the Bush and the Obama administrations have used government control of Fannie and Freddie to implement various policies to try to address rising home foreclosures and falling prices. The firms are a key part of the Obama administration's efforts to refinance mortgages of at-risk homeowners, in some cases making loans for up to 125 percent of the home's current market value.

What's clear is that there will continue to be a need for companies like Fannie and Freddie to keep mortgage costs relatively affordable by packaging loans into securities, placing a guarantee on them, and selling them to investors.

To be very clear, both companies were shareholder-owned, but were established as government-sponsored enterprises. The implicit involvement of the federal government gives investors and those doing business with these firms a sense of financial security. In fact, the government has used these companies as instruments of public policy.

For example, "In 1999, Fannie Mae came under pressure from the Clinton administration to expand mortgage loans to low and moderate income borrowers by increasing the ratios of their loan portfolios in distressed inner city areas."[7]

What is terrifying is the fact that the government-sponsored Freddie Mac and Fannie Mae:

- Have the highest individual losses of any companies as a result of the 2008 financial crisis

- Have become more inefficient by being used as instru-

---

7   See www.residual-rewards.com/fannie-mae-mortgages.html.

ments of public policy

- Have derived no benefit in management or leadership from government ownership, with the exception of reduced borrowing costs, while saving money increased the losses by lending cheaper money to high-risk clients

Apologists are saying that the huge taxpayer-funded losses were both good and necessary!

Is this what is in store for GM? Already there are rumours that certain GM managers feel quite comfortable in their corporate positions. For the first time in years, the company is awash in cash (taxpayers' cash, that is), besides being immune from shareholder and bondholder criticism. With a $57 billion government bailout, you can make a lot of million-dollar mistakes, and nobody will know or care.

From the perspective of the present—September 2011—the governments and the politicians have kept GM at arm's length. The continued political and economic unrest in America and the world has drawn everybody's focus away from GM. GM share values did not rise to where either Canada or the U.S. Treasury could recoup the money they paid for those shares. In fact, all governments have taken significant write-offs on GM shares. However, acting independently, GM cannot yet be considered the long-term leader in the auto business it once was.

29

What GM Achieved

There is a saying: "Be careful what you ask for; you may get it."

In the case of GM, they wanted to destroy the power of the unions. The U.S. and Canadian governments ensured that happened.

GM wanted to weaken the power of the dealers and they wanted the right to ignore the franchise agreements and laws that they were previously bound to abide by. The governments ensured that happened.

GM did not want to honour their financial obligations vis-à-vis pension funds, charitable investors, and other lenders who had supported GM for many years. The governments ensured that happened.

GM wanted to continue operating as it had in the past, with the same basic management operating team and their attitudes of arrogance and impunity. The governments ensured that happened.

In hindsight, GM appears to have gotten everything it wanted, with the assistance of government power and the taxpayers' money. It was able to ignore normal judicial due process and bully its stakeholders into submission. I believe a great injustice has been perpetrated on the people of Canada and the United States, and the well-intentioned U.S. government, in its desire to act quickly and decisively, has fallen into a trap that gives this one multinational company significant advantages not available to any other company in America.

Tragically, for a fortunate few, jobs and lifestyles will be maintained. The retirees who relied on GM bonds and shares for retirement income have been cheated. The losses experienced by the universities and charities that invested in GM stocks and bonds will not be easily replaced, and people will suffer. The dealers and their thousands of employees who committed themselves both financially and emotionally to GM have been destroyed. It goes on and on . . . communities crippled financially, families in crisis, hopes and dreams shattered.

Unfortunately, it appears that the long line of bad decisions continues to emanate from GM Head Office. The overwhelming reality in the demise of GM is the fact that decisions were almost always made with no consideration of the human factor. The process in forming the "new" GM is a continuation of this policy.

It is a sad fact that, with a few exceptions, the people running GM are the same ones who have run it for the past ten years. Richard Wagoner, Jr., was president from June 1, 2000, to March 30, 2009, then followed by Fritz Henderson from March 30, 2009, to December 1, 2009. Wagoner got a wonderful severance package for his corporate service. His firing was also tokenism in that his replacement was Wagoner's right-hand man for many years. Henderson was fired and replaced by the previously retired and government-appointed chairman of the board, Ed Whitacre.

Whitacre at times appears to believe he is the second coming of Lee Iacocca, appearing in commercials, trying his hardest to be charismatic. He ousted Henderson on December 1, 2009, because he wanted all the attention to himself. Whitacre is now paying himself twice what he was paying Henderson, and in February 2010, he hired Henderson back as a consultant. Henderson will be paid $59,000 a month for twenty hours' work each month!

Whiteacre is an immensely rich Texan who made millions in the telecommunications field. When he became chairman of GM, he admitted he did not know much about the car business. When he fired Henderson and made himself Chief Operating Executive, he proved it.

The Future for GM (and Chrysler)

The Canadian and American governments are betting billions of taxpayers' dollars that the future for GM will be rosy. Already, financial analysts' calculations show that GM will be making profits within a couple of years. I would urge extreme caution for the following reasons (as I write this in the summer of 2011, I admit I have the benefit of hindsight).

Future forecasts are horribly unreliable, especially from GM. Remember, in December of 2008, when automakers went to Washington, they initially asked for about $15 billion and then revised the figure later to $34 billion. At this point in time, the governments have committed over $60 billion! That is four times what the auto companies thought they needed just six months previously!

In other countries where there have been significant government bailouts, the auto companies still failed (United Kingdom) or have become nationalized companies managed by the state (France). In both cases, the long-term results have been negative for the taxpayers. Chrysler is for all intents an Italian company run out of Turin.

Both Chrysler and GM have done inestimable—and I believe non-recoverable—damage to their dealer organization, to their union workforce, and to their loyal customers. There are many people who will not even consider buying vehicles produced by GM or Chrysler. This is validated by the great strength and success of the Ford Motor Company, which has surged in sales and profitability.

The competition will be more aggressive than ever in attacking GM market share. Because of the government involvement, GM might be less flexible and less reactive to market situations. At this time, the general tumult in the political and economic world has precluded focusing much attention on GM. However, the same tumult is negatively affecting the U.S. economy, which places an even greater strain on GM's recovery plans.

I believe long-term success in the GM situation is a good probability. GM got into their problems because of arrogance and mismanagement and felt they had a limitless supply of money; they also consistently misread and underestimated the intelligence of the consumer. (That statement in itself describes most governments and their agencies!) Now they have almost limitless money and very little debt. Unfortunately, the Volt, the Cruze, and Buick have not had the sales volume that was predicted or needed.

I believe success will be more difficult in the Fiat–Chrysler alliance. Mercedes–Benz, a company much stronger and with many more resources and expertise than Fiat, failed to put Chrysler on strong enough financial footing to make it profitable in the long run. If Fiat–Chrysler does succeed, that will be an outstanding achievement.

What Should Have Happened?

When GM went hat in hand to the U.S. government in December 2008, the government had to do something. It was responsible for the fiscal collapse of lending institutions, which precipitated the crisis of solvency at GM; and it had to protect the industry and the jobs.

Specifically, the government should have done the following.

The government should have provided GM with all of the funds GM needed quickly; the delays by the Bush and Obama administration and congressional politicians compounded the problems of GM. The longer negotiations took, the higher the price tag grew. GM got almost four times the amount of money they initially asked for.

The funds should have been provided by means of loans and equity investments, and government should have paid off the existing bondholders at 100 cents on the dollar. As it was, the existing bondholders got screwed and likely will never again lend money to GM. The governments also got too few shares for their investment, which ensures that taxpayers will lose every time those shares are sold in the market.

The top layer of GM management (about fifty to one hundred people) should have been terminated with minimal compensation. It would be a great message to management in all companies that if you get a company into such a mess that it needs government help, you should be prepared to pay with your job. I believe this culling of management without golden parachutes should have happened on Wall Street as well after the 2008 banking fiasco. The terminated GM factory workers and dealership employees did not get to keep their jobs or their benefits.

Promote the new management from within, selecting people who know the business. Insist that the focus of management be on making each individual employee a productive, contributing member of the organization. Stress values and character as the new corporate culture; stress the personal responsibility of each employee to the customer and focus on the product.

Well, we all know we cannot change the past, so we will have to live with all the decisions made in the first six months of 2009. To many thousands of men and women in North America, it was a time of anxiety, fear, and sadness. Many lives and lifestyles were destroyed, and many have been permanently scarred.

To some people, the fall of GM was like the fall of Communism twenty years before—an "empire" that did not serve its people well. The old GM contributed tremendous achievements in the world of science and transportation. It helped win wars and improve prosperity and provided transportation for millions. But like Communism, it could not—or would not—respond effectively to its people, the consumers who voted with dollars. (So much for the central planning that both Communism and GM in its later years espoused.)

Communism's intrinsic weakness was its refusal to recognize the individual, instead focusing only on the proletariat. GM, with more and more centralized management, similarly became focused on dollars and cents, numbers and statistics, forgetting or even ignoring the needs of its employees and its consumers.

When consumers asked for reliable cars, GM said their cars were reliable enough, so the consumers bought reliable cars made by the Japanese. When union line workers had to strike to get decent health benefits, the executives were receiving million-dollar bonuses. When the product development needed more money to ensure quality cars would be built, GM made investments instead in foreign companies and foreign countries. They tried to buy solutions with acquisitions such as EDS and Hughes. When the dealers complained about warranty policies and the quality of cars they were receiving, the company blamed the dealers.

30

A Typical Dealership

Car dealerships are a very unique form of a retail small business. What makes them unique is the huge capital investment required to open the doors, the many diverse skill sets required by the employees, and the link to only one inventory supplier.

Let us assume you want to open a car dealership in your local community, and International Motor Car Company has given you the franchise to sell their brands. The first thing you have to do is line up the money; it just so happens you have won five million dollars in the lottery and you think you are ready to go. You go to your bank and set up all the accounts required by International Motor Car to pay them for the new vehicles and parts they will ship to you. Then you get all the government licences and approvals you need to operate a dealership. In Ontario, car dealerships are regulated by about twenty different pieces of government legislation, which is about average for most jurisdictions.

Now that you have all the forms and permits, you need property to operate on. Even a small dealership needs about two acres of property and 10,000 square feet of building. Depending on land values in your community, this will cost on average about three million dollars if you are very prudent in design and construction. That really eats into your lottery windfall, though. Now you have to install all of your service shop equipment, hoists, compressors, benches, exhaust fans, emission equipment, diagnostic computers, brake lathes, alignment machines, tire changers, presses, grinders, welding torches, and on and on. You also will need parts racking, a computer system, a satellite system to communicate with International Motors, office equipment, desks, chairs, and a thousand other sundry items. By now, your lottery windfall is pretty much gone, and you have not even opened the doors of your business.

You go back to the bank because you need "floor plan" money

to pay for the fifty new vehicles that you ordered from International Motors (about one million dollars' worth of vehicles). You also set up a $300,000 "operating line" that will allow you to buy used cars and bulk oil and parts; and to cover the odd negative cash flow situation in which you are paying more cash out than you are bringing in.

You budget about $50,000 for your grand opening promotion and sale and you open the doors. On the first day, you sell three new cars and two used. Life is beautiful.

After being open two months, you have about four million dollars of your own money tied up in your business. You think because you followed the best advice possible, you have a chance at success. Each day, you study the DOC (daily operating control) and discover that the sales manager is not making much gross profit on the new car sales.

When you tell him that $1,000 per unit gross profit is not enough, he replies that the customers are buying only the International Fuelex, and that model, even when sold at full list, has a $1050 margin, so he feels he is doing okay on the eight Fuelex models the staff have sold. You go away grumbling to the service department, only to find the two service advisors, the cashier, and the service manager talking together in a group. You have a mini-stroke at the thought of $150,000 in annual salaries standing around doing nothing. When you confront them, they tell you that since you are a new dealer in town, there are very few International vehicles in the community. Most were bought from Jacksonville International in Jacksonville, thirty miles away, and Jacksonville gives all their customers free lube, oil, and filters for the first five years of ownership, with free valet service to the customer's residence.

You slide an Ativan under your tongue and walk over to check out the used car lot. The lot man has parked the mint Mercedes with only 14,000 miles on it too close to the laneway, and the UPS truck has put a nice brown scuff on it. You want to cry and you walk back to your office.

On your voice mail, there is a message from Ed Grinder. He had new brakes put on his car last week and they are making a squeaking noise. He wants to know what you are going to do about it. He feels you should fix it, he should get a refund of what he paid, and you should compensate him for the loss of a day's pay if he has to bring the car back to your shop. Ed also reminds you that he is a prominent member of the community and expects to be treated right.

You pause for a minute, waiting for the Ativan to kick in.

There is a knock on your door, and it is night receptionist Amber Goodbody and her father. In tears, she tells you that Slim, your top car salesman, was working on the sales floor last night. He and a couple of other salesmen were standing around her desk while there was a lull in customer traffic and they were telling off-colour jokes. When Amber protested to Slim, he said she was being "prissy." Mr. Goodbody then says the only reason he has not launched a sexual harassment lawsuit is because he is a good friend of yours! At this point, you realize that you should have invested your lottery winnings with Bernie Madoff; the end result would have been the same but less stressful.

You promise Mr. Goodbody to investigate the situation. Then in walks Rex Sharp, your International Motors factory rep. Rex tells you he has some great ideas to help you sell more cars. After careful analysis he and headquarters have recognized some weakness in your operation and, based on the "best practices" of other International Motors dealers, he wants to share them with you. First of all, Rex tells you that your dealership is doing way better than anybody expected (faint praise), and with only a few changes, you can move into the big time. (You thought four million of your own money *was* big time.)

First, you should increase the on-hand inventory to seventy-five cars, because today's consumer wants choice. You have to increase your local profile by sponsoring local baseball, football, soccer, basketball, hockey, cheerleaders, and golf events.

You should either make major donations to, or sponsor fundraising events for, Heart and Stroke, MS, the March of Dimes, United Way, the Red Cross, Rotary, Kiwanis, the Cancer Society, the Diabetes Society, the Salvation Army, and several other worthy organizations.

Finally, Rex tells you he had the dealership "mystery shopped" last week, and one of your salesmen could not explain satisfactorily to the shopper the difference between International's patented Cross-Intuitive-Sensing-All-Wheel-Drive Traction System with the Fuzzy Logic Algorithm (ICISAWDTSFL for short) and the competition's inferior four-wheel drive systems.

Rex then tells you how Jacksonville Motors has leased a mud bog and on weekends supplies demonstrators with ICISAWDTS-FL to the public so they can experience first-hand the superb traction of this system. Rex neglects to tell you one car fell into a "sippy hole" and they had to lease a submersible from the U.S. Navy to locate it! The test driver promises not to sue.

You look down at your mail, and you see an envelope from the Human Rights Investigations Board!

The good news is that the company is holding a two-day training course for salesmen in Capitalville next month at minimal cost to the dealership. Rex has enrolled and reserved hotel rooms for all your staff.

After about a year, you feel you now understand the business and have developed some operating procedures and guidelines.

- No matter how many vehicles you have in stock, you never have enough of the right ones.

- No matter how much money you lose, you will have employees who feel underpaid.

- Your best people are being constantly lured away by the competition.

- Your bad people never leave.

- Everybody wants something for free.

After five years, you have a nice little operation going at your International Motors dealership. You run a very successful used-car and all-make leasing operation, and because you paid cash for your land and buildings, your monthly overhead is very reasonable, and the new body shop is doing well. Buck Horney, your latest factory rep, comes in one day, and tells you because of economic concerns at International, they do not want any dealers in towns of less than 50,000 people. It costs too much to service these small-town dealers, and International believes by concentrating on cities of over 200,000, the remaining dealers will be stronger, as will International. By concentrating on these cities, International will have 100 top-flight dealers. Rex tells you he is sorry, and there is no appeal—you are out; your dealer agreement will not be renewed.

In all seriousness, the real key to a profitable car dealership is volume and cost control.

You need to sell lots of cars at a profit, and that usually happens when you are selling cars people want to buy. If people are not interested in your brand, you can have great facilities, great staff, a great location, and great advertising, and you still will not be successful. Unfortunately, the manufacturer has the greatest control over the consumer acceptance of the product, not the dealer. If you ran a grocery store, and people were not buying Sunlight, but buying Tide, you would devote more shelf space to Tide, or even discontinue carrying Sunlight. In a franchise, you are stuck with the brand.

There are only two ways that a brand can be made more desirable to the consumer: Make a better car than your competition; or lower the price so the car becomes a better value. Yugo proved you can sell any car at a low enough price. The cars that always do well in the various magazine comparison tests tend to sell well. Brands that do consistently poorly in these comparisons do not sell well unless they have a significant price advantage.

In 1990, I was privy to some market research that was very enlightening. Mazda had a special sedan built for market testing. The car was not for sale, as it was a prototype of a future model. They put Mazda emblems on the car, and in a controlled situation they had focus groups look at the car, sit in it, and really give it the onceover. They asked the members of the focus group a number of questions, one of which was, "What do you think this car should sell for?" The members of the group all wrote down a number.

They then took off all the Mazda identification, and put on Honda emblems and markings. They brought another large focus group through with the same characteristics and demographics. They asked the same questions. This was done in several cities, and in several states. The result was that the evaluators who believed the car was a Honda model valued it some $1200 more than the group who believed the car was a Mazda!

This is a very telling result; it shows that consumers attribute dollar values to different brands. If your brand is the perceptually undervalued, you will suffer in both sales volume and profitability. If you reduce the price of your brand, your competition can do the same, and you will lose more profit. This ties in nicely with what happened to GM dealers: As people consciously chose other brands over GM, sales per dealer were reduced, and profitability on those remaining sales went down. The absolute worst thing to do in light of these facts would be to reduce both the dealer and brand count. If consumer demand is the problem, reducing consumer choice both in what and where they can buy is counterproductive.

Successful Dealerships Have the Following Attributes:

People
The real and only key to long-term success is the right people. Dealers want working people of character and values. They do not hire people who have quick and easy answers to all the problems, because there are no quick and easy answers. Every employee must understand that the dealership is in the customer creation business. Only by making a successful sale do we have a customer, and a customer we have created will likely deal with us again in the future.

Well-trained salespeople are crucial; they must first have charisma and empathy that the customer identifies and relates to in seconds. If within thirty seconds the customer has not developed a positive opinion of the salesperson, it will be a very tough sell. Usually, technically proficient salespeople are lower in the charisma factor.

The salesman should have special training in negotiation skills, because in most cases the greatest amount of the time spent with a customer is in negotiating the price and the deal.

Financing a vehicle is a very big revenue area. Offer the customers good value and control the finance process in-house. (In a given year, a bank or lending institution will generate more income on car loans than the dealer made in selling the cars!)

Vehicles

It is not a matter of how many vehicles you carry, but how many of the "right ones" you have.

The only reason a car does not sell is the price. Old stock must be dramatically reduced in price to become a "super deal" for the next customer.

Every used car should be reconditioned to a very high level appropriate to its price point. Never pay too much for a trade-in on a new or used car, or it will haunt you. You can stretch on a prime retail piece. The biggest mistake is paying too much for crap.

Service

Give people more than they expect in the service department. The sales department sells the customer—the service department keeps them.

Always return the vehicle cleaner to the customer than it was when they brought it in. Always facilitate their bringing the car in for service. If you cannot get to their car today, schedule an alternative appointment. Be flexible in your rules to accommodate customers; they will appreciate it.

Parts

Give customers choice, if a part is too expensive, offer an alternative. For example, in the case of an alternator that has worn out after 100,000 miles, a GM franchised dealer was supposed only to offer the customer a new GM Delco alternator, or a Delco remanufactured part. Other lower-cost alternatives available from independent garages are offshore-sourced alternators, local rebuilds, or even "wrecker parts." The difference between parts costs in this situation could easily exceed $300. That is how dealers who were forced to sell only factory-approved parts got the reputation of being expensive places to get cars fixed.

Accounting

This department should be of service to the profit-making departments. At all times, it should be facilitating the other departments of the dealership in their accounting functions through training and assistance.

31

Vehicles That Hurt GM

1971–77 Chevrolet Vega (Pontiac Astre)

(Photo courtesy of www.productioncars.com. Used with permission.)

The Vega was GM's first serious entry into the small car market. Attractive and familiar to traditional American buyers, it sold relatively well until serious engine problems due to design innovations reared their head. Not truly refined before introduction to the market, new questionable engine technology utilizing a liner-less aluminum block with iron heads led to engine reliability problems. Styling was attractive, yet the car lacked the refinement in noise harshness and vibration that the contemporary Japanese seemed to have already mastered. As well, the Lordstown, Ohio, assembly plant suffered ongoing labour strife and quality problems.

1976–87 Chevrolet Chevette–Pontiac Acadian—Pontiac T2000

The Chevette and variations were copies of an older old Opel of Germany design. It was a generation behind its Japanese competitors in almost every way; specifically, the brakes were not suited for North American winter climates, giving it poor reliability.

(Photo courtesy of www.productioncars.com. Used with permission.)

By copying the old design, GM saved millions in engineering costs. The dealers had difficulty trying to sell these rear-wheel-drive, noisy, econo-boxes to consumers who could buy much more sophisticated front-wheel cars from the Japanese. The GM objective was to offer a car priced below the Vega that was still profitable to sell. To facilitate this, GM priced the Vega as a step-up vehicle from the Chevette. The problem was the Chevette was such an unremarkable car that the only way GM could generate any volume was by pricing it very low in the market. What resulted was that GM offered two small cars that were not profitable. This is where GM developed the theory that they could not make money on small cars. The fact was they could not make money on bad, small cars.

1980–85 Chevrolet Citation, Chevrolet Nova, Pontiac Phoenix, Buick Skylark, and Oldsmobile Omega

(Photo courtesy of www.productioncars.com. Used with permission.)

The Citation and its siblings had an outstanding design when introduced in 1980; roomy, comfortable, and stylish, with excellent performance. It was truly innovative and advanced and could have led to renewed long-term prosperity for GM. Initial reviews were outstanding—a true world beater. Unfortunately, an incomplete development process resulted in unproven ideas failing in real-world use (a familiar GM error). Serious engine, braking, steering, and transmission problems drove many loyal GM customers away. Problems with the reliability and durability of most mechanical systems, such as engine oil leaks (no-gasket technology), premature rear brake lock-up (to save money while meeting NHTSA standards), and steering rack failures (again to save money) soured many initial buyers on GM products.

There is a theory that Lee Iacocca's success at Chrysler, besides the minivan, was due to the front-wheel-drive "K" car. It is felt that many consumers who wanted an economical front-wheel-drive American car were scared away from GM by the Citation and its clones and bought the K car. The K car, even though it was bland and uninspiring, was relatively reliable and dependable, and scores of versions were produced. For the 1980s, almost all of Chrysler's volume car sales came from K car-based designs.

1981–84 Cadillac Deville

(Photo courtesy of www.productioncars.com. Used with permission.)

The downsized Cadillac Deville introduced in 1977 was a fantastic car and sales success. Using proven Cadillac components from the past in a smaller, lighter chassis provided traditional prestige and comfort, and the fuel economy improved. A real winner. Unfortunately, the Cadillac reputation was seriously damaged when the 4–6–8 V8 and Olds Diesel engine variations were introduced into various Cadillac models beginning in 1978. In order to avoid the "gas-guzzler stigma," GM adopted an Eaton Corporation design that mechanically/hydraulically deactivated cylinders to improve fuel economy. Supposedly, a Cadillac could get four-cylinder fuel economies when low power was required. Eaton had offered the design to Ford for its Lincoln brand, and they passed on it. Cadillac installed it as standard equipment, and eventually the dealers deactivated all the customers' systems because there were so many problems. Fleet customers such as livery companies and airline limousines replaced their 4–6–8 Cadillacs en masse with Lincolns. Another disaster GM produced was a Cadillac powered by an Oldsmobile-derived diesel V8. Whole books have been written about these engines. Singlehandedly, GM turned North American consumers away from diesel fuel-saving technology for decades.

1982–88 Cadillac–Cimarron

(Photo courtesy of www.productioncars.com. Used with permission.)

The Cadillac Cimarron was an unmitigated disaster when this restyled Cavalier — a mediocre econo-box at best — was dressed up with leather seats and a Cadillac-style grille and emblems and then foisted on the public as a Cadillac. To improve fuel economy, the gearing was altered, which reduced performance. In 1981, GM marketed the Cimarron as a competitor to the BMW 3 series. The 3 series is dubbed the Ultimate Driving Machine; with Cavalier components, the Cimarron was the opposite. Under the old divisional system, a Cadillac Division manager would never have let this car see the light of day. A true abomination in every sense of the word, and an insult to everything Cadillac had stood for previously. The dealers dutifully stocked the car, but it was a performance and sales disaster. Unfortunately, it also sent consumers to the imports to buy small, luxurious, fuel-efficient cars.

Buick Regal, Oldsmobile Cutlass Supreme, Pontiac Grand Prix, Chevrolet Lumina

(Photo courtesy of www.productioncars.com. Used with permission.)

Introduced in 1988, but developed in the previous four years under Roger Smith, these were the cars that killed the brands forever, a classic example of "Badge-Engineering" gone horribly wrong. First, to save costs, GM decided that all brands would share the same basic design, with minor styling differences. The media was quick to point out that there was no basic difference between the cars. They had the same engines, transmissions, brakes, suspensions, and tires. The mantra began: "Too many brands selling identical cars from too many dealerships."

On top of this, GM introduced the two-door models first, a much smaller segment of the market (Toyota did not even offer a two-door Camry then). GM delayed the Lumina four-door version of the Chevrolet brand for two years, forcing consumers in the huge, mid-size volume segment to buy the more expensive Oldsmobile, Buick, and Pontiac versions, or buy an import. On top of this, the cars were functional and mechanical disasters. ABS electronic brake controls failed, rear brake calipers seized, digital dashes went blank, steering racks seized, brake rotors wore out regularly. The problems with the automatic transmissions were ongoing. Imagine the experience of an owner of a Citation who then traded it in for a Buick Regal? A GM customer for life? Not likely.

1991–95 Saturn

(Photo courtesy of www.productioncars.com. Used with permission.)

Roger Smith formed the Saturn Car Corporation in 1985. The company came close to revolutionizing the industry, through its dealer organization, its autonomy from GM, its customer relations, and its unique plastic body. Initially a great seller, it was again let down by poor mechanicals and internal jealousy from established GM corporate loyalists who felt money invested in Saturn would have been better used on the traditional brands.

As sales fell and money became short, the brand became starved of new product to keep up with the market. Saturn was to be a grand experiment for a "Different kind of car and a different kind of car company." The differences were the relationship between Saturn and its workers, its dealers, and its customers. The dealers created a different, more positive relationship with its clients.

On the initial Saturn models, there was no GM identification. Unfortunately, there was one common element that Saturns had in common with regular GM products: they had numerous mechanical problems. The customers were patient and loyal, the dealers were overachievers in fixing the problems, and things looked good for the long term. When Saturn became starved of development money, new models were delayed. Even though consumers loved the expensive plastic bodies that gave the Saturn brand much of its cachet, GM wanted to switch to much cheaper steel bodies. So GM started the myth that customers did not like the panel gaps. (Panel gaps are the spaces between body panels such as the fenders and the trunk lid. These gaps were about twice as large on Saturns to allow for expansion and contraction of the plastic in various temperature conditions. Steel does not change its dimensions as much under temperature changes.) Eventually, Saturn ceased to be an individual division; in 2009, it ceased to exist. Created and destroyed by the same GM organization.

1997–2004 Chevrolet Venture, Pontiac Montana, Oldsmobile Silhouette, Buick Rendezvous

(Photo courtesy of www.productioncars.com. Used with permission.)

After introducing the unique and innovative plastic-bodied Lumina APV in 1990 (a.k.a. the "dust buster"), GM replaced it in 1997 with the Venture for Chevrolet, with variations for Pontiac, Oldsmobile, and Buick. Minivans were hot sellers in the eighties and nineties, and GM's second-generation minivan was designed to topple the hot-selling Chrysler minivan from #1 in sales. Even though these minivans were again badge-engineered clones of one another, they were styled uniquely and distinctly enough to appear different to the consumers. They had everything going for them. In most ways, they were excellent vehicles and very successful until the intake manifold gaskets began to leak. If the customer was lucky, this happened during the warranty period, but most often, the warranty had expired. As mentioned previously, failure rate approached 100 percent. Unfortunately, under the metal skin they were mechanically identical and were haunted by the old GM ghosts of steering, transmission, and brake durability problems. These vans were very popular on the used-car market and were often the purchaser's first exposure to GM-built vehicles. If the van had the (probable) intake gasket problem, it was also their last GM vehicle. The customers left in droves. GM does not produce this series of minivan today. Chrysler sold over 215,000 minivans in 2010.

2001–2005 Pontiac Aztek

(Photo courtesy of www.productioncars.com. Used with permission.)

The Pontiac Aztek was an attempt to attract younger buyers to GM vehicles. The Venture minivan chassis gave it an "edgier styling." In real life, the vehicle did not look as attractive as in this picture. Of course, it had all the mechanical difficulties of its siblings.

DEX-COOL Antifreeze

DEX-COOL was a super-extended-life antifreeze developed with

(Author's collection)

Texaco (merged with Chevron in 2001).

GM always tried to be the automotive technological leader. It fact, it is believed GM has had more patents than all of the other carmakers combined. One of the advantages GM saw it had over the imports was the lower cost of service and operation of their vehicles. GM put a real effort into increasing the longevity of various maintenance items.

They introduced spark plugs that would last 100,000 miles and maintenance-free batteries; and, in conjunction with Texaco, developed an ultra-long-life antifreeze called DEX-COOL. The antifreeze was based on organic acid technology, which offered much longer coolant change intervals with no loss of corrosion resistance and coolant protection. It was good for 150,000 miles before needing replacement.

DEX-COOL came into widespread use at the same time as the leaking intake manifolds appeared in GM minivans and other GM vehicles that featured the 3.4-litre V6. The erroneous conclusion by many consumers was that it was the DEX-COOL that was destroying the gaskets and causing the leaks. In fact, some consumers began draining out the DEX-COOL and reinstalling old-fashioned ethylene glycol or propylene glycol coolants (the green stuff). My experience in dealerships was that DEX-COOL was *not* the cause of mechanical failures, especially the intake manifold leaks it was blamed for. Old GM settled a $2.2 million class action suit. The bad publicity cost a lot more. But all along, although GM knew it was not the coolant that was causing the leaks, they never came out openly and honestly to say it was the engine and gasket design that led to the leaks, not the coolant. By this time, the damage to GM's reputation was irreversible. Today recognized as a fine product, all of the major coolant companies offer their version of DEX-COOL.

Most of GM's mechanical reliability problems were based on improper or inadequate testing in the design and pre-production stages. There was an implicit belief by GM that whatever problems occurred could be handled more cheaply at the dealer level after the consumer owned the vehicle. Many poor-quality decisions were consciously made by the "bean-counters" after careful analysis that it would be more profitable to sell substandard and/or defective vehicles and then muddle through with customer complaints. GM also found it much more economical to blame the workers for substandard products than to engineer them correctly from the beginning. Of course, the market share slide and bankruptcy are simple proofs of the fallacy of that thinking.

The Big Three are now the Big Five in America.

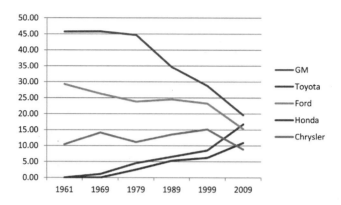

Over five decades, there have been monumental shifts in U.S. market shares from the years when GM, Ford, and Chrysler controlled about 85 percent of the market; in 2009, five companies were in the 10 to 20 percent range each. At its current growth rate, Hyundai may be joining this group.

(Courtesy of Wards Automotive Group)

32

Conclusion, Part 1

GM was successful for many decades because of the divisional system of operational control. As the divisions were emasculated, then eliminated, more power accrued to head office. Head office became focused on Wall Street reviews, share prices and short-term profits, self-perpetuation, and rich pensions.

With the elimination of the divisions, GM became a behemoth that had more inertia than an iceberg. It could not turn or manoeuvre; it might have wanted to do many wonderful things but it just drifted and eventually melted away.

Every company needs creative tension throughout its leadership ranks, to ensure that the best ideas rise to the top. The divisional structure provided that for GM. Many other companies have various organizational structures that ensure the sort of independent and creative leadership that the divisional system provided GM, and they are doing just fine. I believe that another reason for success in Ford's case is that the founding family is still in charge; to the great-grandsons of Henry Ford, it is a hundred-year tradition of effort and achievement they are perpetuating.

Successful companies and successful leaders have been able to facilitate this creative tension in their organizations for the benefit of all. When this creative tension disappears; when the striving for success by individuals disappears; and when arrogance takes hold, falsehoods replace the truth, and blame replaces responsibility, the organization will begin its downward spiral.

A cautionary note: with the onset of protests in North America against the greed and avarice of Wall Street, Big Banks, and Big Business, corporate leaders must develop a moral compass on issues for which they were previously given a "free pass." Most business schools taught that the goal of business was to be profitable, and it was government's responsibility to ensure justice and fairness for all. However, Business learned very well how to co-opt government's role, and we see the results in our economy today with the maldistribution of benefits throughout society. I believe our corporate leaders will have to control greed, avarice, and the hyper-accumulation of wealth and ensure all citizens have an opportunity for fair access to society's benefits.

If corporate leaders do not implement and utilize ethical and moral values in their decision-making, citizens of a democratic society will demand that their elected officials set the standards. Tough legislation was imposed for auto safety and the environment, and it can happen in financial and corporate industry sectors as well.

PART 2

GENERAL MOTORS CANADA

1

GM Canada

In trying to deal with the General Motors saga, because of the vastness of the topic, I felt it was important to get insight into the human level on the impact of the bankruptcy of GM. In much the same way as you can learn more about the British Navy in the Napoleonic wars by studying the operation of one British frigate than by reading all the Admiralty's reports, I have chosen to look into the actions of a small segment of the vast worldwide GM operation during the crisis of 2009. Because of personal familiarity, I chose GM Canada.

At the turn of the twentieth century, brothers Sam and George McLaughlin were, with their father, successful carriage builders in Oshawa, Ontario, Canada. They saw a future in transportation and decided to produce automobiles in Canada. First, they researched the products that were currently available on the market. In 1905, Sam test-drove several automobiles but quickly decided that the Buick was the car he wanted to make in Oshawa.

Sam and George were unable to come to terms on financial arrangements with William Durant, the head of Buick in Flint, Michigan. Sam and George returned home and convinced father Robert to form the McLaughlin Motor Car Company. Production of an original and unique McLaughlin automobile was about to begin when the chief engineer they had hired, American Arthur Milbrath, fell seriously ill with pleurisy. After some hesitation, Sam sent a telegram to Durant and asked to borrow an engineer. The next day, Durant arrived in Oshawa by train with two Buick executives, the original plans for collaboration were resurrected, and in 1908 the plant turned out 154 cars—called McLaughlins—with Buick engines and components. GM of Canada was one of the early divisions of the GM empire.

Canada is economically a world powerhouse, ranking ninth in the world in total GNP in 2005. It is a vast land with only about 34,000,000 residents, 80 percent of whom live within 200 miles of the U.S. border. Canada's economy is integrated with that of the United States and Mexico as a result of the North American Free Trade Agreement of 1994. The new car sales are usually about 7–10 percent of the U.S. annual total. Canadians buy a greater proportion of smaller, more fuel-efficient cars, because purchase taxes and gasoline prices are significantly higher in Canada. The U.S. is still the world's greatest auto market, and more new cars are sold in Greater Los Angeles annually than all of Canada. General Motors has its Canadian head office in Oshawa, Ontario, and a number of plants and supplier plants, mostly in the provinces of Quebec and Ontario. They have regional sales offices throughout the country as well.

The president of GM of Canada (from this point we shall use the short form GMCL, General Motors of Canada Limited) is traditionally a non-Canadian who is usually on temporary assignment to develop skills for the next promotion in the GM worldwide organization. The Canadian president tends not to get involved in the day-to-day issues of making and selling cars, but rather spends most of his time dealing with various levels of Canadian governments, media, and trade associations.

All Canadian management decisions have to be approved in Detroit, and there are no distinct or unique GMCL policies that have not been approved in Detroit. It would be fair to say that the bulk of GM's Canadian top management's time is spent doing Detroit's bidding. This is just the reality in the multinational world we live in now. Over the years, Canada has benefited from GM and its investments and commitment to Canada, and Canadians have been loyal buyers of GM cars for decades. In fact, imports hold a greater share of the U.S. market than in Canada's, and GM lost market share at a much slower rate in Canada than in the U.S. One could say that GMCL was a healthier organization than GM in the U.S. GMCL never asked for bankruptcy protection.

The most influential position in the Canadian GM hierarchy traditionally has been the vice-president of sales. He is ultimately responsible for all aspects of sales in Canada. Nothing related to sales of GM cars in Canada—from national advertising, to who is a dealer, to what a dealer can display in his showroom—occurs without his implicit approval. He is the closest thing to God in the GMCL world.

Dick Conlin held this position from 1997 until 2002. Dick was the son of a car dealer, was very familiar with all aspects of selling GM vehicles in Canada, and was well respected.

Marc Comeau replaced Dick Conlin in 2002 and was not well known by the dealer organization. Comeau is also on the board of directors for GMCL. I saw Marc Comeau for the first time on an HIDL broadcast (HIDL was an interactive satellite communication system, for which the dealers paid, by which GM could provide all sorts of video communications and training to the dealership) and was underwhelmed by his presence and his presentation. Dick Conlin was an impressive man, following in a long line of GMCL excellent sales executives. Comeau did not fit this image. Many assumed he must be some sort of marketing and sales genius to have been promoted to this position. Despite his underwhelming presence, under his leadership, Canadian sales did relatively well, losing market share at a slower rate when compared to U.S. GM sales.

Comeau was a company man through and through. He loved to be in communication with the dealers through the HIDL, but never said anything that was not scripted, edited, or massaged to suit the GM party line. When listening to Comeau, one always wondered what was being withheld. Even when introducing an unpopular program, he would state that it was supported by the dealers. He never said *how many* dealers supported the program; he just said dealers supported it. Many dealers after listening to Marc on HIDL realized that often he did not say anything of substance. He was noted for always telling the dealers how hard he and his staff had been working to develop this great new sales promotion, even if it was last year's program recycled!

You may ask: How did he rise to this auspicious and powerful position? It is obvious he was very astute when it came to corporate politics. He seemed eternally positive that the great GMCL sales rebound was just around the corner. He had no trouble pitching the corporate line to the dealers, no matter how ridiculous it sounded.

The most amazing thing you heard from Comeau was how great things were, how good GM cars were, how GMCL was driving back the competition, and how our market share was rebounding. If you as a dealer were having a rough time, it was your fault—all of the other dealers were doing great.

A confident and assured-looking Marc Comeau prior to GMCL's difficulties to which he contributed in 2009. It has been said that so much of his time is involved in lawsuits that some weeks, he spends two to three days at GMCL's law firm in Toronto and only one or two days at his office in Oshawa.
(Photo courtesy of auto123.com. Used with permission.)

Here are some media interviews that give you some insight into the man.

This is an interview of Marc Comeau from January 23, 2007, by Michel Deslauriers. (My comments are in brackets.)

Q) GM seems transformed compared to just one year ago. What happened?

A) Actually, the change started about three years ago, when Rick Wagoner [fired by Obama in 2009] and Bob Lutz [retired at the end of 2009] decided to focus on design and to address quality shortcomings. We now offer a five-year/160,000 km powertrain warranty. In addition, we're putting the emphasis on our Green concept, offering a diversified range of eco-friendly products.

Q) I'm thinking of your presentation last year in Detroit, as the company only launched big trucks and announced price cuts. We felt that the morale was low at GM. Today, with car and truck of the year, the Volt, the new Malibu . . . the optimism seems to have returned.

A) We're number one in China, and our sales have increased 20 to 30 percent in Latin America, so last year was a good one for us. Since his arrival, Bob Lutz established a new discipline at GM, and we now take the necessary time to do things right. We're going to get back the sales we lost in the last years.

Q) We're seeing several new products for Chevrolet, Saturn [gone in 2009], Buick, Cadillac, and GMC. What should we expect from Pontiac [gone in 2009], and will they also get hybrid models?

*A) Yes. Pontiac will get new products next year and that division has a promising future [**less than two years before cancellation!**] despite certain rumours. Pontiac will also get hybrid vehicles.*

Consider that this interview took place twenty-one months before the same Mr. Wagoner went to Washington to be rescued; Marc Comeau is talking about how great things are going to be! We even hear about great new products from Saturn and Pontiac, two brands that have been eliminated. Twenty-one months before the company heads for bankruptcy, everything is roses!

Here is another media story by Chris Vander Doelen of the *Windsor Star*, published on Tuesday, April 8, 2008 (eight months before the cry for help):

"We haven't seen consumer confidence drop as it has in the United States . . . but there is a little bit of apprehension out there," Comeau said in an interview while describing industry trends evident in the first quarter. "It's digging into confidence."

In addition to affordability, always a dominant issue with Canadian buyers, Canadians are also increasingly worried about long-term debt, Comeau said. That's the message coming back to head office from dealers and sales-people across the country.

"So we're devoting a lot of resources to dealing with that fear. We will manage that." So far, zero percent financing seems to be giving Canadians the confidence they need to help them make up their minds.

GM SALES VP "QUITE HAPPY" ABOUT
ITS MARCH SALES

Despite all the grim reports about March sales last week, GM Canada is still counting on seeing a sales increase of between one percent and 1.5 percent. **[Sales actually fell more than 20 percent for the year!]**

Last week's headlines about the Detroit-based auto-makers were a lot more downbeat than the reality, according to Marc Comeau, vice-president of sales for GM Canada. **[Was Comeau talking to anybody in Detroit before he made this statement?]**

In the U.S., yes, March was an unmitigated disaster for Detroit Big Three sales. But General Motors of Canada was actually "quite happy" about its performance.

Despite a 16.4 percent plunge in sales in March, GM, still the leader in Canada by a wide margin, was up 2 percent for the quarter, Comeau said. **[By 2011, Ford surpassed GMCL as #1 in Canada.]**

Outside of reduced fleet sales to daily rental companies, the main reason for the plunge in GM sales in Canada was the expiry at the end of February of the Wish and Win Contest, which was so successful at the end of 2007 that GM extended it.

The contest, which gave contestants a minimum of $1,000 off any purchase and a chance to win up to $10,000 off, goosed sales so much that GM ended up pulling ahead some March sales.

"I'm not really concerned about March because we knew we were mortgaging March a little bit," Comeau said. "Look at the quarter: we're up two points. All of our new vehicles performed better than we thought." **[Is this "bean-counter" jargon?]**

GM's Canadian sales increased across the segments of the two extremes of the marketplace: compacts and sub-compacts, mid-sized crossovers, and full-size pickup trucks.

The sales of some of GM's Korean-built subcompacts were up as much as 50 percent, and the company believes Canadians will continue to migrate away from SUVs and full-size sedans into more and more small cars.

"I think you're going to continue to see a strong run on small vehicles," Comeau predicted, due to persistently high fuel prices.

That also explains the move to mid-size crossovers, such as the Acadia/Outlook/Enclave, sales of which rose by up to 45 percent last month as sales of SUVs dropped.

Even sales of GM pickup trucks rose 11 percent in Canada last month, despite high gas prices and plunging pickup sales in the United States.

Many U.S. buyers of pickups use them daily for the commute to work; a larger percentage of Canadians buy them because they can't do without them.

"They're a utilitarian vehicle—we simply need them to run our businesses and haul our trailers and our horses," Comeau said.

Based on the Comeau view of the future, most people would have to think twice about following his guidance or advice. I have always believed if you cannot tell the truth, it's better to say nothing; could Comeau possibly believe he was telling the truth? He was contradicting GM of Detroit's warnings.

The issue that is specifically of interest is Comeau's role in eliminating 42 percent of the Canadian dealer organization in one day.

Some Background

For years, GMCL believed and stated that the number of dealerships it had in Canada was a positive. From sea to sea, GMCL was serving customers in every part of the land. They even boasted about their numbers in press releases for years.

"GM of Canada manufactures a variety of vehicles, engines, transmissions, and other components, and markets the full range of General Motors vehicles and related services through 785 dealerships and retailers across Canada. Vehicles sold through this network include Chevrolet, Pontiac, Buick, GMC, Cadillac, Hummer, Saturn, and Saab."[8]

Because Canada has a land mass equivalent in area to that of the U.S., and only about 10 percent of the U.S.'s population, it has a much lower population density, so the dealerships would necessarily be on a smaller scale.

By the end of April and the beginning of May 2009, rumours started to spread throughout the Canadian dealer organization that there would be a mass closing of dealerships. Since everybody knew that the sixty or so Saturn stores were closing, it was believed these and maybe thirty to forty rural or small dealerships that had not completed Image 2000 would be phased out. From a dealer's viewpoint, closing a total of ninety to one hundred dealerships in Canada was a huge number and would be considered an enormous and unprecedented action.

The U.S. Treasury issued the following statement on May 15, 2009, in response to GM's closure announcement in the U.S.

GM's announcement is part of the company's larger effort to restructure to achieve financial viability. The Task Force is continuing to work with GM and all its stakeholders and will stand behind GM during this process to ensure that it emerges as a more competitive, viable business in the long term. As was the case with Chrysler's dealer consolidation plan, the Task Force was not involved in deciding which dealers, or how many dealers, were part of GM's announcement today.

Based on this announcement, most Canadian dealers were relatively sure that their businesses were secure. Yet somebody decided that GMCL had too many dealerships. Who it was, and for how long this decision was contemplated is not known. Most likely, it was a Detroit mandate, but we do not know if Comeau

---

8   Quoted from a GMCL standard press release.

or any Canadians objected—or, like loyal minions, did what they were told. Or possibly Comeau decided himself to whack a large percentage of Canadian dealers.

In a 2010 court document, Comeau stated that in early 2000, GMCL was beginning to be concerned by dealer numbers. However, until it was mentioned by dealers at Dealer Communication Sessions with GMCL in 2008, eight years later, GMCL management never expressed any concern to the dealers about over-dealering!

On May 22, 2009, about 240 Canadian GM dealers were issued convoluted and confusing "Wind-Down Agreements." These agreements stated that GM had selected the dealership to be a non-continuing dealer, and laid out further details. The dealers were given six days to agree.

Days prior to receiving this news, Marc Comeau had addressed the dealers through an HIDL, stating that

a. The Wind-Down agreements were coming.

b. The agreements were in response to Government of Canada requirements.

c. It was important for GMCL's viability that they reduce the dealer numbers.

d. Dealers selected to be non-continuing were carefully chosen by means of a number of key performance criteria.

e. f all the dealers did not sign, the agreement could be withdrawn by GM.

f. If the dealers did not sign, GM of Canada would probably go bankrupt and all dealers would get nothing!

All but twenty dealers signed the Wind-Down Agreement!

This HIDL was shocking to the dealer body, even though they saw the news reports regarding GM in America; a significant number of dealers had believed Comeau's optimistic and positive comments in the past few years. What is very curious was the fact that Comeau stated that it was the government's requirement that dealership counts be reduced. This is a direct contradiction of the lead government agency in auto bailout negotiations, the

U.S. Treasury, and their statement of May 15, 2009. A non-involvement policy in the dealership culling was also stated by the Canadian government some weeks later.

In Canada, under Marc Comeau's leadership, 42 percent of the dealers were told they were terminated by the end of 2009! Considering GM had a better market share in Canada, this does not make sense, unless you believe GM was proportionally "over-dealered" in Canada. But since GM of Canada very carefully monitors and controls the number of dealers, dealer locations, operations, facilities, financials, and operating principals, how could they become "over-dealered"?

Is this not the same as a bigamist pleading poverty in court because he has too many wives and children to support? GM of Canada carefully analyzed and specifically authorized and approved every dealership that operated in Canada.

GMCL implied that the Canadian government insisted that the number of dealers be reduced. We know now this was untrue. I tend to believe that GM of Canada told the Canadian government that they would close inefficient and/or redundant dealers, including sixty or so Saab and Saturn dealerships, and some government bureaucrat likely said "okay, if that is what you need to do."

The fact that the U.S. Treasury issued a specific statement on May 15, 2009, that the task force was not involved in decisions regarding the number of dealers terminated makes it clear that dealer reductions were not on the agenda for the bailout of GM and Chrysler. Think about the implications of that. GM of Canada led its dealers to believe that dealer reductions were a government demand, and GM of Canada knew it was not true.

Marc Comeau, who has already displayed questionable foresight and who could be accused of having a deficient grasp of reality, was ultimately responsible for the culling of Canadian dealerships.

I have already shown the lack of a business case for reducing automobile dealerships. However, under Marc Comeau's leadership, GMCL cancelled approximately 240 dealers in one day. The sixty or so Saturn–Saab franchises that were cancelled were on borrowed time ever since GM in the U.S. stated they were cancelling the Saturn brand. The rest were simply whacked without justification or valid explanation.

> *In response to January 2010 mandate whereby the U.S. Congress ordered GM and Chrysler to give independent arbitration hearings to those terminated American dealers who so request them, General Motors' CEO Ed Whitacre has announced that he expected hundreds of GM dealers to be reinstated.*
>
> *Whitacre cautioned, however, that the number could be as low as 100 and that the company might benefit from some of the dealers being reinstated.*
>
> *Whitacre admitted that GM probably made a few mistakes during the closing process, but that by its very nature, an arbitrary line had to be drawn.*[9]

There were a number of major flaws in the whole process of eliminating dealers, and as Chairman Whitacre stated, there were "mistakes during the closing process." By the summer of 2010, GM under Whitacre reinstated *every* U.S. GM dealer who applied for reinstatement. Obviously, by then GM realized every termination had been a mistake. No Canadian dealers have been reinstated without dealer-initiated legal action.

---

9   January 7, 2010: egmcartech.com.

2

Closing Canadian Dealers

Everybody was fairly upbeat at Sheridan Chevrolet Cadillac Ltd. in Pickering, Ontario, a suburban community just east of Toronto. The previous afternoon, Marc Comeau, vice-president of sales, had advised all the dealers in Canada via a video broadcast that there were going to be significant cutbacks of the dealer body. Each dealer who was slated to be cancelled would receive an email by 10:00 a.m. Wednesday, May 20—the next morning.

Jerry Gazarek, sixty-eight-years old, owner of Sheridan Chevrolet Cadillac, and Lesley, his forty-year-old daughter, operator of Saturn Saab of Pickering, were of mixed emotions. Previously, word had come from GM in the U.S. that the Saturn brand was going to be cancelled (even though Saturn dealers in the U.S. had the highest sales per dealer of all GM brands).

Both Jerry and Lesley knew that their Pickering Saturn dealership franchise was going to be terminated. On the other hand, everybody went home that evening feeling pretty confident about the long-term viability of the Chevrolet Cadillac dealership.

Of the three remaining GM dealerships in Ajax–Pickering, Sheridan was the oldest, having operated thirty-two years at the same location. His was the only dealership that had completed the Image 2000[10] renovations as part of a four-million-dollar expansion and renovation package to the dealership facilities. It had won more Newspaper Reader Choice awards than the two other dealers combined.

The facilities were so excellent that GM had filmed their 2008 spring and summer commercials at the Sheridan facility. The dealership was located on six acres at the busiest intersection in

---

10 The reader will notice the term "Image" is used as both a verb and noun. "Image 2000" was the term GM used for the facilities standards that it demanded of all GM dealers by 2010. GM dealer jargon began to sound like this: Are you Imaged? Are you finished Imaging? Are you going to Image? The author has followed that pattern.

the Durham Region. There were two road frontages; one, Brock Road, was the new main street of the Seaton development (less than two kilometres away), which was under construction and was to have an initial population of more than 30,000 people.

Because of the four-million-dollar debt incurred so as to meet GM's Image 2000 standards, as GM continued to lose market share, Sheridan suffered an erosion of profitability and diminished capital reserves. The question a reader might reasonably ask is: Why did Gazarek initiate such a massive renovation and expansion? He was a loyal GM dealer who believed the speeches and pronouncements of Comeau and other GMCL executives. He'd had a personal relationship with GM for over forty years and was a committed GM person. He backed his loyalty with his dollars.

When comparing themselves with the two nearest GMCL dealerships, the Sheridan managers felt it was obvious that Sheridan should be retained. It was centrally located between the communities of Ajax and Pickering. It was at the entrance of the new community of Seaton. It had the largest, most up-to-date facilities and was already franchised as a Chevrolet Cadillac dealership—the two core brands in GM's future.

In Canada, the loss of dealership jobs far exceeded the GMCL total direct employment in Canada. In reality, both the Ontario provincial and the Canadian federal governments gave GM over $10 billion, and the net result was greater unemployment in Canada than was necessary. Sound fiscal government policy? As well, the losses of municipal tax base on dealership facilities that have been closed far exceed the property taxes GM pays on their Canadian facilities. Similar costs to municipal and state governments occurred in the United States.

Despite the voodoo economics and accounting GM used in their presentations to the governments, the dealership count was not the problem. Some experts will now quote new sales per dealer and dealer profitability statistics to show how far GM was behind their competition in these areas.

(Statistics are dangerous. If a ten-year-old male and an eighty-year-old male are in a room, the average age of the males in the room is forty-five; what are the chances that our average forty-five-year old is married and has two young children?)

When GM had 40 and 50 percent of the market, GM dealers led these sales-per-dealer categories. The dealers did not decide to stop selling GM cars; many went broke trying to be successful. What caused GM's sales drop was the fact that customers stopped buying what GM was building! If GM does not build what customers want, even one dealership will be too many!

Why, for example, cut 42 percent in both Canada and the U.S., as was initially stated by GM, but none in Mexico? In their presentation to the U.S. government, GM proposed a 25 percent reduction in dealer outlets in the U.S. In fact, they claimed they whacked 42 percent of the dealers in the U.S. and Canada. What was the basis for this number? Was it a quick way to get the average sales per dealer on par with the imports? What made this the right number in both Canada and the U.S.? Simple logic suggests that because of the huge geographic and population differences, the "right number" for each country should be different. Why were they the same? Why was Mexico excluded? Its GNP is only a few spots behind Canada's, and there are several GM plants in Mexico. It appears that since Mexico did not participate in the bailout, their dealers were untouched. Some Canadian dealers believed that once the claimed 42 percent figure was selected for the U.S., GM in Detroit felt that Congress would not tolerate any other number for Canada. Of course, GM then voluntarily reinstated well over half of the American dealers and none in Canada, so there is no sense to this argument. In reality, the net result of whacking and reinstating by GM was a reduction of dealers of about 15 percent in the U.S. and 30 percent in Canada, and all· of the dealerships in the U.S. who asked for reinstatement were reinstated. The same was not true for Canada.

Obviously, GMCL would apply sound business principles when choosing dealers to close—would they not?

You would think that dealers who upgraded, improved, or expanded their facilities to meet GMCL's Image 2000 standards would be safe from being whacked.

WRONG. In fact, 70 percent of the dealers who had not upgraded facilities were kept. The complete opposite of the public statements made by GM were true.

You would believe that dealers who had a high community and customer service reputation would stay and the ones with a history of poor customer relations would be gone.

WRONG. In fact, one of the top ten dealers in customer complaints to GMCL was kept.

You would think that the Pontiac dealers who were losing their brand would be cancelled.

WRONG. Actually, it was an advantage to be a Pontiac dealer because since Oldsmobile was cancelled, Chevrolet dealers have lost sales relative to Pontiac Buick stores, and these lower sales volumes were used to justify eliminating Chevrolet dealers.

Pontiac-Buick	Chevrolet
Pontiac Vibe	No entry
Pontiac G5-Sunfire	Cobalt
Pontiac G6-Grand Am	Malibu
Pontiac Gran Prix Buick Allure	No entry
Pontiac Bonneville Buick Lucerne	Impala
Pontiac Solstice	Corvette
Pontiac Buick Rendezvous	Uplander
Pontiac Torrent Buick Enclave	Equinox

Comparison of 2007 Canadian Dealers' product lines. All the Pontiac dealers had the Buick models as well. Not surprisingly, with superior entries, Pontiac-Buick dealers on average outsold Chevrolet dealers in Canada.

You would think that dealers who in the past have expressed a desire to retire would be assisted to do so now.

WRONG. One example exists where a dealer who had asked for several years for financial assistance to wind down was refused then and not cancelled now.

You would think the cuts would be based on the population of the community being served.

WRONG. The Community of Clarington, just east of Marc Comeau's office in Oshawa, has a population of 80,000 with two

GMCL dealers. Just to the west of Oshawa lies the town of Ajax and the city of Pickering, each with over 90,000 residents. Plus, Pickering expects the new Seaton development to bring in 30,000 or more new residents within ten years. These two communities will have one dealer each, after the oldest and most modern was cancelled.

You would think an award-winning dealership would be kept.

WRONG. Marvin Starr Pontiac Buick GMC has won the GM President's Triple Crown award many times. This is the top award a dealer can receive in Canada. Marvin Starr received his letter of acknowledgement for winning the 2009 Triple Crown, signed by the president of General Motors of Canada, the day after he was whacked.

You would think GM was telling the truth when it stated that it selected dealers to be whacked on a pure business basis.

WRONG. GM would not have rescinded any Wind-Down letters had that been true. However, rumours exist that at least three dealers had their terminations withdrawn after certain phone calls were made. It is believed that certain dealers had "side deals" with GMCL that protected their investments.

You would think that there would be no appearance of bias.

WRONG. In fact, 50 percent of the GM dealers in the French-speaking province of Quebec were cancelled, while less than 40 percent were cut in the rest of English Canada. This apparent appearance of bias also occurred in the City of Toronto, where all three of the Jewish-owned dealers were whacked. Toronto has the largest Jewish population in Canada, and Jewish people make up about 7 percent of the city's population. For the record, there are no South Asian, Islamic, or Asian GM dealers in Canada's most cosmopolitan city, which has a population made up of almost 50 percent visible minorities. Maybe instead of whacking dealers, GM should have created a dealer organization that reflects the communities they want to sell cars in.

You would expect that GM had no hidden agendas, but in some of cases, it appears as though certain preferred GM dealer candidates were encouraged to purchase the empty real estate left by whacked dealers at fire sale prices, with the intention to open later on the same site as a newly appointed GM dealer.

You would also expect that GM would ensure there was significant physical distance between retained dealers, so as to serve the consumers effectively. Yet in several instances, two retained dealers are basically across the street from each other.

You would also expect that GMCL would maintain the dealers who did a good job in achieving above market share. The reality is that GMCL's best dealers in terms of retaining market share were strongest in the small, non-urban centres; the import competition was strongest in large, urban centres. Rather than building on their strength, GMCL weakened itself where it was strongest.

3

The Wind-Down Agreement

Most readers will have never heard about the Canadian Wind-Down Agreement and even fewer have actually seen one. (GMCL considers these as confidential and will not release copies to the public.) I would like to explore some of the more intriguing aspects that show the blatant coercion involved in the document. Remember that, prior to dealers' receiving this document, Marc Comeau in his broadcast message said if all the dealers did not sign, the agreement could be withdrawn by GMCL; and if the dealers did not sign, GMCL would probably go bankrupt and all dealers would get nothing! It is my contention that the Wind-Down Agreement was a highly effective bullying tactic used by GMCL to extract acceptance from non-retained dealers, for the least possible cost and effort on the part of GMCL.

It is also my belief that GMCL and Marc Comeau felt that the Wind-Down Agreement would be the most efficient and cost-effective way to eliminate 42 percent of the Canadian dealers.

I would like to address a number of specific clauses in the Wind-Down Agreement that I and most dealers felt were most onerous.

Non-Retained Dealers Acceptance Threshold
GM's offer to the Dealer set forth in this Agreement is conditional upon all of the Non-Retained Dealers accepting the offer (the "Acceptance Threshold Condition"). The parties acknowledge that the Acceptance Threshold Condition is solely for GM's benefit and GM reserves the right, in its discretion, to waive the Acceptance Threshold Condition for any reason whatsoever.

GMCL is saying here that if all non-retained dealers did not sign, GMCL could withdraw this offer. Of the 240 non-retained Canadian dealers, supposedly all but twenty signed. GMCL had expected between 100 and 120 not to sign. If a dealer did not sign the agreement, under his existing Dealer Sales and Service Agreement, the dealer would have the right to resign his franchise and return all of his parts, special tools, and new vehicle inventory to GMCL (assuming GMCL was not bankrupt).

With the Wind-Down Agreement in place, the dealer could not return parts, special tools, or cars. The money being offered to the dealer in the Wind-Down Agreement was considerably less than the value of the parts and new cars the dealer would be stuck with. Since the dealers had been told by Comeau and CADA (Canadian Automobile Dealers Association) legal advisors that GMCL was likely going bankrupt, the Wind-Down Agreement was the dealers' only choice. That is why the vast majority of dealers signed. If a dealer did not sign, the risk was that he would get nothing. From an economic point of view, there was no alternative.

Payment to Dealer

. . . GM shall pay each installment of the Wind Down Payment to the Dealer by crediting Dealer's open account maintained on the GM dealer payment system (the "Open Account") on the Payment Dates, provided the following have occurred or are true, on each Payment Date:

. . . Dealer must not:

(1) be wound up, dissolved, or liquidated under any law or otherwise have its existence terminated or pass any resolution or become subject to any order in connection with any of the foregoing;

(2) make a general assignment for the benefit of its creditors, acknowledge its insolvency or be declared or become bankrupt or insolvent, or cease to carry on or fail in its business;

(3) commit an act of bankruptcy, file a proposal or notice of intention to make a proposal or be issued a notice of intention . . .

GMCL stated that they would pay the non-continuing dealers on an instalment basis; the total amounts of the payments were based on a rate per new vehicle sold the previous year. The amount paid per vehicle was a function of how many vehicles the dealer had sold previously. Large-volume dealers also received more dollars per unit than smaller dealers. What the reasoning was behind different payment rates to dealers of varying sizes was never explained or justified. In GMCL's view, there must have been a difference in the value of a sale, even though they charged all the dealers the same amount to buy the cars. It probably was a method to reduce the total payout, which was estimated at $130 million, which was far less than the dealers had to pay GMCL for the new cars and parts they were forced to keep.

These conditions are most interesting. GMCL is telling the dealer he cannot go bankrupt or cease operating through liquidation (even though there is no such condition on GMCL itself) if the dealer or its creditors want to receive payment from GMCL. I believe that GMCL expected or even hoped a number of non-continuing dealers would be forced into bankruptcy by the dealer's lenders and other creditors. GMCL could expect to save millions if this were to happen, by not paying what they said they were going to pay. To make insolvency more likely for many non-continuing dealers, GMCL told them they were expected to continue operating for another six months.

Complete Waiver of All Termination Assistance Rights

. . . Dealer and Dealer Operator hereby waive all Dealer's rights to receive termination assistance, whether under the Dealer Agreement or applicable laws or otherwise. For greater clarification, the Dealer and Dealer Operator expressly waive provisions of Article 15 of the Dealer Agreement, including any obligation of GM to purchase from Dealer any Motor Vehicles whatsoever; and . . . any obligation of GM to purchase from or accept returns from Dealer of any Parts and/or Accessories whatsoever.

This statement makes it very clear: GMCL is not taking vehicles or parts back. One non-continuing dealer had about $120,000 in parts and $5 million in new vehicle inventory. GMCL was going to pay the dealer under $600,000 in accordance with the Wind-Down Agreement. You may reasonably ask: Why did the dealer agree and sign the agreement? He had no other alternative!

The next paragraphs will likely be debated long and hard in the courts. I am not a lawyer, but common law says that waiving your right to sue is *not valid* if you waived it as a result of being coerced, misinformed, compelled, or deluded by the party requesting the waiver. GMCL (and their major shareholder, the Government of Canada) and the government's law firm (Cassels Brock) all gave the dealers misleading information about the actual bankruptcy status of GM of Canada.

Release; Covenant Not to Sue; Indemnity.

Each of Dealer and Dealer Operator on their own behalf and on behalf of any of their respective Affiliates, members, partners, venturers, shareholders, Dealer Owners, officers, directors, employees, agents, spouses, legal representatives, heirs, administrators, executors, successors, and assigns (collectively, the "Dealer Parties"), hereby absolutely and irrevocably, subject to the conditions set forth in the concluding paragraph of this Section 5(a), releases, settles, cancels, discharges, and acknowledges to be fully satisfied any and all claims, demands, complaints, damages, debts, liabilities, obligations, costs, expenses, liens, actions, and causes of action of every kind and nature whatsoever (including without limiting the generality of the foregoing, negligence), whether known or unknown, foreseen or unforeseen, suspected or unsuspected, in law or in equity ("Claims"), which any of the Dealer Parties may have as of the Effective Date or may thereafter have or acquire at any time against GM, its Affiliates, or any of its or their members, partners, venturers, shareholders, officers, directors, employees, agents, spouses, legal representatives, heirs, administrators, executors, successors, or assigns (collectively, the "GM Entities"), arising out of or relating to:

• The Dealer Agreement, this Agreement or any predecessor agreement(s);

• The National Automobile Arbitration Program;

• The operation of the Subject Dealership Operations, including without limitation any Dealer's employees' severance Claims against any of the Dealer Parties;

• *Any facilities agreements in respect of the Subject Dealership Operations, including without limitation, any claims related to or arising out of dealership facilities, locations, requirements, or image stipends, and any representations or warranties regarding motor vehicle sales or profits associated with Subject Dealership Operations under the Dealer Agreement; or any and all applicable statute, regulation, or other law, including Ontario's Arthur Wishart Act (Franchise Disclosure), 2000, Alberta's Franchises Act, Prince Edward Island's Franchises Act and/or any other similar franchise legislation which may be enacted or proclaimed in force in the future (collectively, the "Acts").*

Dealer and Dealer Operator acknowledge that it has always been and continues to be GM's position that the Acts are not applicable to the Dealer Agreement or the relations between GM and Dealer and/or Dealer Operator. However, if a court were to conclude otherwise, Dealer and Dealer Operator specifically acknowledge that it and they are hereby waiving any and all rights given to it or them under the Acts and are hereby releasing GM and the other GM Entities from any obligation or requirement imposed on GM and/or any of the other GM Entities by the Acts and further acknowledge that they are doing so with full awareness of such rights, obligations and requirements, and intend to waive its and their rights to:

(1) Any Claim for a breach of the duty of fair dealing in the performance or enforcement of or exercise of any right under the Dealer Agreement

(2) Any Claim for GM and/or any of the other GM Entities penalizing, attempting to penalize or threatening to penalize the Dealer and/or the Dealer Operator for associating with other GM dealers or retailers

(3) Any Claim for damages for a misrepresentation contained in a disclosure document or a statement of material change

(4) Any Claim for rescission for failure to provide a disclosure document or a statement of material change as required by the Acts

(5) Any Claim for rescission for failure to provide a dis-closure document or a statement of material change within the time required by the Acts

(f) Any Claim for rescission for providing a deficient disclosure document or statement of material change as required by the Acts.

The Wishart Act is Ontario provincial legislation that regulates the relationship between franchisors and franchisees. GMCL claims that its relationship with its dealerships is not covered by the Wishart Act regulations. Below is the definition used by the Wishart Act.

"[F]ranchise" means a right to engage in a business where the franchisee is required by contract or otherwise to make a payment or continuing payments, whether direct or in-direct, or a commitment to make such payment or pay-ments, to the franchisor, or the franchisor's associate, in the course of operating the business or as a condition of ac-quiring the franchise or commencing operations and [the GMCL dealer makes indirect payments in the process of purchasing of goods from GM for the purpose of resale. He is bound to deal exclusively with GM] (a) in which,

(i) the franchisor grants the franchisee the right to sell, offer for sale or distribute goods or services that are sub-stantially associated with the franchisor's, or the franchi-sor's associate's, trade-mark, service mark, trade name, logo or advertising or other commercial symbol, and

(ii) the franchisor or the franchisor's associate exercises significant control over, or offers significant assistance in, the franchisee's method of operation, including building design and furnishings, locations, business organization, marketing techniques or training, or (b) in which,

(i) the franchisor, or the franchisor's associate, grants the franchisee the representational or distribution rights, wheth-er or not a trade-mark, service mark, trade name, logo or advertising or other commercial symbol is involved, to sell, offer for sale or distribute goods or services supplied by the franchisor or a supplier designated by the franchisor, and

(ii) the franchisor, or the franchisor's associate, or a third person designated by the franchisor, provides location assistance, including securing retail outlets or accounts for the goods or services to be sold, offered for sale or distributed or securing locations or sites for vending machines, display racks or other product sales displays used by the franchisee ("franchise") ...

These conditions apply in the relationship between GMCL and the dealer, and most legal experts in Ontario agree. However, GMCL in the Wind-Down Agreement states that the Wishart Act and other provinces' similar legislation are not applicable to GMCL. But then GMCL says that if the Wishart Act is found applicable by a court, the dealer waives his rights; but again I believe that common law states that waiving your rights is not valid if you waived your rights as a result of being coerced, misinformed, compelled, or deluded by the party requesting the waiver. GMCL, their major shareholder, the government, and the government's law firm all gave the dealers misleading information about the actual bankruptcy status of GM of Canada and other matters relating to the Wind-Down Agreement.

Note: Days before a court hearing in December 2010, GMCL through its lawyers admitted that the relationship between itself and its dealers was a franchise relationship as defined by the Wishart Act. After denying the reality of the franchise relationship for over a year, one wonders how and why GMCL was able to perform this dramatic about-face. One wonders about the quality of the legal team that drew up the Wind-Down Agreement, as they were not able to recognize that the Wishart Act governed the dealer-GMCL relationship. No doubt loyal GM employees following orders.

The fact that GMCL specifically goes into so much detail about the Wishart Act and similar legislation in the Wind-Down Agreement, and states that it is not applicable, and, if found applicable, the dealers waive their rights of protection under the Wishart Act, demonstrates that GMCL believes the Wind-Down Agreement to be legally wrong and injurious to the dealers coerced into signing.

The next section of the Wind-Down Agreement says that the dealer cannot buy any more vehicles from GMCL. Since dealers earn their income from buying vehicles from GMCL and selling them to the public, this was an underhanded way on the part of GM to limit the income a dealer might make and potentially expedite the dealer's insolvency so GMCL would not have to make the payments they promised.

Subject Dealership Operations

From the Effective Date of this Agreement until the Termination Date:

(a) Dealer shall not, and shall have no right to, purchase Motor Vehicles from GM, which rights Dealer hereby waives;

(b) Dealer shall not, and shall have no right to, propose to GM (under Section 12.3 of the Dealer Agreement or otherwise) or consummate a change in Dealer Operator, a change in ownership, or a transfer of the dealership business or its principal assets to any Person . . .

Not exactly what most people would say is dealing in good faith.

This next clause terrified many of the dealers and probably still does. Dealers were worried if they talked to anybody without GMCL's approval, they were at risk of losing their payments.

Confidentiality

Dealer and Dealer Operator hereby agree that, without the prior written consent of GM, they shall not disclose to any person (other than [a] its or their agents or employees having a need to know such information in the conduct of their duties for Dealer or Dealer Operator, or [b] its or their legal, tax or other professional advisors, or [c] representatives of the Canadian Automobile Dealers Association [notice GM specifically okayed speaking with the CADA; GM likely knew CADA was employing Cassels Brock Blackwell LLP as counsel], in each case provided such individuals shall be bound by a similar undertaking of confidentiality) the terms or conditions of this Agreement or any facts relating hereto or to the underlying transactions, except where the disclosure is required pursuant to an order of a court, arbitrator or arbitration panel, administrative tribunal or other body having the power to compel the production of such information. Such disclosure shall be made only to the extent so ordered and provided that Dealer and/or Dealer Operator receiving such an order promptly notifies GM so that it may intervene in response to such order, or if timely notice cannot be given, seeks to obtain a protective order from the court or government for such information.

Of course, GMCL was terrified that this document would get out, and the Canadians would see how underhanded GMCL was with taxpayers' money. The worst possible scenario would be that the opposition parties in both Canadian federal and provincial Parliaments would get hold of this document and start asking questions. It is amazing how the unscrupulous try to avoid the light of scrutiny.

Likely the most devious behaviour of both GMCL and Cassels Brock was the fact that they consciously led the dealers and the public to believe that GM of Canada was at risk of declaring bankruptcy after May 22, 2009, and that the government funding was predicated on GMCL's reducing the number of dealers.

Consider these four related news reports, regarding GMCL bankruptcy—imminent as implied by Marc Comeau to the dealers prior to May 20, 2009. There are four statements to consider:

a. The above was not true once CAW made their concessions.

b. The statement by the U.S. Treasury regarding their non-interest in dealer cuts and statements from Canadian governments support this stand.

c. The statement by President Obama was in regard to the closure of GM dealers in the U.S. only.

d. The statement by General Motors that only GM in the United States was involved in bankruptcy proceedings.

e. Combined together, these statements show:

f. GMCL bankruptcy was never a serious consideration.

g. The closing of dealerships had no impact on government funding.

h. Acceptance of the Wind-Down Agreement by the dealers had no influence if GMCL would declare bankruptcy.

The first news report is dated May 20, 2009, and is by Tony Van Alpen in the *Toronto Star*.

General Motors will probably seek bankruptcy court protection in Canada and the U.S. in its fight for survival, a top union leader warns.

Ken Lewenza, president of the Canadian Auto Workers union, said yesterday the company's worsening financial condition is increasing the likelihood of court protection from creditors in both countries.

"It is very clear General Motors is in serious trouble," he said.

Lewenza said the federal and Ontario governments have issued an ultimatum to the union that if it doesn't agree to significant concessions within the next week, they won't provide billions of dollars in crucial public aid and the company will face liquidation.

"If we don't get a deal, the governments will provide no financing and GM Canada will be liquidated," he said. "Plants will close, jobs will be gone, retiree benefits are gone and the pensions are sacrificed. This is an unbelievable situation."

From these statements by Ken Lewenza, it is obvious that Union concessions were a determinant in the bailout scenario and the potential bankruptcy of GM of Canada. *The CAW agreed to concessions by May 20, 2009, which ensured no bankruptcy for GMCL.*

The second document is dated May 15, 2009, by the U.S. Treasury Department, the lead negotiator for all governments in putting the bailout package together for GM and Chrysler.

As was the case with Chrysler's dealer consolidation plan, the Task Force was not involved in deciding which dealers, or how many dealers, were part of GM's announcement today.

This clearly states the Governments are not involved in which or how many (if any) dealers are being terminated as it is not part of any bailout agreement. Therefore dealer terminations are not a determinant in accessing funds by GM. For GM to say the Government demanded a reduction in dealer numbers is a falsehood.

The third document, dated May 31, was a statement by President Obama in which he detailed the General Motors restructuring. He discusses only General Motors USA's filing for bankruptcy, and in regard to terminated dealers he stated,

There are some dealers that GM has identified that will not continue with GM. It is expected that the terminated deal- ers will be offered an agreement to orderly wind down their operations over the next 18 months.

The issue of dealer numbers is not dealt with in regard to the gov- ernments' restructuring plan. There was no linkage in the plan to fund dealer closures. In fact, several Canadian and American government statements have been issued saying that dealer clo- sures were not on the governments' agenda.

On June 1, 2009, General Motors in Detroit issued a press re- lease outlining their reorganization. A key statement was:

None of GM's operations outside of the U.S. are included in the U.S. court filings or court-supervised process, and these filings have no direct legal impact on GM's plans and operations outside the U.S. GM confirmed that all business operations are continuing without interruption in its Eu- rope; Latin America, Africa and the Middle East; and Asia Pacific regions.

This is the clearest statement possible that General Motors of Canada was *not* considered for bankruptcy.

Any prior statements made or implied by Cassels Brock, the CADA, Marc Comeau, or other General Motors of Canada execu- tives after the CAW agreed to further concessions regarding GM of Canada's bankruptcy were misleading, wrong, and devious.

The least these above-mentioned parties could have done on May 20 after ratification of the CAW–GMCL agreement was to advise all GM of Canada dealers who had received Wind-Down agreements that GMCL bankruptcy was not on the table.

GMCL was very aware that this Wind-Down Agreement was of questionable validity, in whole or in part. One of the ways they hoped to protect themselves was to insist that each signing dealer attest to the fact that they had received independent legal counsel. Most dealers used their regular business lawyers. However, most terminated dealers had been party to the CADA conference call on Sunday, May 25, where the representatives of CADA and representatives for Cassels Brock, the law firm retained by CADA on behalf of the non-retained dealers, were told they really had no alternative to signing the Wind-Down Agreement, and GMCL bankruptcy was a real possibility. It was made perfectly clear that the dealers had no choice but to sign the agreement. The power and influence of this advice resulted in 90 percent of the non-retained dealers' signing the Wind-Down Agreement—a number far in excess of GMCL's expectations.

When asked by various dealers to provide independent legal advice, as required in the GMCL Wind-Down Agreement, representatives of Cassels Brock refused. It was obvious to Cassels Brock's own lawyers that they could not provide independent legal advice to any GMCL dealer because as legal representatives of the Government of Canada in negotiations with GM, any direct or indirect counsel Cassels Brock provided to one or more GMCL dealers was a conflict of interest; the Government of Canada was a shareholder in GM, and the interests of the dealers and the shareholders appeared to be—and were—different.

Summary

- There was no threat of a GMCL bankruptcy once the CAW signed an agreement with GMCL on May 20, 2009.

- No governments were mandating dealer closures, and specifically, dealer closures were not a factor affecting potential GMCL bankruptcy.

- In the U.S., the GM bankruptcy filing did not invalidate the existing dealer sales and service agreements, as GMCL in Canada threatened would happen.

- Neither Obama nor GM, in the U.S., mentioned possible GMCL bankruptcy.

- Cassels Brock knew — or ought to have known — these realities, when on Sunday, May 24, 2009, they counselled terminated GMCL dealers.

- Marc Comeau was aware of these facts when he threatened the dealers in the HIDL of May 19.

4

Non-continuing Dealer Choices and Actions

The non-continuing dealers received their Wind-Down Agreement on Thursday, May 21, or Friday, May 22, and had to return it, signed, to GM by May 26, 2009. In reality, the window of opportunity for careful consideration was non-existent.

A typical scenario: On Thursday afternoon, the dealer is surprised to receive his Wind-Down Agreement and learns he has been whacked. On Friday morning, he gathers his key people and discusses the consequences. He calls his lawyer only to learn that the lawyer will not be back until Monday morning. Calling other dealers, he learns there is to be a CADA-sponsored telephone conference call on Sunday, in which representatives of Cassels Brock, the best law firm for matters dealing with auto franchises, will be giving advice.

The dealer, with his key staff, partakes in the Sunday conference call. He learns that if GMCL goes bankrupt, he will get nothing. The dealer has been told by Comeau already that if GMCL does not get a sufficient number of non-retained dealers to sign the Wind-Down Agreement, GMCL will likely go bankrupt. The dealer sees no alternative to signing the Wind-Down Agreement. On Monday, the dealer meets with his lawyer, who then asks the dealer what guidance he got from CADA and Cassels Brock. Dealer says they advised him to sign; his lawyer responds that he is not able to contradict these experts. Dealer also asks lawyer about severance pays, his other obligations, and numerous issues related to losing the franchise.

The dealer signs the Wind-Down Agreement and has it delivered to GMCL. It is again pertinent to note that the dealers who asked Cassels Brock for independent legal advice, as required in the Wind-Down Agreement, were refused. It is obvious now that

Cassels Brock knew they had insider information, were in a conflict of interest, and could in no way offer any dealer independent legal advice.

On June 1, 2009, General Motors in the United States declares bankruptcy as part of the government funding and reorganization plan. General Motors of Canada does not declare bankruptcy. An important fact to note is in declaring bankruptcy and forming a new GM, all of the dealer agreements for non-terminated dealers were continued. The big threat that Comeau/CADA/Cassels Brock had presented to the Canadian dealers—sign the Wind-Down Agreement or GMCL will go bankrupt and you will get nothing because the Dealer Sales and Service Agreements will not be enforceable—was a fiction.

In the U.S., GM went bankrupt, yet the dealers still had all the continued protection of their DSSAs. For example, Tate Porter Chevrolet in Ripley, West Virginia, resigned its GM franchise in August of 2010 under the terms of their DSSA, even though they had signed their original DSSA with the old bankrupt GM. It is obvious that GMCL and Cassels Brock were making misleading statements to the dealers. GM in the U.S. went bankrupt, and the DSSAs were kept in force.

By June 2, 2010, the Canadian dealers had begun to plan for the future. Most of the whacked "non-continuing" dealers were beginning to come out of the "fog of war" and they became angry as they began reflecting clearly on what had happened in the previous ten days.

Many terminated dealers wanted to continue in the business and sought franchises for alternative brands. Several were very successful in this. In fact, one former Pontiac Buick GMC dealer became a Hyundai dealer and sold more vehicles and was more successful than he had ever been as a GMCL dealer.

A number of dealers planned to continue as independent leasing operations, used-car dealers, and service operations; however, only a few well-capitalized dealers in some locales were successful during the worst economic recession in memory. Most dealers who did not get alternative franchises simply ceased operations after they lost their GMCL franchises.

As over 70 percent of the terminated dealers had completed the Image 2000 upgrades mandated by GMCL, many of them were faced with multi-million-dollar debts related to the upgrades, with no potential income to pay for it. Other dealers planned to sell their commercial real estate and go on with their lives, only to find that realized property values for single-purpose car dealerships have declined in the near-depression economy, to the point that offers to purchase were about 50 percent of the tax assessment value, and in some cases would not cover the existing mortgages.

Once the terminated dealer's banker became aware of the loss of his franchise, to protect its interests, the bank began reducing or cancelling operating lines, loans, and cash flows to the dealer, imposing additional financial pressure.

Many dealers suffered from bouts of depression and anxiety and sought professional help. They were told their feelings of loss were equivalent to the death of a spouse, and they might well experience other psychological symptoms, some of them long-term in nature.

There is a realization by all dealers that the financial payouts under the Wind-Down Agreement are not nearly sufficient to actually wind down the business. For instance, a few dealers were given up to $25,000 for sign removal, but the company that was contracted by GMCL to remove the signs wanted $40,000 in some cases to remove the signs. Information technology companies that had GMCL-mandated contracts with the dealers insisted on payment of full-lease terms. One dealer paid $210,000 to the company that handled the transmission of data between GMCL and his dealership. Dealers who refused to pay were being sued. Dealers discovered that the payout money received from GMCL was often insufficient to pay employees as much as government-mandated severance packages. A number of dealers were sued by ex-employees because the employees felt they had not been treated fairly financially when terminated.

By August 2009, as many dealers began to see the hopelessness of their future and the injustice done to them, they began thinking about their rights. In the United States, the dealers approached Congress and the Obama administration, and the U.S.

government mandated an arbitration process for every dealer who requested it. Over 800 dealers filed for arbitration, over 70 percent of the dealers terminated—double what GM had forecast. By July 2010, GM decided not to fight any dealers in arbitration where GM's chance of success was minimal, and GM reinstated every previously terminated dealer who asked for it. As of the same date, GMCL had not reinstated any dealers.

In Canada, there quickly developed three types of GMCL dealers. Initially, approximately twenty dealers who had been terminated, but did not sign the Wind-Down Agreement, filed a suit against General Motors in November 2009, seeking punitive damages each of $1.5 million, plus actual damages, plus reinstatement as GM dealers.

A second group of initially twelve dealers filed a Class Action Suit on behalf of approximately all of the 220 dealers who were terminated and had signed the Wind-Down Agreement. The suit was for $750 million against General Motors of Canada and Cassels Brock. In the spring of 2011, the dealers *were certified* as a "class." This was a tremendous victory that proved the validity of the dealers' case. Quickly, GMCL and Cassels Brock filed appeals in Divisional Court. On March 23, 2012, the Divisional Court dismissed, in full, the appeals of both GMCL and Cassels Brock. All Canadian dealers in Canada who signed the Wind-Down Agreement would be eligible to receive a share of proceeds of any class action settlement. It is important to note that these dealers do not want to be reinstated. It is their belief that there are so many irreconcilable differences between GMCL and themselves that there never again could be an effective franchise relationship between the parties.

The remaining group of about 470 retained dealers was figuratively drinking champagne and back-slapping each other on their great good fortune to be retained. But reality set in for them quickly. Many expected their dealership sales to double with the elimination of many nearby competitors. That did not happen in the autumn of 2009 and winter of 2010, even though GMCL introduced numerous new products, customer incentives, and heavy media promotion. Many of the remaining dealers could not even match the previous year's dismal sales. The continuing dealers quickly learned that the remaining customers in the market who had bought GMCL cars in the past few years were loyal to their *dealership*, not to GMCL. "If I cannot get my next car from ABC Chevrolet-Cadillac, I might as well go to the nearby Ford dealership."

To give you some idea of the disastrous GMCL policies under the leadership of Marc Comeau, consider this graph:

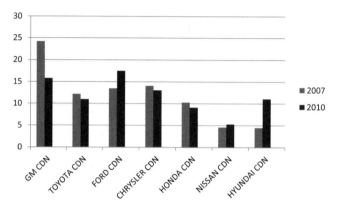

In 2007, GMCL was #1 in sales and share in Canada; the only company to terminate dealers in Canada in 2009. By 2010 they lost 8.4 percent market share, the number one sales position to Ford, and were beset with dealer lawsuits.

Any time you have a one-point share change, it is considered a dramatic and significant event. A loss of 8.4 share points in three years is unfathomable and anxiety-provoking. Just compare the North American lineup in Canada for 2007.

Also, the remaining dealers soon discovered that General Motors was downloading costs to the dealerships more aggressively than ever before. Charges, fees, and costs that added up to thousands of dollars each month were now the dealers' responsibility.

The third shock came when the remaining dealers were advised (remember, most had not upgraded to Image 2000 standards) that they would have to bring their dealerships up to the "new" GM standard. A typical dealer was now faced with a $3–$5 million renovation requirement.

Finally, the remaining dealers, who had been Pontiac Buick dealers, lost the Pontiac brand when it was discontinued by Detroit.

The Pontiac brand in Canada often made up over 75 percent of the new car sales in a typical Pontiac Buick store. Some ex-Pontiac dealers were told they would be given Chevrolet instead, but never were. In many Canadian communities, Pontiac brand outsold Chevrolet, and the gross profits were traditionally much better on Pontiacs. As well, your nearby competitor now was selling exactly the same brands as you were. In some communities, you ran into the situation where there were two dealers, the previously high-volume Pontiac Buick GMC store, and the Chevrolet Cadillac dealer. With the loss of the Pontiac line, that dealer had no volume cars brands to sell, and was begging GMCL to give him the Chevrolet brand. The other dealer, who was always outsold by the strong Pontiac brand, and lost Oldsmobile just a decade ago, did not want to share Chevrolet with his main competitor. Threats started: "If you do not give me Chevrolet, I will sue you for taking Pontiac away." The other dealer says: "I will sue if you give my competitor Chevrolet."

Here is a specific example of a situation that is being faced by dealers throughout Canada. The small city of Lindsay, Ontario, has an urban population of 16,200 as of the 2001 census. After careful study and analysis, GMCL deemed that two dealerships were viable in this community: Lindsay Pontiac Buick and Boyer Chevrolet. Now, these two dealers are 2.9 kilometres (1.8 miles) apart on the north side of the city. What does GM do: leave the Lindsay store a single line Buick dealer—or do they give Lindsay Buick a Chevrolet franchise and say "tough luck" to the Boyer Chevrolet store? Can anybody at GMCL look the owners of these dealerships in the eye and tell them that as dealers they will be more successful due to the reorganization?

In 2010, there is Lindsay Buick and Boyer Chevrolet, both single-line GM dealers with less consumer product choice and fewer sales each than they had before the great GMCL dealer rationalization. Each dealer owner is waiting for the other to go broke. By the way, the nearby city of Peterborough, with a population of over 75,000 based on the census of 2006, has one GM dealership. To be scrupulously honest (something GM is unfamiliar with), in 2001, Lindsay was amalgamated with several other small rural communities into the city of Kawartha Lakes, so as to have a population of 75,000 as well in 2006. However, the actual urban footprint of Peterborough is at least twice as big as Lindsay's.

Several other large urban areas have the same silly situation as Lindsay, where two dealers are either selling the same vehicles or have had 75 percent of their product line removed and are located a short walk from each other! Based on the reality of what has happened to GMCL sales and marketing twelve months after reorganization, the remaining streamlined dealer organization is selling fewer cars and making less money.

Marc Comeau bears ultimate responsibility for the culling of the dealerships. He is responsible directly for the lost jobs, the bankruptcy of individuals and businesses, and all the other social and financial costs involved in the closing of these dealerships.

Why? Because under Marc Comeau's leadership, many dealerships were encouraged (threatened?) to expand, renovate, and improve their facilities. Never were the dealerships cautioned about a GMCL plan (the so-called Plan 2000) to reduce dealer numbers. In fact, GMAC in many cases lent money to these dealers. Of course, GMAC did not know that GMCL was going to terminate the very dealers for whom GMAC was providing capital financing. Because Marc Comeau must have had some inkling that this culling was being contemplated, he had a moral obligation to advise the dealer body of the possibility.

Alternatively, if this plan for eliminating dealers was sprung on Marc Comeau as a last-minute surprise, he had the authority and the power as a member of the GMCL board of directors to question its validity, its justice, and the business sense of such an action. To give him the benefit of the doubt, GM Detroit may have told Comeau, "Either you do as you are told or get out." We all can assume that Comeau was faced with a moral dilemma; however, based on his past actions, Marc just followed orders regardless of the impact on others. Probably he even believed it was the right thing to do, just as he had believed his words twelve months before bankruptcy — that everything was wonderful with GM.

5

Secret Deals, Subsidies, and Agreements with GMCL Dealers

One of the most surprising revelations that came about after June 1, 2009, when terminated dealers for the first time began to speak to each other without fear (What was GMCL going to do, take away their franchise?), was the number of secret and confidential agreements and understandings that GMCL had undertaken with various dealers.

What was most shocking to most dealers was the fact that official GMCL policy was that every dealer was treated equally and fairly, with no special deals or side arrangements for anybody.

What a shock when it was discovered that various individual dealers were getting financial subsidies of all kinds to maintain their profitability.

On the east side of Toronto are two border communities, Scarborough in the city of Toronto and Ajax–Pickering in the region of Durham. Scarborough, except for its most easterly border area, was a steady growth area, while the eastern border area of Scarborough and all of the Pickering and Durham region had continually experienced strong economic growth over the years. Located in the Eastern Scarborough/Pickering geographic area (about fifteen miles by ten miles) were five Chevrolet dealers and four Pontiac Buick dealers. All these, with two exceptions, had been opened in the 1970s and before. One of these was Trillium Pontiac Buick, which was opened in 1989. Of course, at that time GMCL did its normal due diligence prior to approving this new franchise.

That year, 1989, was the onset of economic hard times for the auto industry again in Canada. In 2010, while filing affidavits in a lawsuit, GMCL admitted it gave Trillium over $6,900,000 dollars in direct and indirect financial support!

This is the company that refused nearby dealers who wanted

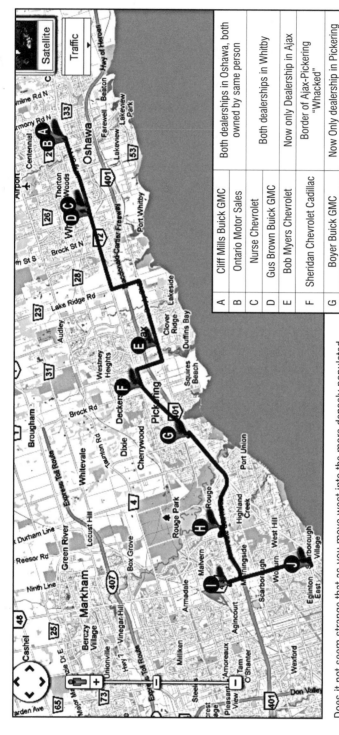

A	Cliff Mills Buick GMC	Both dealerships in Oshawa, both owned by same person
B	Ontario Motor Sales	
C	Nurse Chevrolet	Both dealerships in Whitby
D	Gus Brown Buick GMC	
E	Bob Myers Chevrolet	Now only Dealership in Ajax
F	Sheridan Chevrolet Cadillac	Border of Ajax-Pickering "Whacked"
G	Boyer Buick GMC	Now Only dealership in Pickering
H	Trillium Pontiac Buick	"Whacked"
I	Hogan Chevrolet	All nearby competition eliminated
J	Marvin Starr Pontiac Buick	"Whacked," no GM representation south of 401 and east of Victoria Park

Does it not seem strange that as you move west into the more densely populated areas of the greater Toronto Area, GMCL representation would be reduced?

This map shows dealership locations west of Oshawa. The community of Clarington which is east of Oshawa also has two GMCL dealerships

(Map data copyright Google 2011)

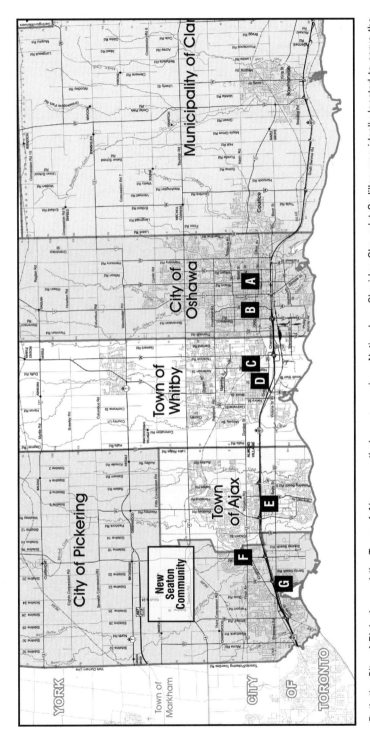

Both the City of Pickering and the Town of Ajax currently have approximately the same 90,000 population. The new community of Seaton is expected over time to grow to 80,000. Almost all the new growth in both communities is north of the 401 (black band).

Notice how Sheridan Chevrolet Cadillac was ideally located to serve the joint communities. One can understand the shock when Sheridan was terminated.

(Courtesy Regional Municipality of Durham)

financial assistance for Image 2000 renovations.

This is a company that stated it had no money to facilitate a dealer consolidation.

Bob Myers, a former pro football star and the owner of the Bob Myers Chevrolet dealership in nearby Ajax, was rumoured as wanting to retire after 2005. Supposedly, discussions with the dealer principals of Sheridan, Myers, and Boyer led to a request for financial assistance from GMCL to supplant the two remaining dealers' financial contributions so that Bob could retire and the dealership, Bob Myers Chevrolet, could close. This request was rejected summarily, as it was stated GMCL had no funds to close or consolidate dealers. This contradicts Marc Comeau's statement in 2010 that GMCL had been actively trying to reduce the dealer count since 2000. Less than a year later, GMCL had $135 million to facilitate the closing of dealers.

Bob Myers did not perform Image 2000, as he had no desire to invest more capital in his facility. It was thought by some that Myers might be terminated in May 2009. In fact, the nearby Sheridan Chevrolet Cadillac — which had just taken out a mortgage of $4 million to perform an expansion and Image 2000 renovations, was a chronologically older dealership, and had larger and better facilities with a Cadillac franchise — was closed instead.

In 1989, GM of Canada decided that this geographic area could support another Pontiac Buick GMC dealership, to be called Trillium Pontiac Buick. They had an applicant, Lynt Hurdman, who agreed to acquire land, build a new dealership facility, and begin operating. The land to be acquired was in a new "auto mall" facility that GMCL felt that they should be represented in. To ensure that the new dealer would be financially viable, GM of Canada gave Trillium financial support! The general consensus by us in the trade was that this new dealership would not be financially viable, and there was no economic justification for its opening.

According to recent court documents, GMCL has stated:

> In response to these competitive challenges, during the 1990s, GM and GMCL introduced a program known as Project 2000 ("P2000"), the goal of which was to reduce the size of GM's and GMCL's respective dealer networks

and to ensure their brands were properly aligned. Prior to introducing P2000, GMCL had relied on normal attrition to reduce the size of the GMCL Dealer Network, but under P2000, GMCL assessed the long-term viability of individual Dealers and communicated those assessments to Dealers by way of the Market Evaluation Summary.

Most, if not all, Dealers were aware of the challenges to GMCL's competitive position and the need to rationalize the GMCL Dealer Network over time. As the presence of too many Dealers in a local or regional market directly affects Dealers' profitability, "over-dealering" was a significant concern to Dealers. In 2007, for example, CADA conducted a survey of Dealers and found that "over-dealering" was the second most serious concern of Dealers.

This is GMCL's statement, but in reality, GMCL was opening and supporting dealers who were not financially viable and refusing to financially assist dealers who wanted to close their dealerships.

After Trillium was operating, with the millions in financial backing from GM, two of the nearby existing dealerships ceased operations: Alex Irvine Chevrolet and Bob Johnson Chevrolet. These two established dealerships never appeared to overcome the loss of the Oldsmobile brand in 2000 that had made up to 40 percent of their sales. As well, the additional GM store (Trillium) in their trading area surely had a negative effect. This reduced the normal dealer count by 33 percent by normal attrition (normal if you disregard the fact GMCL was subsidizing their competitor).

In May of 2009, GM terminated Marvin Starr Pontiac Buick Cadillac, Trillium Pontiac Buick, and Sheridan Chevrolet Cadillac. This left two dealerships serving communities where a few short years previously GM felt that five dealers were not sufficient. What is especially curious: where there were two Cadillac dealers in this area, there were none after June 2009.

GM of Canada and Marc Comeau specifically pride themselves on their planning and forecasting skills and speak of right-sizing the dealer organization. But in a matter of twenty years, they start with eight dealerships and add a ninth that they financially subsidize to the detriment of other nearby GM dealers. Three dealers then closed because they were not successful and viable (normal attrition in the retail auto industry); then GM whacks three more dealers in May 2009 because GM does not feel they are viable, even though the two GMCL was not subsidizing were profitable until their termination.

This example creates the appearance that by the turn of the century, GMCL had no idea what they were doing in terms of operating a dealer organization. Subsidizing new dealerships while nearby GM dealers are closing; forecasting great sales growth while supposedly realizing they are over-dealered; designating Cadillac as a core brand then closing both Cadillac retailers in a 150-square-mile urban area!

In the Class Action suit involving the 220 dealers who did sign the Wind-Down Agreement, Trillium Pontiac Buick GMC and its owner, Lynton Hurdman, is the lead plaintiff in the legal action. Besides the claims already laid out in the lawsuit, Hurdman could claim that contrary to his DSSA and the other agreements he had with GMCL, GMCL was trying to renege on their financial commitments to him. Once Hurdman was no longer a dealer, all GMCL's financial commitments expired. How cute. We subsidize a dealer to open and operate for twenty years, to the detriment of his nearby GMCL competitors; then in order to avoid our future responsibility and commitments, we use the false threat of GMCL bankruptcy to terminate him.

In its statements of defence, GMCL has stated that Trillium was terminated because it was not viable and GMCL had to subsidize it to such a great extent. The point could be made that it was not viable from the day it was opened, as that was when the GMCL subsidies were commenced, and continued for twenty years. In fact, GMCL only terminated Trillium to avoid continuing subsidy payments they were obligated by contract to make.

6

What GMCL Should Have Done

Many readers still may feel there was no alternative for GMCL other than to cull the dealer organization. Question is: What would have been a better and more effective way to reduce the number of dealers? (Not that I believe there was any benefit to GMCL by radically eliminating dealers.) We now know the strategy used was strong-arm tactics, and in the U.S., the terminations have all essentially been reversed. In Canada, there was no appeal, no asking for reconsideration, not even the ability to request a time delay or even an explanation.

Careful Study and Analysis of the Markets

Especially in Canada, the dealers chosen to be culled appear to have been selected based on non-business factors. GM should have carefully developed a strategy to come up with the target number of dealers required to serve the various communities. They should have considered a large number of tangible and intangible factors such as demographics, future growth patterns, and the plans and expectations of the existing dealers. Only then should a target closure level have been selected. (Why was 42 percent in Canada the right number? Why not 51 percent or 33 percent or 5 percent? What scientific or business rationale was used to arrive at 42 percent?) Once the target was set, then there were potentially a number of alternative approaches GM could have used.

Collaborative Approach

First of all, you could have a collaborative approach. For example, in our community of Ajax–Pickering, GMCL could have had their district sales manager meet with the local dealers. The district manager could have explained that GMCL wants (for example) only two dealers in Ajax–Pickering. In our case, one of the dealers had wanted to retire for several years and would have loved to be bought out! GMCL could have offered him a buyout, and the other dealers would have taken his vehicle and parts inventory and absorbed the closing dealer's staff. Everybody would have been happy, and it would not have cost GMCL much money. This same collaborative approach could have been used all across Canada. I am sure this would have been very effective.

In other cases, GMCL could have used their government money to facilitate mergers and acquisitions that would have been fair and equitable. Let us say, however, that when it comes to working with dealers, GMCL is not into the collegial collaborative style. They have the power and are going to do what they want regardless.

Imaged Dealers Kept or Compensated for Expense to Image

The greatest injustice to the tyrannical method GMCL used to close dealerships was the fact that compensation offered to the dealers did not take into account the investment the dealer had made to meet GMCL-mandated facility standards. The dealers who had implemented GMCL's Image 2000 standards were committed to GMCL over a long term. But the fact that they had facilities to Image 2000 standards had no effect on the culling. Dealers who Imaged were whacked and dealers who did not Image were kept. The dealers who made millions of dollars in facility investments were offered the same compensation as dealers who had done nothing. It is important to note that 70 percent of the non-Imaged dealers were kept, even though dealers had been told if they did not make the Image upgrades and improvements, they would not be renewed as dealers. In fact, several Cadillac dealers who had been told they had to Image prior to 2005 and had not done so were not terminated!

GMCL should have gone to the dealers who had made facilities expansions and improvements to their dealerships at GMCL's behest and compensated the dealer for those costs. GMCL had line-by-line veto on all dealership improvements; so morally and ethically, they had authorized the expenditure by the dealers, and GMCL should have compensated them when they whacked them.

Five- or Ten-year Phase-out Plan

GM could have utilized a five- or ten-year phase-out process; since having fewer dealers would not save GM money, there would be no rush to crush dealers. All dealers who wish could wind down by November 2010, as the GM Wind-Down Agreement stated, but GM would take cars and parts back as per the Master GM Dealer Agreement (this would be the appropriate choice for Saturn and Hummer dealers) and be compensated fairly in relation to actual closing and investment costs.

All other dealers would be given further five-year agreements, with another five-year option to 2020. This would allow the dealers up to ten years to recoup their investments and develop a closing strategy. Dealers would be encouraged to work together to rationalize the dealer count. GMCL would create a buyout fund to facilitate these closings. This would reduce the dealer count and, combined with the Saturn closings, would achieve a sensible dealer size. Funding would come from the estimated $135 million spent on the signed Wind-downs and avoid another billion dollars defending and settling legal suits. In fact, with judicious planning, I believe GMCL could have effectively and peaceably "right-sized" their dealer organization for less than $50 million. Right-sizing would have resulted in a reduction of maybe 5 to 10 percent of the dealer body, plus Saturn and Hummer dealerships.

GMCL authorized the opening of every one of the dealerships they closed. GMCL spent countless hours and effort in selecting these dealers on a long-term basis. To cancel so many so quickly really brings into question GMCL's judgment again.

No doubt there are some GMCL apologists who believe GMCL did what they had to do in the most financially prudent way. I disagree. First of all, GMCL was using taxpayers' money; the justification GM used to get taxpayers' money was to save jobs. The closing of all these dealerships throughout the U.S. and Canada *increased unemployment levels.* It increased all levels of government's expenditures for job loss benefits and social assistance payments. Many communities suffered a loss of property tax payments, and the federal deficits in both Canada and the U.S. increased. GM had no right to do this to the citizens of North America. It was not a business decision they made but a public policy decision where the taxpayers were not represented. Feel free to ask your elected representative how this was allowed to happen. At least GM, in the U.S., by reinstating all the dealers who requested it, mitigated some of the job losses. In Canada, no such easing of job losses occurred.

I believe that the governments should have assisted GM and Chrysler, but they should have carefully watched what management was doing with the taxpayers' money.

The chickens have come home to roost in 2011. In every case where there was a significant "whacking" of dealers by GM and Chrysler, they lost significant market share and sales. These market share points will not be easy to regain in the tough economic and competitive environment that exists in North America today.

7

The Duplicity of the CADA

When planning this book, I had an open attitude toward the CADA, the Canadian Automobile Dealers Association. After I reviewed its positions and stances on the issues and crisis in 2009, even though I did not agree with their decisions and actions, I believed they were doing what they thought was best.

Subsequently, I have had to re-evaluate my position, based on recent actions of the CADA vis-à-vis this author. In a letter dated March 5, 2010, Richard R.C. (Rick) Gauthier, president and CEO of the CADA, asked Marc Comeau to reinstate the terminated Canadian GMCL dealers, as was being done in the U.S.

This letter was posted for all to see on the CADA website at http://www.cada.ca/site/content/letter-marc-comeau.

I felt this letter showed leadership and character and was a positive action by the CADA and its CEO. To that end, I asked the CADA for permission to use the letter in my book. I was refused, even though the letter was posted on their website, and Mr. Gauthier had discussed this letter often in the media.

I was told by a representative of the CADA:

"Unfortunately, we are unable to consent to your request to use this material in your book. This letter, as is the case generally with our CADA materials, letters and other documents, is not intended for individual business activities such as your book, but rather for the specific association activity for which it was created."

I then wrote back to the CADA:

"The letter is also published on your website and is available to anybody. As well, several other websites have links to your site to access the letter. I believe the letter was a very positive action and it stands on its own merit. If there is something you are particularly concerned with, I would be happy to discuss it with you."

After two more follow-up emails and a phone call on my part, I received the same response from the CADA as before.

It should be noted that the NADA (the U.S. dealer organization) gave permission to use similar material.

Based on their lack of co-operation and response, I can only assume that the CADA (a) is not interested in getting their side of the story out; (b) has acted inappropriately and does not want any exposure on this matter; and (c) fears that actions, guidance, counsel, and advice that they have given or not given regarding the GMCL terminations leaves them susceptible to legal action.

The CADA purports to be the organization that represents the nation's new car dealers. Organizations such as the CADA can react in two different ways when a portion of their membership is attacked, such as in the case of the widespread dealer terminations by GMCL in May 2009. (Chrysler Canada did not terminate any dealers in Canada.)

One alternative would be an appeasement policy: If some members are threatened or attacked, before the CADA comes to their unconditional assistance, they will be pragmatic and weigh the pros and cons, consider the risks, and strive to keep the bulk of the members safe. In 1937, France and England sacrificed Czechoslovakia to appease Nazi Germany and avoid a European war. In that case, the appeasement policy was a disaster. Unfortunately, the CADA followed the same policy in May 2009.

The other alternative for the CADA was to recognize that each and every member is important, and an attack on one member is considered to be an attack on all members. This is the NATO policy: Hurt one member of the alliance and you will have to deal with the full power and might of all the members of the alliance. CADA had selected the firm Cassels Brock in April 2009 to represent GMCL dealers in the event of GMCL reorganization. Cassels Brock was selected because of their experience in franchise and dealership matters and Cassels made a commitment to the CADA that they would vigorously defend the rights of terminated CADA members.

On May 4, 2009, CADA sent a memorandum to all GMCL dealers, CADA members or not, stating that they had selected Cassels Brock to represent the dealers collectively in restructuring or insolvency by GMCL. Dealers were urged to fill in a form and send at least $2,500 in to the "Cassels Legal Fund," which would pay for the dealer's legal representation. Truly the CADA was showing initiative and an egalitarian attitude. A similar memo was sent on May 13 by CADA to all GMCL dealers, again voicing the importance of acting together as one body. So far, so good.

All those dealers who signed on and paid the fee felt well represented by the CADA and Cassels Brock. What the dealers did not know and the CADA did not learn while retaining Cassels Brock, and what Cassels Brock did not disclose, was that Cassels Brock was representing the Government of Canada in the bailout negotiations with GM!

The Government of Canada was about to take on a significant investment and shareholding role in General Motors, and was using Cassels Brock as their legal firm.

The conflict that should have been so apparent to the CADA at the time was: Cassels Brock was representing a large GM shareholder (the Canadian government) that would directly benefit from any and all cost reductions GM could achieve. For months, GM had been saying publicly that slashing the dealers would yield great savings and logically benefit its shareholders, one being the Government of Canada. If cutting dealers benefits the shareholders and hurts the dealers, how can the same law firm represent both parties? What was Cassels Brock trying to accomplish beyond more billings? Why did CADA tolerate this?

When GMCL issued their Wind-Down agreements on May 20, instantly dealers contacted CADA, and CADA reacted to the crisis with a very watered-down response. On May 22, the CADA sent a memorandum to the GMCL dealers with a summary of the contents of the Wind-Down Agreement. The memorandum offered no advice or recommendations other than the consequences of signing or not signing. The CADA memo did not propose unified dealer action, there was no suggestion of CADA's leading legal action, and, in fact, it recommended that the affected dealers get their own independent legal advice. Rather than leading the affected dealers with a unified voice, it was telling the dealers to act independently. It is believed that Cassels Brock approved this memo, which was a significant reversal of the May 4 memo, where the CADA was showing true leadership. The May 22 email did not address the fact that the Wind-Down Agreement appeared to violate various legislative acts regarding franchise law (a supposed Cassels Brock specialty). In fact, the dealers were not given any real valuable legal advice or guidance.

The CADA scheduled a national telephone conference call for Sunday, May 24, 2009. Many affected dealers felt this was where the leadership of CADA and the crack legal minds of Cassels Brock would come to the forefront. Previously, there was talk of injunctions against GMCL; CADA-led negotiations with GMCL; requests for government intervention; and mass refusal to sign the Wind-Down agreements among the dealers, all before the conference call began.

Once the conference call began, the CADA staff and the lawyers from Cassels Brock made it very clear that each dealer was on his own. They offered no hope, no encouragement in any way that the terms of the Wind-Down Agreement could be altered, modified, or renegotiated.

I was privy to the call, and after listening to the "experts," I believed their consensus advice was that if you do not sign, you will likely get nothing. GMCL has de facto terminated you and it will declare bankruptcy and void the Dealer Sales and Service agreements, and you will get nothing.

The dealers were not told of the possibility that a bankruptcy judge could rule that the Dealer Sales and Service agreements remain in force after bankruptcy, which is exactly what happened in the U.S.

The dealers were not told that the CADA could or would petition the bankruptcy judge on behalf of all GMCL dealers to keep the DSSA in force.

I was flabbergasted. I had never heard lawyers who specialized in litigation offer no options, no leadership, no alternatives, and no hope. Over 200 dealers who signed the Wind-Down Agreement believed there was no alternative option.

In court testimony, where Cassels Brock was defending itself against the charges of "conflict of interest," they claimed they were not representing or acting for the CADA or any of the GMCL dealers and therefore they could not be in conflict of interest.

The judge asked piercingly, "If Cassels Brock was not representing or not acting for the dealers and CADA, what were they doing taking part in the conference call?" Of course, there was no answer, because the truth of the matter was that Cassels Brock *was* acting on behalf of the CADA and the terminated dealers. It seems apparent that if the client (the dealers taking part in the conference call) believes a law firm (Cassels Brock) is representing them, and the law firm acts like it is representing the client and provides the client with opinions, guidance, counsel, representation, or advice, then the law firm is acting for the client.

One other thing did strike me as odd when I heard it later: A dealer asked the Cassels Brock lawyer if he would sign as independent legal advisor. He was told to get some other lawyer to sign. I thought that was very strange; why would Cassels Brock turn down another billing opportunity?

Very strange, but of course we all know now why Cassels Brock could not sign as independent legal counsel. Cassels Brock knew that if they signed, GMCL would instantly recognize Cassels Brock was not and could not be an independent legal advisor for a dealer, as they: (a) had acted for the Government of Canada in dealings with GM and GMCL, and (b) had acted for the CADA and could not very well act now for an individual terminated dealer.

Another blunder by CADA and Cassels Brock was the "steering committee" set up after the May 4 memo by CADA. After May 20, this committee had both continuing and non-continuing GMCL dealers as members. It became instantly apparent after May 20 that the goals and aims of the two groups of GMCL dealers were diametrically opposite. The dealers selected by GMCL to continue had no interest in the welfare of the dealers being terminated. From the continuing dealers' point of view, the fewer dealers there were, the better, and GMCL should not give them another moment's thought. It became obvious by their actions that CADA's interest lay with the continuing dealers and maintaining a good relationship with GMCL. The continuing dealers could continue to be members of CADA and pay dues. The terminated dealers, who had no future with CADA, were cut free. (CADA's logic appeared to be: If the dealer is terminated, he cannot be a member of CADA; why should we be concerned with non-members?)

CADA accepted the fact that a strong GMCL was in its best interests and that it should encourage as many affected dealers as possible to sign the Wind-Down Agreement—a radical change in attitude just sixteen days after the May 4 memo was issued.

On May 28, two days after the Wind-Down Agreement deadline, CADA sent another memo to all of the dealers that had contributed to the Cassels Brock Legal Fund, initiated by the May 4 CADA memo, and told the dealers that CADA had not retained Cassels Brock, and the fund had been set up only in case GM declared bankruptcy in Canada. Of course, this was a direct contradiction of the May 4 memo. It is believed this latest memo was a response to the fact that numerous dealers had contacted CADA about the poor representation that Cassels Brock had shown during the period of the Wind-Down Agreement.

From this time on, the CADA ceased pretending to act in the best interests of all of its dealer members. One can only wonder what pressure was applied on the leadership of the CADA and by whom, to abandon over 200 paid-up CADA members in good standing. Like Czechoslovakia after the Munich conference, the terminated dealers could only watch as jackals (many being fellow CADA members) came to pick over the bones of their dealerships at cents on the dollar.

By comparison, John McEleney, chairman of the National Automobile Dealers Association—the U.S. equivalent to the CADA—was actively protecting the interests of U.S. dealers in June of 2009.

> WASHINGTON (June 3, 2009)—John McEleney, chairman of the National Automobile Dealers Association, commended a Senate committee today for focusing on the unfair treatment of the General Motors and Chrysler dealers. Also, McEleney expressed grave concerns about GM's plan to require all of its surviving dealers to sign a one-sided, open-ended operating agreement as a condition for remaining a GM dealer.[11]

11 NADA 2009 Press Release.

There is no record of CADA's lobbying on behalf of GM dealers in Ottawa at this time.

Many months later, Richard Gauthier, the president of the CADA, appeared to flip-flop on representation and involvement with terminated dealerships. In fact, on March 5, 2010, he sent a letter to Marc Comeau, which CADA has refused permission to print in this book.

This letter was the result of the reinstatement of U.S. GM dealers and seems a reasonable approach. There were other examples of Gauthier's speaking with the media in support of reinstatement of Canadian dealers. Some pundits felt that this flip-flop was the result of the CADA's studying its activities with Cassels Brock in May 2009 and realizing that they did not act in the best interests of the terminated dealers they had promised to represent. The CADA also realized they could be potential defendants in any lawsuit brought forward by the terminated GMCL dealers who had signed the Wind-Down Agreement. The basis for such a lawsuit might be:

- CADA had a duty and an obligation to represent the terminated dealers and lead the fight against the terminations. CADA did not do this.

- CADA had an obligation to retain a law firm that was not in a position of conflict with the terminated dealers' objectives. CADA did not do this.

- CADA as a national organization had an obligation to use its political influence with the Canadian government to either mandate arbitration or reinstatement of terminated dealers, as was done in the U.S. CADA did not do this.

It should be also noted that Marc Comeau publicly responded to Rick Gauthier's letter as written by Greg Keenan and reported in the Globe and Mail March 12, 2010:

General Motors of Canada Ltd. has rejected calls to follow its parent company's example and voluntarily reinstate dealers who were terminated when the automaker restructured its operations last year, saying courts and arbitrators should rule on demands by some dealers that their businesses be restored.

"We cannot rewrite history," Marc Comeau, GM Canada's vice-president of sales and marketing, said in a letter to Canadian Automobile Dealers Association (CADA) president Rick Gauthier and the company's remaining Canadian dealers.

That answer to Mr. Gauthier's recommendation did not sit well with the head of the dealers' group and could escalate the tension between CADA and GM Canada, whose U.S. parent agreed last week to reinstate 661 of about 2,000 dealers who were terminated.

"That's not a satisfactory response," Mr. Gauthier said yesterday, adding that the group is assessing what further actions to take.

GM Canada is already embroiled in two lawsuits over the dealer restructuring. One is a class-action suit by dealers who signed wind-down agreements last year; the other is a court action by 20 dealers across the country who did not sign the agreements and are seeking compensation and restoration.

CADA has asked its 3,000 members nationally to contribute to a special fund to help cover legal costs for the 20 GM dealers.

Alexandre Saillant, who signed a wind-down agreement when his family's Pontiac-Buick-GMC-Cadillac-Hummer dealership in Quebec City was terminated last year, said he plans to launch a separate lawsuit.

"We were—most of the time—the most profitable dealership in the province of Quebec," Mr. Saillant said. "We were a flagship for GM." The dealership is now selling Mazdas.

Mr. Comeau said the company's distribution network in Canada is different than the U.S. setup.

"To suggest that we reinstate all the dealers that were offered a wind-down agreement is not practical and, with respect, it would condemn both GM Canada and its dealers to an uncompetitive distribution network," he wrote.

The company was able to avoid going into restructuring under the Companies' Creditors Arrangement Act in Canada in part because of agreements with "a sufficient number of dealers," Mr. Comeau wrote.

General Motors Corp. slid into Chapter 11 bankruptcy protection in the United States and was bailed out with about $60 billion (U.S.) of taxpayer money from the U.S., Canadian, and Ontario governments.

The original viability plan for GM Canada included a modest cut in its 700-plus dealership network, Mr. Comeau wrote, but that plan was rejected by the federal and Ontario governments.

Documents filed in one of the GM Canada dealership lawsuits, however, include a letter from Ontario Premier Dalton McGuinty saying that neither Ontario nor Ottawa ordered the automaker to slash its dealership network in Canada during negotiations on the $10.5 billion provided by those governments for the bailout.

GM has applied to the Ontario Superior Court to rule on each of the 20 terminations involved in that action individually, or dismiss it and send each case to a dealer-automaker arbitration system called the National Automobile Dealer Arbitration Plan.

Notice at even this late date of March of 2010, Comeau is flippant and untruthful to the point that Greg Keenan, the reporter, corrects Comeau's allegation that the governments forced GMCL to slash its dealership network in Canada.

8

GMCL's Relationship
with Canadian Governments

For decades, General Motors saw itself and the success of the
United States' and Canadian economies closely intertwined. Historically, the Big Three were always fighting the government over
increased legislation, regulation, and involvement in the auto industry. In the early 1970s, the U.S. government had introduced
tough (for the times) safety and emission standards. All of the Big
Three took the U.S. government to court to have it delay, defer, or
rescind the standards. Their argument was based on the fact that
the current technology available would not allow the carmakers
meet the standards.

At the time, Honda was a really minor player in the automotive world. They had a pretty good history with motorcycles but
no redeeming virtues as a carmaker. In 1972, Honda introduced a
car called the Civic, pretty basic transportation but with features
and build quality superior to the Big Three's offerings. In 1973, the
Oil Crisis hit, and the future of the 1169cc-powered Honda was
assured. In 1975, Honda introduced a CVCC version of the Civic.
This vehicle's engines met and surpassed all current and future
emission standards of the time. While the Big Three were in court
spending millions trying to prove that the required technology
was impossible, Honda was selling the technology to the public!

This contributed to the rapid rise of the Japanese car industry
in North America.

Eventually, GM seemed to learn that "you cannot fight city
hall" and then spent millions trying to influence it. When I began to research lobbying activities in Canada by GMCL, I was as-
tounded; it seemed all the top executives of GMCL were lobbyists!

Below is a list of GMCL corporate lobbyists registered with
the Canadian government in 2008. This does not include private

firms and individuals retained on a contract basis to lobby on GMCL's behalf as well. These individuals have declared that they spend more than 20 percent of their time as employees of General Motors of Canada lobbying the Canadian government.

	GMLC Corporate Lobbyists	
1	Arturo Elias	President and Managing Director
2	Marc Comeau	Vice-president, VSSM
3	John Stapleton	Vice-president, Finance and CFO
4	Marc Boismenu	Manager, R & D Programs
5	Glenn Bryksaw	Vehicle Environmental Programs
6	Miriam Christie	Manager, Government Relations
7	Christina Cuthbert	Lawyer
8	Jason Easton	Corporate Affairs Analyst
9	Marianne Emig Munro	Counsel
10	Nicole Gibson	Manager Strategic Studies, Planning, and Product Allocation
11	Tammy Giroux	Senior Environmental Analyst
12	Heather Innes	Counsel
13	Louise Kevins	Vehicle Safety Liaison
14	Sam Lusty	Manager, Business Control Services and Dealer Audit
15	Neil Macdonald	Vice-president; General Counsel
16	Anjela Mitra	Supervisor, Risk and Compliance Management
17	Terry Ostan	Manager, Vehicle Automotive Regulatory Activities
18	Greg Parker	Manager, Engineering and Product Planning
19	Phillip Petsinis	Manager, Government Relations
20	Faye Roberts	Manager, Government Relations
21	David Stainton	Analyst, Risk
22	Bryan Swift	Director, Environmental Affairs

With so many top-echelon staff that GMCL has listed as registered lobbyists, one wonders who is running the company or the government. Remember, GMCL would also have hired lobbyists, association lobbyists, and law firms to represent them to government.

It would be reasonable to believe that in the U.S., a proportional amount of the executives were acting as lobbyists as well.

From a Canadian perspective, things become self-evident. GM is a multinational corporation with its main interest being the success of itself. GM will do and say anything to governments to receive an edge for itself. GM has received over $10 billion from various levels of Canadian governments alone in the bailout process. The decision to cull Canadian dealers was facilitated by these funds.

If the decision to terminate Canadian dealers was made in Detroit, then the Canadian government was duped by a foreign multinational—unless it gave prior assent to the decision.

If the decision was made by GMCL, the taxpayers should know who in the Canadian government signed off in agreement. Who in Ottawa had the knowledge and awareness? Who analyzed the benefits and costs to Canada and its job situation and said, yes, GMCL, take our money and close all these dealerships because it is good for Canada, and this is how we should spend the taxpayer's money?

I believe Ottawa was misled, and the closing of Canadian dealers was a U.S. decision; Canada spent $10 billion propping up an American multinational that sees its biggest growth potential in China!

Speaking of money, GMCL has its hands full with dealer-based legal actions: the twenty-one dealers who did not sign the WDA and who sued and then successfully settled out of court. GMCL also has approximately 220 dealers who are making excellent progress with their class action suit, which we will discuss later. There also has been a number of other individual dealers who have launched suits and also settled successfully, based on the GMCL's actions in May 2009. Finally, there appears to be a new groundswell of legal action happening over the retained dealerships. To be straightforward, business has been very, very poor for the remaining GMCL dealers, especially the Buick GMC franchises, which, when they lost the Pontiac franchises, lost up to 75 percent of their car sales volume. Even internal GM statistics report that only 36 percent of the owners of Pontiac, Saturn, and Hummer are staying in the GM family at their next purchase time. They are losing over six out of ten customers.

The Canadian Buick dealers are speaking of suing GMCL on the basis that the Buick franchise is not viable without the

Chevrolet car line, and either GMCL should award them Chevrolet franchises or compensate them appropriately. The problem is: Where GMCL has given Chevrolet franchises to the local Buick dealer, the existing Chevrolet franchisee has sued GMCL for violating the Dealer Sales and Service Agreement. So GMCL is stuck between a rock and a hard place. Please the Buick dealers and get sued by the Chevrolet dealers, or the reverse happens.

9

The Major Lawsuits

It should be noted that GMCL has not publicly released any lists of the names of dealerships terminated, their owners' names, who did or did not sign the Wind-Down Agreement, who have lawsuits pending, who have settled lawsuits, and who have been reinstated. For this reason, there often are discrepancies in the numbers. For sake of consistency in this book, we will use the number 240 as the total number terminated, 215 as the number who did sign and 25 who did not sign the Wind-Down Agreement.

Car dealers tend to be tough, determined individuals. They are resilient and do not accept defeat readily. After the June reorganization of General Motors in the U.S., the terminated Canadian dealers began hearing stories and reports that were confusing and contradictory:

- Why had the CADA flip-flopped from their initial position of fighting GMCL?

- Why did it appear to everyone that Cassels Brock was weak and ineffective?

- Why did not Cassels Brock advise dealers of their rights and options?

- Why did GM of Canada and Marc Comeau mislead the dealers?

- Was GM of Canada's bankruptcy ever an option after the CAW renegotiated?

- Why did there appear to be no consistent business pattern to the selection process of dealers chosen for termination?

Besides these and many more questions, more rumours began to fly, such as:

- GMCL had exerted pressure on CADA through retained GM dealers to abandon the terminated dealers.

- Since Cassels Brock was representing Canada in negotiations with GMCL, it was in their client's (the government) best interest for the dealers to sign the Wind-Down Agreement.

- The governments had no interest in when or how many; if any dealerships were closed, it was GMCL's idea to blame the governments.

- GMCL had used the Wind-Down Agreement to punish enemies and reward friends and to ensure the dealer body became suitably subservient.

Terminated dealers began to speak more openly among themselves and they were not happy.

Lawsuit #1, launched November 25, 2009

More than a couple of dealers were angry and were not going to take it anymore. The first group was twelve dealers who had not signed the Wind-Down Agreement.

Key Points in these dealers' claims were:

- They all were long-term dealers

- They all were key components of their communities

- They all had been renewed automatically every five years in the past

- They all upgraded their facilities based on GM's requests and GM's promises to the effect that they would be dealers in the long term

- None of them would have invested in facilities upgrades if they had not been assured of their viability — especially recognizing the turbulent times GM was facing after the year 2000.

The Statement of Claim, which is excerpted here, contained the details of each individual dealership.

With one or two exceptions, these dealerships were located in small communities. The reality was that GMCL had their best market share and sales percentages in small communities. While their GMCL market share had collapsed to less than 10 percent in large urban communities, in many rural communities, GMCL still had share ratings in the 40- to 50- percent range. Why would GMCL force a dealer closure where the dealer had a dominant market share and was profitable?

Those small-town, family-owned dealerships that had refused to sign the Wind-Down Agreement on May 26, 2009, retained McCarthy Tetrault LLP (Limited Liability Partnership), who filed in the Ontario Supreme Court on November 26, 2009, a claim for the following (summarized in layman's language):

> General Motors is to declare the Dealer Agreements are in effect until at least October 31, 2015. The twelve dealers want to be normal GM dealers for at least another five years.
>
> GMCL is forbidden from terminating or in any way interfering in the dealerships.
>
> GMCL is to comply with the Dealer Agreement, including the renewal option in the Agreement.
>
> GMCL is to treat these twelve dealers equally to all other dealers.
>
> GMCL is to cancel the termination notices issued to these dealers.
>
> GMCL is to compensate for losses, costs, and damages incurred by these dealers as a result of GM's actions.
>
> Punitive damages of $1,500,000 are to be granted to each dealer.

It appears that these twelve dealers wish to be reinstated, compensated for damages, and continue on as if nothing had happened. There is a lot of validity in their claim, and McCarthy Tetrault is the type of high-profile firm that does not bother with nuisance suits.

This action having been launched, the only way I think the twelve dealers could lose is if GMCL could convince the judge that a) GMCL acted fairly, justly, and equitably in offering each selected dealer a Wind-Down Agreement, based on requirements GMCL had to meet for government money; b) the fact that these twelve dealers chose not to accept GMCL's Wind-Down Agreement should not incur a burden on GMCL in trying to restructure its operations in North America; and c) GMCL has the right and obligation to operate its business for the benefit of its shareholders (the government mainly), and to be compelled by the courts to alter its business plans to suit individual dealers would be counterproductive and just wrong.

This suit has two aspects: reinstatement and compensation. Reinstatement will be very difficult for GMCL to agree to. GMCL supposedly had a master plan in mind when they whacked all the dealerships. How valid or sensible that master plan was is highly debatable, but GMCL is not likely to deviate from it. Fortunately, because of government funding, GMCL is awash with billions in cash—and cash can cover a lot of sins and a lot of pain. I envision a confidential out-of-court settlement where each of the parties receives an amount equal to their dealership investments in Image, plus several million for the loss of the franchise plus legal costs.

Rarely in Canada do cases like this ever go before a trial judge, and GMCL is not going to want to take that risk. They probably can make this case go away for about $50 million or less, and all will be forgotten. The final decision on how this case is resolved will take place in Detroit, and GMCL's traditional pattern is not to settle but to drag a case out as long as possible, to wear out the claimants. No doubt this will be GMCL's initial plan. However, Canadian courts do not like the delaying tactics and procedural battles that are so common in the U.S. Canadian courts also actively urge out-of-court settlements to keep the process streamlined.

The Players

Robert Slessor Pontiac Buick, Inc.

Located in the town of Grimsby, Ontario, with a population of 23,000. Currently operated by Robert Slessor, the dealership has been continuously operated by the Slessor family for fifty-five years. In 2002–2003, at GMCL's request, Slessor invested $3.5 million in Imaged facilities.

As stated before, certain values such as character, integrity, and justice seemed to have disappeared from GMCL. However, many of the dealers who were whacked did possess these virtues. One example is Robert Slessor, who did not sign the Wind-Down Agreement and was one of the first dealers to voice his opinion publicly regarding General Motors of Canada's actions.

Grimsby is a regional farming centre located between the cities of Hamilton and St. Catharines, Ontario, in the heart of the tender-fruit farming region. For decades, family farms have been growing peaches, plums, pears, and cherries. In the past twenty years, grapes have become a very prominent crop through the entire Niagara Region, and Grimsby has benefited from the viniculture growth. (Grimsby is about thirty minutes by car west of Niagara Falls.) The local farmers and agri-businesses rely on Grimsby for many specialized shops and services.

Robert's father started the dealership in 1955, and, in later years, his uncles opened dealerships in Newmarket and Milton. Robert began working full time in the family dealership when he finished high school and took over operating the business when his father retired. Robert is a religious man who believes in Christian values. Being brought up in a family of GMCL dealers imbued him with loyalty, trust, and belief in General Motors, which is something that permeates most of the GMCL dealers' families. Rob Slessor and his family were committed to General Motors. He put his money where his mouth was, when he spent $3.5 million dollars on Image 2000 upgrades.

What was doubly hard for Rob was the fact Sandra Voitka, Central Region manager under Marc Comeau, and someone directly involved in the selection of dealers to be whacked, had been Rob Slessor's factory representative in her early years at

General Motors. Rob considered Sandra an ethical and honourable compatriot on the GMCL team. Upon learning of Sandra's involvement in the dealer terminations, Rob felt betrayed by her; that she had sold him out for "thirty pieces of silver." When Sandra was confronted with this accusation, she blamed the government for insisting the dealerships be closed. The hurt was compounded when Robert soon discovered—as has been disclosed in this book—that no Canadian government or U.S. government agency mandated the dealership closings. The government bailout funds or potential bankruptcy for GM and GMCL had no linkage to dealership terminations at all. The fact that GM's reinstating over 600 dealers in the U.S. had no impact on their bailout money proves this point. Dealership closings were not on the government agenda.

A significant bit of history is that since the Slessor family has owned and operated the Pontiac Buick GMC dealership in Grimsby, there have been thirteen different Chevrolet dealers in Grimsby. The twelve previous ones failed at operating successfully and closed. The current operator is the Wills family—fine and experienced dealer operators. Wills took over in 2003 and has struggled in the tough economy.

In 2003, after the twelfth Chevrolet dealer failed, and prior to Wills's opening, Robert Slessor went to GMCL and stated that statistics and history had proven that Grimsby could support only one GMCL dealership. History also showed that the Slessor family had earned the right to be that dealer. (If GMCL had been honestly following Plan 2000, they would have agreed and not given the Chevrolet franchise to anybody else.) GMCL's response was to install a new Chevrolet dealer. Terminating Slessor's is one way GMCL can try to ensure that the thirteenth Chevrolet dealer in Grimsby will be successful.

As over 90 percent of the GMCL dealers who were whacked signed the Wind-Down Agreement, I was curious as to why Robert Slessor had not. So he told me his story.

"I got a phone call from a senior GMCL manager advising me that I was being terminated as a GMCL dealer. I was an emotional wreck on hearing the news. My father was with me when I got the call and he could not believe it either, after all our family loyalty and commitment to GMCL for so many years."

After reading the Wind-Down Agreement, Slessor was disgusted and angry for the following reasons:

- The amount of money offered by GMCL was "insulting" and it in no way compensated Slessor for the goodwill and customer base the family had developed over fifty-five years.

- The fact that GMCL was insisting that the dealers sign off all their rights that had been enshrined in the Dealer Sales and Service Agreement was morally wrong. If GMCL was going to do this, why have a Dealer Sales and Service Agreement in the first place?

- The fact that GMCL was refusing to take back vehicle inventory, parts, and special tools was extremely irritating and financially costly.

- The "non-disclosure" clauses hit him as a violation of the fundamental right of free speech.

- The fact that GM wanted a quick answer in four business days sealed his rejection. "If you want a fast answer, the answer is NO!"

Rob Slessor went to his own lawyer with the unsigned Wind-Down Agreement and had his lawyer shred the document! He did not want to waver in his beliefs and convictions even if pressure were applied to him.

Of course, on May 26, 2009, pressure was applied to Rob with phone calls from GMCL. GMCL wanted Rob to sign. When Rob mentioned the injustice and unfairness of the document and the process, he was told, "The government made us do it."

On June 1, GMCL did not declare bankruptcy, and Rob began trying to get his dealership reinstated. According to the termination letter, and since he did not sign the Wind-Down Agreement, he would cease to be a GM dealer on October 31, 2010. He then wrote the first of seven letters to Marc Comeau requesting a face-to-face meeting and requesting that the criteria for Slessor's termination be provided. Seven times, Rob was called back by a subordinate of Marc Comeau's who stated Marc was too busy, and they would be happy to do a review with Rob. Of course, Rob knew that unless he met with Comeau, there would be no chance of a positive outcome.

. Finally, Comeau caved and agreed to meet with Rob Slessor in the General Motors of Canada's Oshawa head office on October 17, 2009, almost six months after his initial request. Slessor asked for, and was given, permission to record the meeting; the recording is now filed with the courts as part of the lawsuit. Comeau arrived late and read a prepared statement. Rob made his presentation. With little comment other than being told flippantly, "We have a lot of money in our legal defence fund" (kindly provided by taxpayers), he was escorted out of the building. A number of weeks later, he received a letter stating his requests had been denied.

Prior to launching the suit, the twelve dealers had requested that GMCL go to arbitration as a group under the National Automobile Dealer Arbitration Program. GMCL refused, as they would not allow the twelve dealers to act as an "association." On October 26, 2009, Rob Slessor and eleven other terminated dealers filed suit in the Ontario Superior Court of Justice.

Robinson Pontiac Buick Ltd.

Located in Guelph, Ontario, population 110,000. Cindy Robinson is the current owner/operator. Her father, Howard Robinson, had operated the dealership since 1965. Cindy Robinson had a similar experience to that of Robert Slessor. In 2008, she had received permission from GMCL to replace her father as dealer operator, on the condition that the dealership upgrade their facilities to the Image 2000 standards. Two million dollars later, the work had just been completed when Cindy received her termination notice and Wind-Down Agreement; she was very angry. What was especially galling to Cindy was that she had developed her used-car retail and wholesale sales operation to the point where they were generating significant profits. Even with the dramatic decline in GM's new vehicle sales in the previous two years, the dealership was financially doing very well.

Cindy also spoke to her Member of Parliament, and he supported her belief that GMCL was not going to declare bankruptcy in Canada; that reinforced her decision not to sign. (NB: In every recorded case where a dealer asked his/her elected Member of Parliament, the parliamentarian did not expect bankruptcy; however, GMCL was constantly waving the "red flag" of bankruptcy in front of the dealers.)

Cindy's frustration with GMCL stemmed from the fact that she and her family did everything GMCL had asked them to do. She operated a profitable and respected dealership in her community, and there was no logical reason for her dealership to be terminated. She honestly believed the termination of her dealership was unjustified and erroneous.

E.L. Fordham Motors Ltd.

Located in the farming hamlet of Rodney, Ontario, the company is owned and operated by Ronald Fordham. The Fordham family has continuously operated a GM dealership in Rodney since 1936. In 2006, the Fordhams spent $1,000,000 Imaging their facilities, after they had been assured by GMCL that Fordham would remain a long-term dealership.

Fifty-four-year-old Ron Fordham is a third-generation dealer. His grandfather started selling General Motors vehicles in 1933, when Alfred Sloan was running GM in the U.S. and Sam McLaughlin was the head of GM Canada. Over the years, the Fordham family has been loyal and supportive of GMCL in every way. Other rural small-town dealers nearby had closed, and Fordham's in Rodney was the only GM dealer in a twenty-five-mile radius. With GMCL's supposed commitment to maintaining a strong presence in farming communities at that time, Ron Fordham undertook a million-dollar renovation and upgrade to his facilities in 2007–2008.

When Ron received his termination notice, he was shocked and felt a tremendous sense of betrayal. His immediate reaction to the Wind-Down Agreement was that he was not signing. He did not believe that General Motors in Canada was going bankrupt, and now he did not believe anything that GMCL said. He quickly got on the phone and spoke to a number of fellow dealers in the area. There was no clear consensus of what the majority was going to do. Many dealers were not going to make a decision until the Sunday CADA telephone conference. Ron, on the other hand, had his mind made up and decided not to take advantage the CADA/Cassels Brock advice and guidance. On Monday, when talking to a few dealers, he was surprised how many had gone from "not signing" and "undecided about signing" to signing, based on the CADA Cassels Brock teleconference.

Ron did not waver from his decision, and on Monday he got calls from GMCL. He was unavailable to speak to anybody from GMCL until Tuesday afternoon, when his receptionist was told in an aggressive manner by a GMCL manager that it was "imperative" that Ron sign the Agreement. Ron took exception to the tone and manner of the message and called the GMCL manager back; he clearly expressed his feelings about GMCL and its Wind-Down Agreement, and repeated that under no circumstances would he sign such a document.

Ron's son was graduating from university, and was the fourth-generation Fordham to work in the dealership, and Ron was not about to let the family's heritage just fade away. He retained an area lawyer to advocate for him but, a few months later, joined Rob Slessor and the other dealers who did not sign the Wind-Down Agreement in initiating a lawsuit against General Motors of Canada.

The point that Ron reiterated was the sense of betrayal and abandonment he felt upon receiving the Termination Letter and Wind-Down Agreement. As with so many dealers I spoke to, Ron had a strong emotional attachment to being a GMCL dealer; he had always done what GMCL had asked; spent millions on facilities, training, equipment, and his own personal commitment to GMCL. All Ron ever wanted was to be treated honestly and fairly by GMCL, and GMCL abandoned him.

Niagara Motors Ltd.

Located in the village of Virgil, Ontario, about five kilometres from the city of Niagara on the Lake (population 14,000). Virgil is in the heart of an intensive agricultural area, and there are no other new-car dealers located near it or in the city of Niagara on the Lake. Owned by David Dick, the Dick family has operated a GM dealership in Virgil since 1953. Based on GM commitments, David Dick invested $4.2 million in Imaged facilities.

Giles Chevrolet Ltd.

Located in Stouffville, Ontario, which is rapidly transitioning from a rural to a suburban community. Owned and operated by Duncan Giles, the Giles family has operated GM dealerships since the 1920s. One of GMCL's oldest continuing dealers, Giles was able to meet GMCL's Image standards with an investment of only $90,000. New facilities in a new location were contemplated in the future. In 2008, the dealership had been given commitments by GMCL executives that they would continue in the long term as a GMCL dealer.

Upper Canada Motor Sales Ltd.

Located in Morrisburg, Ontario, on the St. Lawrence River, this is the only GMCL dealer in a radius of about fifty kilometres and 10,000 people. Owned and operated by Paul Goupil since 1971, in 2006, the dealership invested $1.6 million in Image upgrades and renovations.

Dave Hitchcock Chevrolet Ltd.

Located in Essex, Ontario, a mixed suburban farming community of 20,000 people. It has been owned and operated by Dave Hitchcock since 1973; David was a former GMCL sales management employee. Hitchcock Chevrolet was a Triple Crown-winning dealer, one of the top 100 dealers in Canada!

Lanoue Chevrolet, Inc.

Located in Tilbury, Ontario, with a population of 4,500 people. Craig Lanoue began operating Lanoue Chevrolet in 2009. He also owned the local Pontiac Buick GMC dealership, and GMCL actively encouraged Craig Lanoue to take over the faltering Chevrolet franchise from its existing operator. Based on promises of being a long-term Chevrolet dealer, financial agreements were finalized, and Craig began operating the Chevrolet dealership as Lanoue Chevrolet in 2009, only to be told on May 21 the dealership was terminated. The fact that Lanoue owned and operated both GMCL dealerships in Tilbury was an example of the type of rationalization and consolidation that was supposed to be achieved. Why did GMCL then terminate one of Lanoue's stores after he had just acquired it on their advice?

Bud Rier Chevrolet Ltd.

Located in the hamlet of Paisley, Ontario, and has been owned and operated by Bud Rier since 1975. In 2008, GMCL mandated that Bud Rier spend $250,000 to Image his facilities by 2010 in order to continue as a GMCL dealer.

Island Chevrolet Cadillac Ltd.

Located in Charlottetown, Prince Edward Island, it is owned and operated by the Brett family. The Brett family has been operating GM dealerships since 1967. In 2006, the Bretts acquired Island Chevrolet with GMCL's encouragement. Island Chevrolet was on the verge of bankruptcy at that time, partly because they had just spent $1 million to Image their facilities. Based on commitments made by GM, the Brett family spent approximately $4 million to acquire the Charlottetown dealership. The fact that Chevrolet and Cadillac were "core" brands as designated by General Motors must have had little influence on who got whacked.

Stoneleigh Motors Ltd.

Located in Midland, Ontario, a city of approximately 16,000 citizens; owned and operated by Mike Stone and his son Matthew. The Stone family operated the dealership continually for thirty-seven years and since 1972 have had their Dealer Agreement with GMCL automatically renewed. In 2002, at GMCL's request, Stoneleigh invested $400,000 in renovations to bring the facilities to the Image 2000 standards.

Slessor Motors (Newmarket 1979) Ltd.

Located in Newmarket, Ontario, population 75,000. Owned and operated by John Slessor, cousin of Robert Slessor; members of the Slessor family have been GMCL dealers in Newmarket since 1957. Based on commitments from GMCL, Slessor spent $1.3

DENNIS GAZAREK

million on Imaging in 1997–98. They were one of the first dealers in Canada to do so. Both Robert's and John's dealerships refused to sign the Wind-Down agreements when asked to, and tried to operate under the terms of their Dealer Agreement with GMCL.

The Newmarket situation is most curious; it has a population about the size of Santa Fe, New Mexico, and, as of 2011, had two GM dealers. *Both* dealerships in town were terminated, so there was no GMCL representation in this large community. It made no sense at the time.

Neither Les Kensit, owner of Colonial Chevrolet, nor John Slessor, owner of Slessor Motors, signed the Wind-Down Agreement.

Les Kensit, who could not be reached for an interview, was not active in any of the groups involved overturning GMCL's termination decision.

A number of months later, Kensit sold his dealership property, for what was considered an extremely lucrative price, to a company controlled by the Croxon family called Newland Chevrolet, Buick, Cadillac. The Croxon family owns a chain of dealerships, one of which was the terminated North York Chevrolet.

The Croxon family's North York Chevrolet dealership was located next to Foss Pontiac Buick GMC, a very large GMCL dealership and part of a large national leasing and automobile chain.

The rumour is that the Foss family eliminated their biggest competitor, the Croxon family got a big new dealership in a growing community, and Kensit received a windfall on the sale of his property. All transactions supposedly were facilitated financially or in other ways by GMCL. The story goes on to say that when Marc Comeau retires from GMCL, he will have a senior position within the Foss organization.

The point that this group will have to prove in their claim to win in court is:

- General Motors of Canada does not have the right to terminate dealers without cause, according to the Dealer Sales and Service Agreement, which is in effect until

274

October 31, 2010.

Section 13.1 of the Agreement states that termination can only occur in the event of: *"the following acts or events which are within the control of the Dealer or originate from action taken by the Dealer or its management"* and then lists fifteen clauses of acts for which the dealer will be liable for termination.

Nowhere does the DSSA state that "unprecedented economic conditions" are justification for dealer termination—which was the justification given in the termination notices dated May 20, 2009. The GM Dealer Sales and Service Agreement states, *"[T]he dealer is assured the opportunity to enter into a new Dealer Agreement with GM at the expiration date if GM determines Dealer has fulfilled its obligations under this agreement."*

It will be difficult for a judge to not find in favour of the claimant dealers (eventually twenty-one dealers joined the suit), as the Dealer Agreement is quite specific as to what reasons for which Dealers can be terminated, and economic conditions is not one of them. One strategy GMCL lawyers may use is to convince the trial judge that the economic times that GM was facing were so unusual that the DSSA could not envision them and therefore should not be binding on GMCL. However, if GMCL wanted to avoid the constraints of the DSSA, all they had to do was declare bankruptcy in Canada and hope the bankruptcy judge would revoke the DSSA.

General Motors of Canada lawyers are taking the typical GMCL tack in their approach to this case: delay, deny, divide. They have continuously brought motions forward to frustrate the claimants' right to their day in court. For example, GM has asked that the Superior Court stay the claim and insist that the dealers individually submit to arbitration under the NADAP (the National Automobile Dealer Arbitration Program). Of course, GMCL's lawyers knew that the twelve dealers had asked collectively for arbitration prior to launching the suit, and GMCL rejected it.

It is heartwarming for Slessor and the original twelve that nine more dealers who did not sign the Wind-Down Agreement have come forward to join their group. GMCL still refuses to issue the list of dealers who were terminated and those who signed the Wind-Down agreements, and as a result there are motions before the courts that this information be released. Of course, GMCL is fighting these requests.

Rob Slessor is a determined man of character and values. He believes the whole dealer termination process was unnecessary, unjust, unfair, and handled despicably by GMCL. He believes the dealers have to stand up to this injustice perpetrated by GMCL, and since GMCL has avoided behaving with the dealers in a responsible way, the courts are the only way GMCL will be brought to their senses.

As an active dealer who has been given his termination notice that his dealership will be gone as of October 31, 2010, Rob is faced with challenges. He has to be a good dealer and actively promote GM cars. Even though he is part of a lawsuit against GMCL, he has to communicate with them daily for parts, new vehicle inventory, and so on. Already he has found this relationship strained and finds it difficult to have sold orders built for customers. He is confident the lawsuit will be successful because to him all the secrecy, obfuscation, and concealment by GMCL to date validates that they did something very wrong and have something to hide, and court proceedings will bring it to light.

VICTORY

At least 10 General Motors of Canada Ltd. dealerships that had been scheduled to close as part of the automaker's restructuring will remain open as part of a settlement in a lawsuit between the company and 21 of its Canadian dealers.

(Globe and Mail, *Published on Monday, Aug. 23, 2010*)

The lawsuit was settled by GMCL and the twenty-one dealers who did not sign the Wind-Down Agreement, because GMCL probably saw the futility of their position: Opposition members in the Canadian Parliament were questioning the government's lack of support for the dealers, and GMCL realized it would be cheaper to settle now. Plus, GMCL and their legal team must have realized that their chances of success in a trial were very poor.

What did the twenty-one get? There is an extremely tight "gag" order on all participants. None of the parties with whom

I spoke would even hint at details. There are some interesting rumours circulating that seem to have some validity:

GMCL refused reinstatement of certain dealers as part of the deal. Some dealers who all along had wanted to continue to be GM dealers were denied. Both Slessor dealerships will not continue. It is believed they are being punished, as they were ringleaders/instigators of the legal action. It is estimated the dealers who are closing will receive four to five times more money than they would have received if they had signed the Wind-Down Agreement. So that was a big win for those dealers who did not want to continue.

The dealers who are continuing got what they wanted.

Overall, it was smart for the twenty-one dealers to not sign the Wind-Down Agreement in May of 2009 and take GMCL to court. It cost GMCL a lot of money and GMCL gained nothing.

10

Sheridan Chevrolet Cadillac Ltd.

As good as the probability of the suit launched by the dealers who did not sign the Wind-Down Agreement had of success (they won in August 2010), the second suit, initially launched by one dealer on behalf of all the dealers who *did* sign the Wind-Down Agreement, looks even more winnable.

The second suit has a much more seamy side, with implications of collusion, conflict of interest, duplicitous actions, false disclosures, and bad counsel.

As a senior manager at Sheridan Chevrolet Cadillac, a whacked dealership, I was privy to all the key discussions when our dealership received the Termination Letter and Wind-Down Agreement. Based on the statements and verbal commitments of Marc Comeau and other GMCL managers over the previous months and years, and based on the criteria GMCL purported to be using in selecting dealers to stay, I was relatively confident we were secure and not to be terminated; so when the termination came, all the staff were shocked.

I believed that for the following reasons Sheridan Chevrolet Cadillac was going to be safe: The communities of Ajax and Pickering are almost unified geographically. In fact, the town of Ajax was cleaved out of the old Pickering Township lands to build a munitions plant during WW II. For various reasons, they are two distinct political entities, but in the minds of many residents, the communities are one. At the end of 2008, there was a Bob Myers Chevrolet and a Bissell Pontiac Buick GMC dealership in Ajax, and a Boyer Pontiac Buick GMC dealership and a Sheridan Chevrolet Cadillac dealership in Pickering, plus a Saturn Saab dealership operated by my niece, the daughter of my brother Jerry Gazarek and the operator of Sheridan Chevrolet Cadillac. Bissell Pontiac Buick GMC had moved to a larger location with a brand-new building built to Image standards in 2008. Unfortunately,

Gord Mott, the owner, died, and even though his family tried to continue, they resigned their franchise in March 2009.

That left the Myers Chevrolet dealership in Ajax and the three GM stores in Pickering. It was acknowledged the Saturn store was doomed, with GM's announcement of cancelling the Saturn and Saab brands. If GMCL was truly interested in maximizing the dealership throughput and efficiency, now there was a great opportunity for them to act creatively and boldly.

The remaining Ajax dealer, Bob Myers Chevrolet, had been expressing his desire to retire for several years. He was in his seventies and suffered from injuries incurred during his previous illustrious pro-football career. He had never undertaken the upgrades and renovations required for Image, as he was not sure how long he would own the dealership, and was not interested in spending money on the next owner's behalf.

Boyer Pontiac Buick, initially opened by Michael Boyer, was in transition, too. Michael was spending weeks every year in Florida. He, with his sons and family, owned five dealerships, and Mike left the day-to-day operations to his family. He had not done the renovations and upgrades to these facilities, either. It was speculated that his property was the ideal site for a major hotel that was needed in the west end of Pickering.

Sheridan Chevrolet Cadillac had the largest land area, had the largest facilities in terms of square footage, and was located in the geographic centre of the communities of Ajax and Pickering. Even more remarkable, Sheridan had 700-foot frontage at the busiest intersection in Durham Region, and was the only dealership located on an artery that connected the two major expressways in Durham. This arterial road was also going to be the main gateway to the new community of Seaton in the City of Pickering.

It was felt at the time that if GMCL wanted to be innovative and creative, they would have given Buick to Sheridan, as Sheridan had core brands Chevrolet and Cadillac already and they would have one superstore serving an urban community of 200,000 people, plus the planned 80,000 in Seaton north of the Sheridan site. This store would have the throughput of the single Toyota store that services the same community, but in much larger facilities. According to previous GMCL statements, this was exactly what GMCL wanted to achieve in their reorganization. Now they have two dealers selling the same products located about eight minutes or less than six miles away from each other, both about as far away from the central planned growth areas as is possible.

It should also be noted that Sheridan had been at its location for thirty-one years, while both Boyer and Myers had arrived at their nearby locations approximately fifteen years later. What GMCL actually did was to close the dealership with two core brands, new and upgraded facilities, in the centre of the growth area of these two communities. They kept one dealership ostensibly because it had frontage on an expressway; and the dealership in Ajax also was kept, but nobody knows why for sure. The result is that they now have two dealerships serving the same area that Ford, Toyota, Honda, and Hyundai all serve with one dealership. In fact, all these competitors have more throughput than either GMCL store. So much for GMCL's professed objectives of increasing the efficiency of its retail dealers.

If GMCL had done any type of serious market and demographic studies, they would have discovered that the best place for the "GM Superstore" ready to grow with the new GMCL was Sheridan. Most of the population and almost all future growth is taking place north of the 401 expressway, as Lake Ontario limits further expansion south. Communities to the east and west were well-served with GMCL dealerships, and a centrally located GMCL dealer midpoint on the Ajax-Pickering border would allow GMCL dealerships in the adjacent communities of Whitby and Scarborough room to grow as well.

Sheridan had good CSI numbers, and the main area where they were weak was in Chevrolet sales—but all Chevrolet sales were weak throughout Canada, as compared to Pontiac numbers. Sheridan had been a much stronger dealership prior to the year 2000, when the Oldsmobile brand was cancelled. Oldsmobile had contributed 40 percent of the sales volume and a greater percentage of profits. Cadillac sales were above standard. The dealership was profitable and never received any special or additional financial support from GMCL. Because Sheridan had a $4 million debt due to expansion and Image renovations, it was less profitable than it should have been. Again, when $50,000 a month was going to service the mortgage, poor profitability is understandable. Of course the expansion, renovations, and resultant debt were due to GMCL's encouragement.

Another key fact impacting on all GMCL dealers in May of 2009 was the tightening of credit for auto dealers by all Canadian banks. The banks had heard so much negativity from and about GM and its future, they systematically began reducing operating lines and other credit sources both at the dealer level and the consumer level. This impacted dealers two ways: they could not get their customers financed and they were finding that cash to operate their business was getting scarce. Of course the banks asked each dealer if he had received a termination letter, and if the answer was yes, the bank tightened the "screws" some more.

In the case of Sheridan, the receipt of the termination letter by Jerry Gazarek for Sheridan Chevrolet Cadillac, and Lesley Gazarek, his daughter, for Saturn Saab of Pickering, was a tremendous blow. In many ways, it was worse than the death of Jerry's son Gerald John, the previous summer, from multiple sclerosis. I say that because Gerald John had been sick for years, and in the last year of his life he had been deteriorating rapidly. The termination of the Saturn dealership had been expected, but the end of Sheridan was a total shock.

After receiving the letter, Jerry met with his daughter, Lesley, and son, Brent, and other senior staff of the dealerships to discuss alternative actions. On Friday, he first went to see his doctor, as Jerry was experiencing physical symptoms of extreme stress. These stress reactions were a common denominator of almost every dealer operator that I have spoken with.

What were the stressors for Jerry Gazarek?

- He would have three empty dealership buildings (Jaguar, which leased a building next to Saturn, had vacated it and had only months to go on their lease).

- Property taxes per year were close to $400,000 annually on the land and buildings, and there was $4 million in mortgages on the property. Without dealerships operating and generating revenue, Gazarek had no way of making the monthly payments. If the payments were not made, the mortgage lender could seize the land and buildings worth $12 million.

- The North American economic crisis, which was real estate-based, ensured that it would be extremely difficult to sell his real estate in a reasonable time.

- Brent and Lesley, Jerry's two children, had spent their entire lives in the automotive business and would be out of work.

- The approximately 100 employees of the two dealerships, many who had been with Jerry for over ten years, would lose their jobs.

- The amount of money provided by GMCL in the Wind-Down Agreement was way short of the amount of money required to pay the employees anything more than required by the government. It in no way compensated the dealers for their investment in parts, special tools, or new vehicles they had already paid for but could not return to GMCL.

- The millions Jerry had invested in facilities were a total write-off, as many real estate experts stated there was a surplus of dealership facilities. Most dealerships are single-purpose buildings with little other commercial use.

Some employees initially counselled Jerry not to sign the Wind-Down Agreement. Jerry spoke to a number of dealers regarding their intent. (As Jerry had previously been president of the GM National Dealer Council, he was well-known and well-connected with the dealer body.) The consensus was that there was not a lot of choice for the dealers, but they should try and act as a group under CADA leadership. As we know, the CADA scheduled a national teleconference call for Sunday, May 24, 2009, where all dealers would be able to speak, and where lawyers from Cassels Brock would give expert advice.

I was hopeful CADA and the lawyers would launch some sort of legal activity that would allow the terminated dealers time to plan and organize a strategy. The Sunday afternoon telephone conference was not at all what I expected. Personally, I believed that the CADA, with the Cassels Brock lawyers, would come up with a strategy that would halt the termination and Wind-Down Agreement process. I honestly believed that a plan of action would be put forward that would involve the following steps.

- CADA with Cassels Brock would file for an injunction in court the next day that would freeze the termination letters and the deadline in the Wind-Down Agreement, the reason being that the contents and the complexity of the two documents required serious and in-depth study that was not available to the dealers within the deadlines set by GMCL.

- Cassels Brock would request that the court ensure that GMCL abide by the terms of the Dealer Sales and Service Agreement that was in force.

- Cassels Brock would ask for documentation from the Canadian government that it specified the closure of 240 GMCL dealerships as GMCL officials were stating.

I believed action by Cassels Brock and the CADA would allow GMCL and the dealers to carefully review their positions and develop a collaborative approach to the challenges that faced both parties. In reality, Cassels Brock and the CADA fielded questions from the dealers then delivered a summary that basically stated:

> The terminations are a result of pressure that GMCL is getting from the government. The Wind-Down Agreement is really not a good offer, but if you do not sign it and GMCL goes bankrupt, you will get nothing. "Talk to your own lawyer and do what is best for your own dealership situation."

This *something or nothing* alternative weighed very heavily on all the dealers. It was implied to the dealers there was no alternative to dealing with the offer that was presented by GMCL. There was no legal means to stop the process, and GMCL held all the cards. After this telephone conference, based on the information supplied by CADA and Cassels Brock, the matter was settled for most dealers, with the result that almost 90 percent of the terminated dealers signed the Wind-Down Agreement. There is no doubt in my mind and in many dealers' minds that this teleconference swayed the vast majority of dealers to sign. I also believe that if the CADA and Cassels Brock had voiced the desire and leadership to provide spirited opposition and legal action against GMCL on this matter, very few of the dealers would have signed. The 90-percent results exceeded even GMCL's highest expectations.

After the teleconference was over, there was very little more discussion at our dealership. We all felt that the CADA and Cassels Brock were the best resource for advice and information available, and they were giving the dealers sound and valid counsel; and that recommendation sure sounded like "you'd better sign."

At the Sunday meeting, I had contemplated speaking up against signing the Wind-Down Agreement for Sheridan. As it stood, I would have to go against the advice CADA and Cassels Brock had just given. None of the other managers seemed to see another way out, so I agreed with the consensus. It was a very defeated management team that left the dealership that Sunday.

After signing the Wind-Down Agreement and having it delivered to GMCL, Jerry set out on a three-part plan:

Find another brand of automobile to sell from the existing facility(s)
Find another dealer to buy or lease the facility(s)
Find an alternative use for the facility(s)

The first step Jerry took was to contact his long-time good friend, real estate broker Bob Oldham. Bob is one of those extraordinary gentlemen who is very successful in the cutthroat world of real estate development while being humble and genuinely concerned for others. When Jerry first told Bob the news of the dealership terminations, Bob ascertained that Jerry would have cash flow concerns and without being asked sent Jerry a substantial sum of money to help him through the tough times that were coming. Without any contracts or written agreements, Bob put his full efforts into finding alternative uses for the facilities and had come up with a plan to redevelop the Sheridan site for retail uses. Unfortunately, the economic downturn has left a surplus of existing vacant retail facilities available in the area.

The economic reality of June 2009 was that most of the major automakers were well represented in the Ajax–Pickering area. Several factory representatives made visits to the Sheridan facility, and for a time there was a belief that Chrysler was seriously contemplating offering a franchise to Sheridan. In the end, Chrysler realized that due to their financial and business difficulties, adding a dealership could be perceived negatively at the time.

Two of Ajax–Pickering's existing dealers considered upgrading to better facilities owned by Gazarek. The first was Boyer Pontiac! The existing Sheridan facility, as we saw from the urban geography point of view, was ideal to house the Boyer Chevrolet Buick Cadillac dealership. Plus, from the Boyer point of view, they would not have to spend millions performing Image upgrades to their old facility. The Sheridan facility had all the interior designs for both Chevrolet and Cadillac that the Boyer facility would need. Finally, the Sheridan facility was larger both in land and building area. Boyer's existing location had very positive hotel/condo development potential. Plus there was a willing buyer and a willing seller.

General Motors of Canada said NO! They did not want Boyer to move from his existing location—and under the Dealer Sales and Service Agreement they had that right.

I believe this refusal by GMCL was based on political realities. The only possible reason that Boyer was not whacked was the fact that he had expressway frontage. If GMCL allowed Boyer now to move to a whacked dealer's location, what justification was there for not whacking Boyer in the first place and keeping Sheridan?

The local Volkswagen dealer, overcrowded in their existing facility, seriously considered purchasing the Saturn facility. Unfortunately, because of their lack of confidence in future economic recovery, they were unable to make an offer on the property that was adequate to make a deal.

By August 2009, when these two alternatives were falling by

the wayside, and the redevelopment process had already started, the decision was made to begin winding down the operations of Sheridan Chevrolet Cadillac and Saturn Saab of Pickering. Sheridan Chevrolet Cadillac ceased at the end of August 2009 and Saturn Saab of Pickering officially ceased operations early in October 2009.

It is significant to be able to see how an individual and a small group working together can make a change in the course of business history. Jerry Gazarek did not start out to be a "dealer champion" or a knight on a white horse who would save the oppressed. However, through a combination of events, he was a member of a small group that commenced the largest lawsuit by dealers against an automaker in the world.

In discussions with Jerry, I learned the story of the lawsuit.

Upon receiving his termination letter, Jerry felt betrayed, abandoned, and used. The reality of the situation after June 1 was he was $4 million in debt and his only source of revenue—his and his daughter's dealerships—were closing.

The second shock was the approach of banks and suppliers who were now demanding much stiffer credit terms. Suppliers did not want to be caught with receivables from a defunct dealership and were demanding cash payments. Even the local plumber, who had worked for Jerry for years, demanded payment on delivery.

The third shock was when the company that had long-term leases with Sheridan and Saturn of Pickering for Information Technology services demanded to be paid out. Probably the most insensitive supplier company was ADP.[12] Part of the DSSA with GMCL stated that each dealer had to use a GMCL-selected contractor to perform all the dealer's IT activities with GMCL. These IT contracts cost the dealer about $100,000 a year.

When the dealerships closed and Jerry explained to ADP that it was GMCL's decision that he be terminated and that he did not need IT services to communicate with GMCL and GMCL did not want to communicate with him, these explanations fell on deaf ears. Jerry explained to ADP, when ADP threatened a lawsuit, that if he received another franchise from a different manufacturer, he

---

12   Automated Data Processing, a huge IT services company.

would be happy to continue his relationship with ADP. ADP is now suing Jerry for $200,000!

By this time, Jerry had started feeling that GMCL did not want an orderly and quiet wind-down of dealerships. He believed that GMCL wanted the terminated dealers to quickly wither away and go bankrupt from a lack of cash before GMCL made their final payments under the Wind-Down Agreement. He came to this conclusion based on the following facts.

- Once the dealer signed the Wind-Down Agreement, he could not order 2010 products; his primary source of revenue was gone, and the end was near.

- GMCL was making it difficult for retained GMCL dealers to buy parts inventory from terminated dealers. In Jerry's case, he had over $250,000 in new parts, with no market for them.

- Terminated dealers had millions of dollars of new car inventory they were responsible to sell and were paying interest on.

- Because of GMCL's public announcements, both suppliers and lenders were clamping down on terminated dealers in terms of credit sources.

- Retained dealers were advertising the fact that they were "here to stay" in an attempt to lure customers away from terminated dealers.

- GMCL was aware that suppliers with long-term leases to dealers would demand immediate payouts.

- GMCL allowance for sign removal was less than half of what the GMCL-stipulated sign company demanded in payment.

Clearly, it would be in GMCL's best financial interest if each terminated dealer in Canada declared bankruptcy before he/she received his/her final payments under the Wind-Down Agreement, as the Wind-Down Agreement stated GMCL would not pay if the dealer went bankrupt.

Speaking to other dealers in June, Jerry learned that a number of them had contacted various lawyers in the hope there was some escape from this GMCL-engineered financial trap.

At this time, Jerry had read an article written by John Sotos, of Sotos LLP, about the small group of dealers who had not signed the WDA and maintained their right to sue. (This was the group led by Rob Slessor, who launched the first legal action.) Jerry picked up the phone and called John Sotos and told him about his situation and that of the 200-plus dealers who had signed the WDA.

At that time, Cassels Brock had a statement posted on their website showing their areas of expertise and experience. In fact, in February 2012, they continue to state that they:

- Played a significant role in the recent North American automotive industry restructuring, acting for the Federal Government of Canada, through Industry Canada. In connection with the court-supervised sale of both General Motors and Chrysler, the transaction involved over US $12.5B of new Canadian Government financing and included a host of extremely time-sensitive issues, including cross-border bankruptcy, M&A, financing, and litigation

- Acted for the Canadian Automotive Dealer Association

This was exactly the conflict the dealers had experienced.

Jerry arranged for the first group of five dealers to meet with David Stearns and John Sotos at Sotos LLP's offices.

11

Lawsuit #2,
Launched February 12, 2010

There was a great sense of injustice that grew among all the dealers who had been given termination letters. After June 1, 2009, as the dealers started coping with the shock of the termination and their general economic plight, discussions among dealers became more focused and questioning. The questions and discussions were centred on the following topics.

- What were the parameters for selecting the dealers for termination? The further the dealers analyzed the selections, the more political the GMCL process seemed.

- Was there any legal recourse for the dealers, with the termination letters and the Wind-Down agreements so coercive and draconian?

- Why did the Wind-Down agreements try to restrict the dealers' right to associate, the right to free speech, and the right to seek recourse in the courts? What was GMCL hiding? What was GMCL hiding from?

- Why was GMCL so insistent in the Wind-Down Agreement that dealers were not franchises as defined by the Arthur Wishart Act?

- Was it true that the government forced GMCL to whack dealers?

- Was the threat by GMCL to go bankrupt in Canada valid?

- Why had CADA reversed its stand that it was going to support the terminated dealers?

- Why did not Cassels Brock act proactively to help the terminated dealers?

- Why did Cassels Brock refuse to act for any dealer's Wind-Down Agreement as an "independent legal advisor"?

- Why did GMCL terminate dealers in Canada, while Chrysler Canada did not terminate any? Were they not under the same governmental mandates?

- Why was the stated 42 percent termination factor the same in Canada and the U.S.? GM does relatively better in Canada than the U.S. in terms of market share; Canada is a much different geographical and political entity than the U.S.

As experienced businessmen, many dealers felt there had to be some sort of legal recourse to the conundrum they were faced with. True, some dealers felt they would just wind up their businesses and get on with their lives, having no taste for legal confrontations. Those dealers who did not sign the Wind-Down Agreement and who made formal appeals to GMCL for reinstatement knew that the courts were available to them.

A dilemma was that the dealers who signed the Wind-Down Agreement after having received independent legal advice had agreed not to initiate legal action against GMCL concerning the Wind-Down Agreement. That creates the paradox, how can a dealer disagree with an agreement he has already agreed to? He had independent legal advice (insisted upon by GMCL); he has received in some cases hundreds of thousands of dollars from them for signing the Wind-Down Agreement.

The following is a definition of a legal contract in Canada.

> *To form a legal contract, certain essential elements must be present; they are the following:*
>
> *Offer—a party has promised to perform specified acts on certain terms.*
>
> *Acceptance—another party indicates an unqualified willingness to enter into a contract based on the offer.*
>
> *Consideration—each party commits to provide something to the other party; if Party A offers to cut Party B's lawn, Party B commits to pay $200 for Party A's service.*
>
> *Intent—If the first three elements are present, then it*

will be assumed (by a court) the parties intended to create
a legal contract.

On the other hand, if the Wind-Down Agreement was not a valid contract, then the fact the dealer has signed it is irrelevant and the contract is invalid. Why could the Wind-Down Agreement be considered invalid? It has to do with "Acceptance": **an unqualified willingness to enter into the contract based on the offer.**

Dealers signed the Wind-Down Agreement because of one or more of the pieces of (mis)information they received from General Motors of Canada, the CADA, and Blake Cassels prior to the May 26 deadline date, as follows:

- The Government of Canada mandated GMCL to make dealer cuts.

- GMCL said there was a strong probability they would declare bankruptcy if a large proportion of dealers did not sign the Wind-Down Agreement; in which case, the dealers would get nothing.

- There were no legal remedies to counter GMCL's termination letters and Wind-Down Agreement (because none were suggested by Cassels).

- If the dealer did not sign, his future as a GMCL dealer was limited to October 31, 2010 and he would receive no compensation.

- The dealers knew it was a bad deal but it was the only alternative.

On the other hand, one can imagine if upon receiving the termination letters and Wind-Down agreements on May 20, 2009, the dealers knew the following facts would prove to be true:

- General Motors was not declaring bankruptcy in Canada.

- Neither the Canadian nor the U.S. governments had any interest in the number of GMCL dealers or if there was any reduction in their number. Chrysler did not terminate any dealers in Canada.

- The Wind-Down Agreement was in violation of one or more provincial statutes and was not valid, not legal, and not enforceable for that reason alone.

- Cassels Brock & Blackwell LLP[13] was retained by the Government of Canada in the negotiations with GM, and therefore, as representatives for the shareholders of GM, were biased and in conflict when advising the dealers and when dealing with GMCL.

- Comments Cassels made at the conference call on Sunday, May 24, were going to be declared not to be legal opinions by Cassels Brock, and therefore should have no relevance to the dealers' decision-making process; in other words, the dealers should have disregarded what Cassels Brock said.

Lawsuit #2 involves several complex legal issues and has stakes that are many times higher for GMCL because of the sheer numbers of dealers involved (about 220). The key points are:

- Can the dealers who signed the Wind-Down Agreement, therefore agreeing not to sue GMCL, renege on their contract and sue GMCL after all?

- Can GMCL cancel the Dealer Service and Sales Agreement unilaterally for reasons not listed in the DSSA?

- Can dealers be asked to sign away rights and protections that have been established by government legislation?

- Are contracts and agreements binding on dealers if the dealers signed them based on misrepresentations, misstatements, and erroneous information provided by GMCL?

---

13 Cassels Brock & Blackwell LLP is a Toronto-based law firm. According to their website, they have a staff of more than 200 lawyers focused on serving the transaction, advocacy, and advisory needs of Canada's most dynamic business sectors. They claim to be one of the largest business law practices in Canada, serving multinational, national, and mid-market entities and dedicated to value-driven public and private M&A, financing, and other transactional work. They also assert they consistently ranked at or near the top of Bloomberg and Thomson Financial deals league tables for M&A and equity offerings and are cited as market leaders by *Chambers Global, ALM 500, Best Lawyers, Lexpert, Global Counsel,* and others.

- If a law firm represents a major shareholder of GMCL, is that law firm not in conflict of interest if they provide guidance, information, and opinions to another group (the dealers) negotiating with GMCL? The concept being that what benefits GMCL and its shareholders will likely not be in the best interest of the CADA and the dealers. In Canada, the law firm does not have to "act" in a conflicting way; only the appearance of, or potential for, conflict is enough to create the question of the legal validity of the matter in hand.

All dealers who signed the Wind-Down Agreement agreed to cease operating as GMCL dealerships. It is believed that only a very few, if any, will ask to be reinstated as GMCL dealers. What is at stake is a financial settlement, and the suit asks initially for $750 million. In Canada, the courts will order only actual financial damages, and it is estimated that the total actual loss suffered by all the terminated dealers could exceed $1.0 billion.

GMCL is being very aggressive in trying to take the position that the terminated dealers are not a homogenous group and they should not be certified as a class in the legal sense. GMCL desperately does not want this group of dealers to be certified as a class. A court date was set for December 15–17, 2010, where a judge was to hear evidence and make a specific ruling on this point.

GMCL has made statements that all 220 dealers in this action are independent businessmen and are different, unique, and do not in any way fit the legal definition of a class. This position contradicts long-standing GMCL policies and procedures.

For many years, the only written form of official communication to dealers regarding General Motors sales and service policies has been through "Home Office Letters." All written communication to dealers regarding programs, incentives, warranty policies, and all other matters relating to dealership operations is communicated through these letters. In fact, the Home Office Letters are used to settle disputes between GMCL and dealerships. For example, they control the sale of vehicles for export from Canada, specifying the incentives and which customers are entitled to them. Home Office Letters regulate the sale of vehicles to

GMCL employees. The use of these Home Office Letters was the common and codified means of formal communication between GMCL and all its dealers. In this way, GMCL was recognizing the unity, commonality, and homogenous nature of the dealer body.

GMCL National Sales Manager Marc Comeau also communicated to all the dealers via the HIDL system on a regular basis, and these were broadcasts in the true sense of the word. From coast to coast, every dealer received exactly the same presentation and message in their language of choice. There were no unique or individual presentations for any dealers.

The emails sent to the terminated dealers with the Wind-Down agreements were identical with the exceptions of names and addresses and dollar amounts mentioned. All dealers were offered financial settlements in the Wind-Down agreements based on uniform calculations. There was no allowance for unique or unusual dealership situations.

Cassels Brock & Blackwell LLP and GMCL are taking a slightly different approach to their defence in this suit. It appears that Cassels Brock & Blackwell LLP is not disputing whether the dealers are a class. They claim that there is no conflict of interest because they were never retained by, or on behalf of, the terminated dealers. They claim they did not provide any legal services of any type to the terminated dealers.

This is a key paragraph at the beginning of the termination letter portion of the Wind-Down Agreement.

"The unprecedented economic conditions in the United States and Canada and in our industry have made it necessary for us to restructure our business and operations significantly. The restructuring plan also includes addressing GM Canada's dealer network in order to maintain GM Canada's long-term viability. Part of that restructuring is a planned reduction in the number of GM Canada dealerships. As we have communicated to all dealers, our revised restructuring plan is a result of GM being challenged to move more aggressively and faster in its restructuring efforts."

It is the justification being put forward by GMCL to rescind the terms of the GMCL Dealer Sales and Service Agreement that all the dealers had signed and was in force. I firmly believe the "unprecedented economic conditions" were not a valid justification under the DSSA to terminate any dealers in Canada as the economic conditions that were "unprecedented" were confined almost exclusively to the United States of America.

There was no economic reason to terminate dealers in Canada, and it was a political "lock-step" decision mandated by General Motors in the U.S.

- There were no bank failures in Canada.

- No Canadian financial institutions had to be rescued by the government.

- There was no equivalent to a TARP program in Canada.

- There was no collapse of the Canadian mortgage or housing market.

- The Canadian government initiated an "economic action plan" quickly to prevent the economy from spiralling into a recession created by U.S. banking failures.

- The Canadian government was not draining their treasury fighting a war in Iraq and had only 2,000 soldiers in Afghanistan—which they were planning to withdraw.

- It is believed by some that the majority of increase in Canada's unemployment statistics was a result of General Motors of Canada's terminating 240 dealers and their 13,000 employees simultaneously.

GM in the U.S. had a problem there, not in Canada. Canadian GM market share traditionally was and continued to be higher in Canada than in the U.S. Nowhere else in the world did GM terminate dealers because of the U.S. economic crisis; why was Canada so favoured?

The economic "hiccup" Canada experienced was due to the fact that 80 percent of Canada's exports go to the U.S., and any economic recession in the U.S. will negatively affect Canadian businesses. This is especially true of lumber exports for the American housing market. The Canadian economy was one of the soundest in the world, with controls on its financial institutions that prevented the "Wild West Credit Binge and Bust" attitude that permeated Wall Street. The reality was that in Canada there were NO economic conditions that were similar to what the United States was experiencing. Even Chrysler, which erroneously slashed dealers in the U.S., did not do so in Canada.

12

Certification Hearing, December 15, 2010

On January 21, 2010, the class action lawsuit seeking $750 million in damages on behalf of 220 Canadian GM auto dealers terminated by General Motors of Canada was launched in the Ontario Superior Court of Justice.

On December 15, 2010, a hearing was scheduled before Judge George Strathy of the Ontario Superior Court at Osgoode Hall in downtown Toronto. Judge Strathy is considered one of the most knowledgeable justices in the area of franchise and corporate law in Canada. In these hearings, lawyers for all parties make presentations and arguments to the judge. The judge is free to ask questions of any lawyer. No witnesses are presented or cross-examined.

General Motors of Canada was represented by the huge law firm of Osler Hoskin & Harcourt LLP, established in 1862, and with over 500 lawyers on staff. Truly the giant Goliath facing the relatively puny David: Sotos LLP, representing the dealers, is a small firm with twelve staff lawyers. Representing Cassels Brock was the firm Lenczner Slaght Royce Smith Griffin LLP. "Lenczner Slaght is Ontario's premier litigation practice" is how they describe themselves on their website. With forty-plus lawyers on staff, Lenczner is a small firm compared to their client, Cassels Brock, which has 200-plus lawyers on staff. But one can see that the resources of GMCL and Cassels far exceed that of the resources of the dealers.

On the first day of the hearing, the courtroom was jammed with affected dealers and the press. The main issue to be resolved at this hearing was: "Did the 220 dealers who signed the Wind-Down Agreement have enough common interests to be considered a 'class' under the class action laws of Ontario?"

Also intertwined were issues regarding the Wishart Act. Specifically, did GMCL violate the provisions of the Wishart Act when they issued terminations and Wind-Down agreements?

Since GMCL had, only ten days before, declared that the terminated dealers were franchises, GMCL was implicitly agreeing that the dealers were covered by the Wishart Act; but GMCL did not violate any provisions of the Act. This reversal of its position by GMCL regarding application of the Wishart Act to its dealers was a significant about-face after years of denial. Also, GMCL was claiming that the dealer and dealerships were all unique in so many ways that there was no possible way the judge could consider them as a "class." Cassels Brock wanted the action "stayed"[14] because they were claiming they had no involvement with the terminated dealers in any way.

I attended the hearing and what follows is based on my notes.

DAY 1

One of the first questions Judge Strathy asked David Finley, a dealer lawyer, was regarding the provision of the Wishart Act that requires disclosure of specific information when there is a material change to the franchise agreement.

Finley replied, *"If a fundamental or material change is being made to the franchise agreement, that changes the relationship between the parties. As in the Wind-Down Agreement, legislation dictates a disclosure document is required."*

I believe I heard the judge comment, *"What could be more of a material change to a franchise agreement than a document such as the Wind-Down Agreement?"*

GMCL's defence says that it is exempt from providing a disclosure statement because of the one-year rule in the Act, which refers to franchise agreements that have a term less than a year. GMCL claims the Wind-Down Agreement has been in effect less than a year (May 2009–October 2009). However, it is stated in court that the Wind-Down Agreement has a survivability clause in it that extends it for longer than a year, which destroys this weak argument.

David Stearns is the lead lawyer on this case for Sotos, and is stating that because there was not proper disclosure under the terms of the Wishart Act, the dealers suffered. GMCL's lawyer

---

14 A stay of proceedings: a discontinuation of the administrative process pending the outcome of a judicial review or a statutory appeal.

responds: *"If we did everything by rules of Wishart, and some deal-ers were happy to sign before, how does Stearns know if there had been disclosure under Wishart, the same number would not have signed anyway?* GMCL appears to be saying: *"Some guys were happy to sign the Wind-Down Agreement; how can Sotos prove they would not still have signed if they received proper disclosure?"*

When you think about it, GMCL is saying: *"Even if we had given disclosure according to the Wishart Act, nobody knows if the results would have been any different."* To me, that is the equiva-lent of saying that even if the U.S. had had twenty-four hours' warning before September 11, 2001, the results could have been the same. It is an illogical statement about a hypothetical situa-tion that makes no sense.

Stearns goes on to say that the dealers could have negotiated a better deal, because everybody else—unions, bondholders, etc.—was in line, and GMCL needed the dealers in line to get the government funding (according to GMCL). To get government money, GMCL had to negotiate a deal with the dealers. This ap-pears to counter the defence's "pressure from government" claim and is an interesting twist. If GMCL is saying they needed the dealers on board to get government funding, the dealers would have been in a great bargaining position if GMCL had followed the Wishart Act. By not following the Wishart Act, the dealers were severally disadvantaged. Now it is going to be very difficult for GMCL to say we were not pressured by the government.

Judge Strathy asks our lawyers about financial remedies un-der the Wishart Act. Our lawyer states: *"Dealers suffered a loss of unknown amount because they could not negotiate; the loss is unknown but likely in the millions."*

Cassels claims they were retained by CADA on a "collective group" retainer and only in the case of GMCL bankruptcy, and therefore should not be involved in the action. However, evi-dence is brought forward by the Sotos lawyers that the CADA told the dealers Cassels was for GMCL's "restructuring."

Cassels does not provide a defence to the conflict of interest issue because they claim they were never acting for the dealers or CADA, therefore no conflict could have occurred. Cassels also states the dealers did not suffer as a result of Cassels' actions; therefore, the dealers have no claims against Cassels. Cassels Brock is not denying they would have a conflict of interest if they acted for the CADA or the dealers.

The dealers' lawyers state that since Cassels did not act vigorously and aggressively, the dealers have suffered.

While listening to Cassels' argument about not being retained, I remember the Duck Rule: "If it looks like a duck, walks like a duck, and quacks like a duck, it must be a duck!" I think the judge believes in the same rule.

Cassels Brock asked to be retained and solicited money from CADA/dealers.

Money was collected on their behalf by the CADA from the dealers.

Cassels Brock acted like lawyers and behaved like lawyers in the Sunday, May 24 teleconference.

Therefore, they must be lawyers who have been retained.

GMCL lawyers are fighting class certification with great fervour and emotion. *"Big damages are involved, yet in class action, GMCL will not be able to examine each dealer's situation . . . There might be mitigating circumstances that preclude an individual dealer's receiving some damages GMCL will never know*[15] *. . . In individual actions, GMCL will have a right to discovery, in class action they will not. GMCL will be denied their rights."*

GMCL is fighting desperately against a class action because GMCL knows that most of the 220 dealers do not have the emotional or financial resources to fight GMCL and its huge law firm. GMCL could settle with the weakest dealer and use that pattern as a take-it-or-leave-it choice for any other dealers who wish to take it on.

One of GMCL's lawyers states self-righteously: *"Dealer organization is a legacy issue from the times when GM had large market share. GM has been trying for years to rationalize the dealer organization."* As the reader knows, this is not true, as GMCL often had a chance to rationalize the dealer organization and did not.

Another false statement: *"GM had to terminate dealers because the U.S. government rejected an initial restructuring plan."* The

---

15   GMCL would never know the results unless a separate trial were to take place for each dealer.

initial GM restructuring plan presented to the U.S. government, dated February 17, 2009, included dealer cuts by GM. This restructuring plan was rejected mainly because there were too many SUVs in the sales forecast. The rejection had nothing to do with dealer cuts, as confirmed later by several government statements.

The GMCL/Cassels Brock lawyers state: *"They all had independent legal advice."* The defendants are trying to convince the judge that the dealers had independent legal advice and the dealers decided to sign or not sign based on that guidance. Those dealers who signed should not be taking legal action because they now regret what they did in hindsight.

Judge Strathy rejects this claim and says: *"If the dealers had collectively received different advice, they all might have acted differently."* He appears to believe that Cassels Brock were acting as legal advisors for the dealers, and their advice, action, and non-action at the teleconference had a huge impact on the actions of the dealers.

GMCL lawyers begin speaking about *". . . how much time and how much information, guidance, and access to other dealers and advisors the terminated dealers had prior to signing the Wind-Down Agreement. There was no pressure, no coercion from GMCL, and each dealer had a fair and open opportunity to consider the alternatives before accepting or rejecting the Wind-Down Agreement."*

The judge now became somewhat incensed and asked to the effect, *"If everything was so open, why was the Confidentiality Clause so prominent in the Wind-Down Agreement?. . . Truly GMCL was not interested in wide disclosure and open discussion by the dealers."*

DAY TWO

Another windy, damp, and cool December day in Toronto, and in response to the overwhelming dealer audience, GMCL brought in about a dozen staffers to fill their side of the courtroom.

A GMCL lawyer begins by stating that no disclosure was required under the Wishart Act, as the Wind-Down Agreement did not grant a franchise, and was not a material change to the franchise agreement. The lawyer says the Wishart Act requires disclosure only for prospective franchisees.

The judge interrupts the lawyer and says, *"The Wishart Act has a broader application than just prospective franchisees; and the termination of a franchise agreement as specified in the Wind-Down Agreement is a material change."* It appears Judge Strathy has had enough of the defendants' lawyers interpreting laws and statutes to their clients' purposes and making statements that appear true when they are not.

When questioned by the judge, the lawyer for GMCL agrees that the Wind-Down Agreement takes away rights from the franchisees (taking away rights can be easily considered a material change in a franchise relationship). The lawyer for GMCL is having all her points refuted by the judge.

Judge keeps questioning the lawyer about the Wind-Down Agreement, *"If it does not constitute a material change in the relationship, what does it do?"* Lawyer is flummoxed and does not answer clearly.

The lawyer keeps trying to constrict the Wishart Act, giving it a very narrow scope, applying it only to the "granting of franchises" and "prospective franchisees." She quotes Judge Strathy's previous rulings in other cases to support her arguments. The judge takes great exception to these quotes, which are out of context. While retaining his composure, Judge Strathy states that *"Termination is a major and material change to the existing franchise agreement."* The judge again questions the lawyer on her narrow view of the Wishart Act.

The lawyer pushes on with the Wind-Down Agreement's being an amendment to the DSSA, not a material change. The judge does not appear to be buying this argument. From a civilian's point of view, this has been great legal sparring. The lawyer is trying to use the judge's own words to prove her point. The judge will have none of it, especially when it appears she is trying to "school" him on his own rulings.

Continuing on, the lawyer states, *"GMCL is **not** a franchisor under the Wishart Act."* The judge stops her immediately and asks if they are a franchisor as declared by GMCL itself previously in court documents or not, as the lawyer just said. She reverses herself, and now says they *are* a franchisor. This lawyer and her arguments appear to have lost all credibility with the judge.

Judge Strathy later asks her again about the Wishart Act: "*By the fact that GMCL invited Trillium (representative of the Class) to sign the Wind-Down Agreement, which in itself is a major change in relationship between the franchisor and franchisee, does that not trigger disclosure as required by the Wishart Act?*"

Judge Strathy also states: "*The Wishart Act is inclusive, not exclusive legislation, and the lawyer with her arguments is not going to get him [Judge Strathy] to change previously accepted interpretations of the language and definitions of the Act.*" He is concerned that she is attempting to redefine statute law to suit her clients.

The judge questions the lawyer about the fact that Wishart in its definitions section gives a wide definition of agreements. The lawyer for GMCL says that Trillium incurred no costs due to the Wind-Down Agreement. Another falsehood, as eventually, at a later date, Trillium will declare bankruptcy.

GMCL's lawyer wants individual lawsuits so they can have individual hearings discovery. In Canadian civil law, each party is allowed to interview their opponent under oath to "discover" pertinent information related to each case. One can imagine how many years 200 dealers' individual lawyers would need to interview the key players at GMCL on an individual basis with this approach!

As stated before, it is imperative from GMCL's position that this case *not* be certified as a class action. In order to have the dealers not ruled as a "class," GMCL will have to convince Judge Strathy that no, or an insignificant number of, common issues exist that would bind the group of dealers into a "class."

Under the Class Proceedings Act of 1992, the definition of a motion can be certified as a Class on the following bases:

> The court shall certify a class proceeding on a motion under section 2, 3 or 4 if the pleadings or the notice of application discloses a cause of action.
>
> **Not in dispute by the parties in this case.**

> There is an identifiable class of two or more persons that would be represented by the representative plaintiff or defendant.

Not in dispute by the parties in this case.

The claims or defences of the class members raise common issues.

GMCL is fighting to prove a lack of common issues for all dealers.

A class proceeding would be the preferable procedure for the resolution of the common issues.

GMCL is saying there are no common issues, so the case should be handled on a dealer-by-dealer basis.

There is a representative plaintiff or defendant who

(i) Would fairly and adequately represent the interests of the class

(ii) Has produced a plan for the proceeding that sets out a workable method of advancing the proceeding on behalf of the class and of notifying class members of the proceeding

(iii) Does not have, on the common issues for the class, an interest in conflict with the interests of other class members.[16]

GMCL is saying that other dealers are very different than Trillium Pontiac Buick GMC.

Note: "common issues" means, (a) common, but not necessarily identical, issues of fact, or (b) common, but not necessarily identical, issues of law that arise from common but not necessarily identical facts.

GMCL's lawyer further challenges the existence of common issues to all dealers. The arguments follow the same pattern. *"Dealers are all different; all have different damage scenarios . . . Five dealers did not sign the Wind-Down Agreement until months after May 26; why should they be in the Class?. . . 100 dealers signed before the deadline date; how they can say they did not have enough time and be in this Class?. . . This group is inappropriate for a Class proceeding."*

Judge Strathy stops the lawyer and disputes the lawyer's ar-

---

16   1992, c. 6, s. 5 (1).

gument about how a class is made up. The lawyer speaks about the fact the dealers are unique but were allowed by GMCL to associate. I find this an interesting concept, that of "uniqueness." In all its dealing with dealers over the years, GMCL has treated dealers as a uniform and consistently common group.

The lawyer now starts rambling about the difficulty a trial judge hearing this case would have, trying to assess or calculate damages. It is the lawyer's belief because of the complexity of assessing and calculating damages, certification as a class is not possible.

Judge Strathy stops the lawyer with this statement: *"Few actions go to trial, so stop arguing how hard damage calculations will be in a trial."* Judge Strathy does not want to hear about damage calculations that may never happen as a reason to prevent certification as a class.

When the issue of the dealers' signing releases not to sue GMCL comes up, Judge Strathy states that he believes these releases in the Wind-Down Agreement are invalid under the Wishart Act.

GMCL's lawyers again claim there are no common issues of fact or law that exist to bind these dealers together under the Class Proceedings Act. Even though GMCL's lawyers constantly state to the judge this opinion, common sense is against GMCL for the following reasons:

- They were all operating GMCL dealers in good standing.

- They all had current Dealer Sales and Service Agreements with GMCL.

- They were all terminated by GMCL in May 2009.

- They all signed Wind-Down agreements tendered to them by GMCL.

Where in the world is there a group or collection of entities that had these four common denominators?

Peter Griffin, lawyer for Cassels Brock, repeats: *"We were never retained,"* and the two cases, GMCL and Cassels, are incompatible, so Cassels' action should be stayed.

Judge Strathy asks, *"If Cassels was only dealing with bankruptcy issues, why were they involved with the May 24 teleconference?"*

While Cassels Brock's lawyers continually speak of "no expressed retainer," Judge Strathy questions, *"What about an implied retainer, though?"* Judge Strathy is very aware that Canadian law has set a precedent where lawyers have been held liable on the basis of an implied retainer. The judge then asks: *"If there is a retainer, does the law firm have a fiduciary duty to the client?"* The lawyer says, *"Yes."*

The key question the judge has to determine is *if there was in fact a retainer.* Cassels says that since there was no retainer, they do not have to be concerned with any of the other issues.

Judge Strathy discusses the Sunday teleconference, where Cassels Brock lawyers were advising the dealers, even though GMCL was not bankrupt (which Cassels states was the only basis on which they were retained), which then implies that Cassels Brock had a fiduciary duty. Judge Strathy further states, *"Cassels could have given them advice on how to fight the Wind-Down Agreement."*

Cassels Brock lawyer replies, *"We were not retained."*

Judge Strathy pointedly says, *"Then what were you doing at the conference call?"*

Judge further asks why Cassels Brock is fighting the certification: *"Why would they want the dealers not certified as a class and rather face 220 individual lawsuits?"*

When the Sotos lawyer speaks, he explains that Cassels Brock were retained by the dealers, and this is supported by the fact that dealers sent money to the CADA for the Cassels Brock legal fund. If this is not a retainer by the dealers, what is? Even though Cassels Brock claim they were only involved in the event of GMCL's bankruptcy, Cassels Brock had a copy of the Wind-Down Agreement and had reviewed it with the CADA staff. This proves that the firm of Cassels Brock was active and involved in the whole GMCL restructuring process and in the whacking of the dealers. They were involved because they knew they had been retained.

The Ruling

Judge Strathy released his ruling on March 1, 2011. It was a tremendous body blow to the defendants, GMCL and Cassels Brock, and an unmitigated victory for Sotos LLP and their clients, the 220-plus terminated dealers who signed the Wind-Down Agreement.

The ruling was sixty-nine pages in length and is available at: http://www.sotosllp.com/wp-content/uploads/2011/03/reasons-for-decision-certification.pdf.

However, I will discuss the key points in the ruling.

First, based on law and precedent, Judge Strathy notes that franchise relationships, as in the case of the dealers and GMCL, are particularly well-suited for a class action proceeding, due to the nature of franchise relationships (paragraph 59).

Judge Strathy does not accept GMCL's narrow interpretation of the Arthur Wishart Act. GMCL has stated that they did not have to meet the disclosure rules of the Wishart Act because the Act applies only to prospective franchisees, not existing dealers; and/or the Wind-Down Agreement is not an amendment to the Franchise Agreement; and/or if the Wind-Down Agreement is an amendment to the Franchise agreement, since its term is less than one year, the Wishart Act is not applicable.

The judge finds GMCL's pleadings a "novel issue" and rules in favour of the dealers. (Paragraph 78.)

In the issues regarding Cassels Brock, again the judge rules for the dealers: *"that the plaintiff has met the cause of action requirement in s.5 (1) (a)"* of the Class Proceedings Act.

The judge deals with the claim of GMCL that aggregate damages for the class will not be easily calculated, so for that reason alone the class should not be certified. *"In my view, this is not a case in which certification of the action hinges on the availability of an aggregate assessment. If damages have to be dealt with individually, the task will not be insurmountable. On the other hand, depending on the findings of the common issues judge, there may be a basis for an aggregate assessment of damages against either GMCL or Cassels. I therefore leave the issue of aggregate assessment to the common issues judge."* (Paragraph 120.)

Next, the judge deals with the claims of GMCL and Cassels Brock that there are insufficient common issues that bind the dealers together. The judge writes twenty paragraphs of discussion and finally states: "*In summary, for the above reasons I find that this proceeding meets the requirements of s.5 (1)(a) of the CPA, in that the claims of the class members against GMCL and Cassels raise common issues.*" (Paragraph 141.)

Judge Strathy then deals with the arguments of GMCL and Cassels Brock, who claim that the case cannot go to trial as a class action because it is not capable of resolution in that manner. The judge deals with these arguments in the next twenty-three paragraphs and concludes: "*I am satisfied that the common issues are capable of resolution in a fair, efficient, and manageable way. In view of the size of the class, joinder* [joining or grouping two or more similar legal issues] *would not be a practical alternative. Individual proceedings would not be realistic. Only a class proceeding will advance the aims of the CPA.*" (Paragraph 164.)

The issue Judge Strathy deals with before rendering his final ruling is that of Cassels' requesting a stay of proceedings against them. Basically, Cassels Brock is claiming that they should not be linked with GMCL in this case, as the issues are different; that if GMCL wins, there is no action possible against Cassels Brock, and the case of GMCL should go alone first. Judge Strathy is considerate in the next fifteen paragraphs but concludes: "*I accept that this action may be oppressive and onerous to Cassels, and an embarrassment to its partners. A lawsuit, particularly one involving a claim for $750 million, is necessarily so. It cannot be in the interests of the limited liability partnership, or its partners who are individually sued, to have litigation of this magnitude hanging over their heads for many years awaiting the outcome of a proceeding . . . it would be more advantageous to enable them to participate from the outset.*" (Paragraph 179.)

Regarding the claims against Cassels, the judge commented, "*[T]his is not a typical solicitor's negligence case*" and that the case raises "*important issues concerning lawyers' duties to their clients, particularly in the context of group retainers.*"

With that, Judge Strathy declined the stay to Cassels Brock.

Concluding that justice would best be served by allowing the dealers to proceed as a class action, Justice Strathy remarked: *"It is not realistic to think that an individual franchisee, who has experienced the loss of their business, is financially or psychologically equipped to engage in protracted, complicated, and very expensive litigation with one of the largest corporations in North America and a major Canadian law firm."*

In summary, the judge certified the action for a class proceeding, and the dealers were awarded costs.

The Leave to Appeal

Bear in mind that with Judge Strathy's ruling for certification, we are now talking about the real possibility of the defendants' having to pay damages of $750 million dollars or more. We are talking about the largest class action suit in Canadian history. The stakes are huge for everybody. GMCL, if they have to pay, will have a lot of explaining to do to GM in Detroit. If GMCL loses, the senior decision-makers of May 19, 2009, will likely have their careers ended. Cassels Brock does not likely have the resources or the insurance to fund even a $100 million settlement, so losing this case could lead to bankruptcy and the end of the firm, plus professional ruin for some or all partners. You can bet people other than the terminated dealers were losing sleep now.

To put the amount of money at play in context, the largest personal injury settlement in Canada to date was $24 million. A national food contamination case was settled for $27 million. The largest environmental class action suit in Canada was settled for $36 million. So in the context of these settlements, the $750 million involved in this case is mega-huge.

Of course, one could expect that GMCL and Cassels Brock were crushed on hearing the results. They lost on almost every point they raised with Judge Strathy. However, our legal system includes a means to appeal almost everything. In Ontario, GMCL and Cassels Brock would have to find a judge to give them a hearing and ask that judge to rule that Judge Strathy could have made some errors and grant the defendant a "leave to appeal" to Divisional Court, which then would review and rule on Judge Strathy's rulings.

Madame Justice J. Low of the Divisional Court of Ontario heard arguments on May 19, 2011. The defendants moved for leave to appeal in respect of some, but not all, of the questions certified as common issues. Judge Strathy had certified thirteen questions as common issues. GMCL and Cassels Brock disputed only the following seven.

GMCL's Questions for Appeal

- Did GMCL breach its duty of fair dealing with all class members? (*Justice Low's ruling, "No Leave to Appeal"*) **Win for dealers.**

- Is the Waiver and Release found in section 5 of the Wind-Down Agreement null, void, and unenforceable under the terms of the Wishart Act? (*Justice Low's ruling, "No Leave to Appeal"*) **Win for dealers.**

- Did the class members have a right to associate, and did GMCL interfere with this right? (*Justice Low's ruling, "Allowed Leave to Appeal"*)

- Did GMCL breach its duty to disclose material facts at the time of the Wind-Down Agreement? (*Justice Low's ruling, "Allowed Leave to Appeal"*)

Cassels Brock's Questions for Appeal

- Did Cassels Brock owe contractual duties to some or all of the class members? (*Justice Low's ruling, "Allowed Leave to Appeal"*)

- Did Cassels Brock owe fiduciary duties to some or all of the class members? (*Justice Low's ruling, "Allowed Leave to Appeal"*)

- Did Cassels Brock owe duties of care to some or all of the class members? (*Justice Low's ruling, "Allowed Leave to Appeal"*)

In reading Justice Low's ruling of June 22, 2011,[17] it becomes clear that she studied and researched Judge Strathy's rulings very carefully and supported him on every point except where there

---

17   See the link http://www.sotosllp.com/wp-content/uploads/2011/06/decision-of-justice-low.pdf.

was some grey area or some interpretation on Judge Strathy's part.

My feeling is that while trying to be scrupulously fair to the defendants, Judge Low appears to say that most of the issues are clear-cut and obvious and cannot be appealed. However, on some issues, both sides have some validity, and although she is not disagreeing with Judge Strathy's decisions, she feels the questions warrant a second consideration by an appeals judge.

First, overall, Judge Low's rulings could be considered a victory for the dealers. Cassels Brock is still part of the action. The class ruling of Judge Strathy will not likely be overturned, as there are still enough questions for common elements to satisfy the Class Proceedings Act.

Second, Judge Strathy has laid out his decisions for his rulings that will be appealed in such a way that even though there might be some validity in opposing arguments, in this case, after careful analysis, it is not likely the appeals judge will overrule them.

The specific points the appeals judge will have to deal with and overrule Judge Strathy's ruling are:

- **Did the class members have a right to associate, and did GMCL interfere with this right?** By limiting the amount of time each dealer had to decide, and by having an extremely stringent confidentiality clause, it is obvious GMCL interfered with the dealers' right to associate.

- **Did GMCL breach its duty to disclose material facts at the time of the Wind-Down Agreement?** Of course it did. And besides not disclosing pertinent facts, they disclosed misinformation and false facts, such as that GMCL needed all terminated dealers to sign the Wind-Down Agreement; that it was the government making GMCL terminate dealers; and if the dealers did not agree, GMCL would likely go bankrupt.

The Cassels Brock situation deals with the duties of a law firm; Judge Strathy has ruled yes to each of these questions. To overrule, the appeals judge will have to disregard that a significant number of the dealers believed that Cassels Brock were acting on the dealer's behalf.

- Did Cassels Brock owe contractual duties to some or all of the class members?

- Did Cassels Brock owe fiduciary duties to some or all of the class members?

- Did Cassels Brock owe duties of care to some or all of the class members?

As Judge Strathy stated, if Cassels Brock were not acting for the CADA and the dealers at the teleconference, what were they doing?

It can be expected that GMCL will delay, and slow the legal process as much as possible to take advantage of two realities: The suing dealers are older people, and with time may lose their desire for a long, drawn-out legal process. Second, no doubt both General Motors of Canada and Cassels Brock are aware of the tenuous legal position they hold, and any delay they can create in reaching settlement might save them money.

It will be in the early winter of 2012 before the appeal will be heard. Then, depending upon the rulings of the Appeals Judge, the case may go to trial sometime in 2012–13. In all likelihood, after the appeals hearing and rulings, out-of-court discussions to reach a financial settlement will begin.

What the settlement amount will be is unknown, but some dealers feel their individual situation merits settlements in the area of $10–20 million. If the case were to go to trial, I believe the trial judge could be presented with an aggregate damages total exceeding $1.5 billion! If that scenario were to become reality at trial, it is in GMCL's and Cassels Brock's best interest to begin settlement negotiations as soon as possible and use the $750 million number as an upper limit to begin negotiating from.

So far, the dealers are in a very strong legal position; nothing on the horizon looks to weaken their case. Even if they lose all of the current appeals, they still have a very strong case going forward to trial with a strong class action.

Of course, various external forces can have a great impact on the process. General Motors in Detroit definitely does not like the idea of a 750-million-dollar lawsuit hanging over their subsidiary's head. In reality, it will only take a simple phone call from either one of the highest officials of GM in Detroit and/or the government to say, "Do the right thing and settle." To put the settlement in context, GM made a $3.2 billion profit in the first three months of 2011. So in reality, the settlement requested by the dealers is quite doable in terms GM's ability to generate profits.

GM shareholders, including the governments of Canada and the U.S., are aware that this lawsuit can affect future share prices and values. The reorganization of General Motors was to get rid of all these "messy" problems—and yet, GMCL created this one.

U.S. Total Vehicle Sales Market Share by Company, 1961–2009.

Company	1961	1969	1979	1989	1999	2009
GM	45.71	45.79	44.68	34.65	28.76	19.58
Toyota	0.00	1.13	4.51	6.49	8.48	16.73
Ford	29.26	26.26	23.81	24.49	23.20	15.29
Honda	0.00	0.00	2.50	5.28	6.18	10.86
Chrysler	10.37	14.13	11.09	13.52	15.15	8.79
Nissan	0.00	0.79	4.06	4.49	3.91	7.27
Hyundai	0.00	0.00	0.00	1.23	0.94	4.10
Kia Motors	0.00	0.00	0.00	0.00	0.77	2.83
Volkswagen	2.97	4.79	2.37	1.03	2.19	2.79
Daimler	0.19	0.19	0.45	0.71	1.98	2.43
BMW	0.00	0.10	0.24	0.44	0.89	2.28
Subaru	0.00	0.00	0.91	0.92	0.90	2.04
Mazda	0.00	0.00	1.17	2.30	1.40	1.96
Volvo (car)	0.19	0.32	0.40	0.69	0.67	0.58
Mitsubishi	0.00	0.00	0.00	1.01	1.50	0.51
International	1.70	1.20	0.87	0.53	0.64	0.50
Suzuki	0.00	0.00	0.00	0.20	0.29	0.36
PACCAR	0.03	0.08	0.17	0.24	0.34	0.28
Land Rover	0.00	0.00	0.00	0.03	0.17	0.25
Porsche	0.00	0.05	0.10	0.06	0.12	0.19
Volvo Truck	0.13	0.14	0.22	0.28	0.37	0.14
Jaguar	0.00	0.00	0.00	0.13	0.20	0.11
Saab	0.00	0.10	0.11	0.21	0.23	0.08
Isuzu	0.00	0.00	0.00	0.86	0.71	0.05
Other	9.45	4.94	2.33	0.20	0.01	0.00
Total Vehicles	100.00	100.00	100.00	100.00	100.00	100.00

(Courtesy of Wards Automotive Group)

13

Conclusion Part 2

Over the past twenty years, in terms of market share, GM of Canada was a more successful retailer of automobiles than GM in the United States. After whacking the dealers in Canada and continuing to refuse to reinstate those dealers, as was done in the U.S., GMCL has set itself on a very precarious course. It is wasting millions of dollars (taxpayers' dollars, however) fighting a losing battle in the courts. As of March 2012, GMCL had lost its latest appeal against the dealer class action, and the stage is set for the trial to begin. With a continued drop in sales and market share in Canada, the morale of the remaining dealers is very low. There are stand-alone Buick dealers trying to exist with 25 percent of their previous car line sales. The botched realignment of remaining dealerships has created confusion and chaos in the dealers' and consumer's minds. GMCL is no longer the sales leader in Canada; it has lost first place to Ford.

GM of Canada's executives appear to have become much more insular and hunkered down. Rarely does Marc Comeau give juicy interviews to the media as in the past. The appearance that these GMCL leaders are just trying to hold on and survive until they can retire is probably very accurate.

Canada has gone from one of General Motor's most secure markets worldwide to one that is in considerable flux. Things are not rosy for GM in Canada, and remember, from GM's Detroit offices, you can see Canada!

What will happen next? No one knows.

That is what makes the car business exciting.

Appendix A

Legislation and Rulings

The following pieces of legislation can be accessed as follows:

Arthur Wishart Act: http://www.elaws.gov.on.ca/html/source/ statutes/english/2000/elaws_src_s00003_e.htm

Class Proceedings Act:

http://www.e-laws.gov.on.ca/html/statutes/english/elaws_ statutes_92c06_e.htm

Available from the Sotos LLP website are other GMCL case related documents:

http://www.sotosllp.com/class-actions/gm-dealers-claim/

At these sites are copies of the GM Restructuring Plan submitted to the U.S. government:

http://www.scribd.com/doc/40404439/GM-2009-%E2%80%93-2014-Restructuring-Plan-REPORT-TO-TREASURY

Appendix B

Premier: Dealer Cuts Not Our Idea

Tony Van Alphen
Toronto Star **Business Reporter**
February 11, 2010

Ontario Premier Dalton McGuinty has denied General Motors' claims that the federal and provincial governments asked the teetering automaker to slash its dealer network so the company could gain a multibillion-dollar bailout.

McGuinty says in a letter to an eastern Ontario dealer that GM of Canada Ltd. made the decision to drastically reduce its retail network last year, not the two governments.

"Please know that the government of Ontario and the government of Canada did not ask GM to reduce their dealer network," McGuinty wrote in the July 10, 2009, letter that surfaced in a court case on Wednesday.

The federal and Ontario governments provided GM with about $10.6 billion in taxpayer aid to restructure operations and stay alive during the recession and market downturn.

Federal Industry Minister Tony Clement and a senior official in his office could not be reached for comment on McGuinty's letter and Ottawa's position on dealer cuts and GM aid.

The letter contradicts numerous GM statements last year that it needed to cut the dealer network further as part of a survival plan after government requests.

GM disclosed on May 20, 2009, it had advised dealers of a consolidation plan and who would lose franchises at the behest of the governments.

"GM Canada, at the request of the federal and Ontario governments, accelerated its restructuring and released a revised, more aggressive operating plan on April 27, which included plans to reduce the number of GM dealerships in Canada by approximately 42 percent," the company added in a statement.

"Today, GM Canada will advise Canadian dealers of the specifics of our network consolidation plan including the identification of dealers whose sales and service agreement would not be renewed following expiry in Oct. 2010."

GM gave notice to more than 240 dealers who received a few days to decide whether to accept "wind-down agreements" and close before the end of last year, or continue operating until this fall with no compensation. Most dealers accepted the agreements and some money to help cover shutdown costs.

GM spokesman Tony LaRocca said Wednesday that aid was contingent on a second company plan that demonstrated better viability.

"It was up to GM to deliver what restructuring was necessary to achieve that," LaRocca said. "Rationalizing the dealer network to align with our four brands was one component of that plan."

McGuinty's letter appears as an exhibit in court filings supporting a statement of claim by twelve holdout dealers who sued GM last November for millions of dollars in alleged contract breaches.

They are also seeking a court injunction to stop GM from terminating their agreements for another five years.

GM submitted a motion to move the case from the court to individual hearings under the Automobile Dealers Arbitration Program.

McGuinty sent his letter to Paul Goupil, president of Upper Canada Motor Sales in Morrisburg, who complained to local MPP Jim Brownell about GM's decision to close his profitable store after the company received money from the provincial government.

Goupil, one of the plaintiffs, pressed the government to ask GM to reverse its decision.

In noting that the province did not ask for the closings, McGuinty said in the letter that "my colleagues and I are concerned about the workers, families, and communities affected by the closures."

The latest filings include statements by a senior GM of Canada executive who told retailers in a webcast in March 2009 that the company "plans to work closely with its Canadian dealers on further consolidation and rationalization . . ."

But less than a month later, without further consultation, GM announced the plan to cut the network by about 42 percent, according to the claim.

Glossary

Arthur Wishart Act: Also known as the Wishart Act, the act requires fair dealing between parties to franchise agreements, to ensure that franchisees have the right to associate and to impose disclosure obligations on franchisors.

Bankrupt/Bankruptcy: Generic term to describe an insolvent business, or a business unable to meet its financial obligations. In the U.S., bankruptcy filings are under federal jurisdiction and protect troubled businesses and provide for orderly distributions to business creditors through reorganization or liquidations. The vast majority of the business cases in the U.S. are filed under chapter 11 of the Bankruptcy Code, as did General Motors on June 1, 2009, in the U.S.

In Canada, the legislation dealing with bankruptcy is called the Companies' Creditors Arrangement Act. General Motors did not file for bankruptcy in Canada. In most cases, bankruptcy is the result of not having enough cash to pay current obligations.

Bean-counter: A person who is a whiz with numbers, accounting, statistics, and forecasting. Especially useful in top management, in that he/she can add any two or more numbers together and always get the number desired, regardless of mathematical reality. Example $2+2 = 3$, or 4, or 5, or whatever number you are looking for. Bean-counter is not a synonym for accountant, and should not be construed as such.

Car Guy: The self-professed genius of the auto industry, the creative intelligence who produces great automobiles. Unfortunately, history shows that every car guy will eventually be fired, go bankrupt, go insane, be imprisoned, die prematurely, or some combination of all the above.

Class Proceedings Act (CPA): The law in Ontario governing class actions; the full text is available at this website:
http://www.e-laws.gov.on.ca/html/statutes/english/elaws_statutes_92c06_e.htm

Company: Companies are organizations. Organizations are groups of individuals for a common purpose. At GM, this common purpose tended to be: self-preservation; expansion; and wealth generation.

Consumers: Buyers of automobiles. There are millions of them, and every company feels its products suit the consumer best. Especially confusing are the various subsets of consumers and the vehicles they buy. Manufacturers tend to classify the vehicles then study the consumers who buy vehicles in those categories. Unfortunately, it is very difficult to understand the consumer completely because humans are so complex.

Dealer: The intermediary between the carmaker and the consumer. The dealer is held responsible by both the consumer and the manufacturer for everything that goes wrong in the automotive business. It is the dealer's fault when he makes a lot of money and it is the dealer's fault when he goes bankrupt. The dealer buys and pays for the cars the factory produces even if there are no customers. The dealers make it possible for consumers to have service maintenance and warranty repair. Dealers facilitate the sale of new vehicles by assisting in the financing process, buying the customers' trade-ins, and carrying millions of dollars in vehicle inventory to provide the customer with choice. Without dealers, there would be no auto industry.

Divisional System: Developed by Arthur Sloan, CEO of GM from the 1920s on. The objective was that each division would concentrate on a specific market segment. The result was five carmaking divisions, led by a dynamic and relatively autonomous division manager, that were ultra-competitive with each other in every way, striving to produce the best automobiles in the world. The creative tension that existed between the divisions resulted in vehicles that dominated the North American sales charts. Unfortunately, from an accounting point of view, the divisional system appears to be expensive, due to apparent duplication in many areas. Financial gurus at GM were always able to show millions and millions of savings in eliminating all vestiges of the divisional system—until the company went bankrupt.

Factory Rep: Believed by many to be a mythical entity like a unicorn. Rarely seen by the dealership or the public, sightings at dealerships occur when the factory wants to sell the dealer something or charge the dealer for something. Factory representatives, except in a very few instances, have no power, authority, or responsibility, other than to follow orders from above.

General Motors (GM): The multinational automobile company headquartered in Detroit, Michigan, that declared bankruptcy on June 1, 2009. GM has corporate divisions in numerous countries and the European Union. China is said to be GM's growth area.

General Motors of Canada (GMCL): Based in Oshawa, Ontario, GMCL is one of the numerous international production and sales divisions that is responsible for GM's business in Canada.

Highly Interactive Distance Learning (HIDL): The satellite communication system that connected GMCL with its dealers in real time with both audio and video transmissions.

Image: Also known as Image 2000, the redesign of GMCL dealership facilities to have a consistent and consumer-friendly interior and exterior design and style. Uniformity of facilities in terms of appearance was a key goal.

NIH: "Not Invented Here." The great reluctance by American industry in general, the Big Three especially, to consider, let alone embrace, technical ideas and methods from other countries or other cultures. Most citizens believe America invented the modern technological world, and other countries have nothing to offer. This NIH thinking has partially resulted in American consumers' buying more foreign goods than any other nation.

NUMMI: New United Motor Manufacturing, Inc. In 1984, GM and Toyota formed a joint venture to produce automobiles in an existing GM plant in Fremont, California. The plant was managed and operated by Toyota with GM managers assigned to learn Toyota systems and operations. The workers were existing GM workers represented by the UAW. The plant produced over eight million cars for GM and Toyota until 2010.

Plan 2000: A plan by GMCL to supposedly address over-dealering and encourage consolidation of Canadian GM dealers. It is doubtful that this plan was ever finalized or implemented. There is evidence that GMCL refused to provide financial assistance to dealers willing to consolidate while Plan 2000 was in effect.

Store: A euphemism for a dealership, or its facilities. As in, "How many stores does he have?" or, "Where is his store?"

United Auto Workers / Canadian Auto Workers (UAW/CAW): The main autoworkers union founded in 1935 enjoyed its greatest prosperity from 1946 on under Walter Reuther. In every case, the Big Three resisted the organization of its workers by the UAW, and only agreed after strikes and/or government mediation. The UAW was the first union to allow persons of colour to be members, and allowed workers to become middle-class members of society. The CAW, an offshoot of the UAW, has represented Canadian autoworkers since 1984.

Voodoo Economics / Accounting: This is a term stolen from the Reagan administration. The art of using numbers to justify any conclusion, action, or result desired—what you get when a Witch Doctor and a Bean-Counter get together to produce a report. Usually the report will have just enough mathematical validity to make sense to a media reporter or an elected official. "Our studies show that with fewer dealers, we will sell the same number of cars."

Whacked: An underworld slang term borrowed by Canadian dealers to describe terminated franchises, as in, "Both Jerry's stores were whacked." The Mob whacks people for three main reasons: They displeased someone in the hierarchy; they are in the way; or to teach others lessons. General Motors of Canada whacked dealers for the same reasons.

What Consumers Want: Despite spending millions on research, nobody is quite sure what the consumer wants to buy until after the product is introduced to the market. SUVs are a classic example, in that nobody in any of the car companies envisioned the growth and size and the profitability of vehicles in this segment until it was happening.

Witch Doctor (a.k.a. "a Flak"): Those person(s) who are the spokespeople for the auto company are experts in dealing with the media and government. Sometimes it is the chief executive, sometimes it is another corporate specialist. They use buzz-words, smoke, mirrors, rattles, incantations, and song-and-dance routines to get their message across. These are the charismatic (hopefully) public persona of the company. Their goal is to convince the media, the public, and elected officials that the company's latest products and activities are in the best interest of the listener. They work hand in hand with Voodoo Economics / Bean-counters.

Worldwide Overproduction: The sum total of all the automotive production capacity in the world always exceeds the actual number of potential customers. The biggest fear of all automotive marketing departments is to not have enough vehicles to meet demand; therefore, overcapacity is the usual result.

Bibliography

Iacocca, Lee, and William Novak. *Iacocca.* New York: Bantam, 2007.

Ingrassia, Paul. *Crash Course: The American Automobile Industry's Road to Bankruptcy and Bailout—and Beyond.* New York: Random House Trade Paperbacks, 2011.

Johnson, Richard A. *Six Men Who Built the Modern Auto Industry.* Minneapolis, MN: Motorbooks, 2005.

Keller, Mary Ann. *Rude Awakening: The Rise, Fall, and Struggle for Recovery of General Motors.* New York: HarperCollins, 1990.

Lutz, Bob. *Car Guys vs. Bean-counters: The Battle for the Soul of American Business.* New York: Portfolio Hardcover, 2011.

Stewart, Ian. *Does God Play Dice? The New Mathematics of Chaos.* Second edition. Toronto: Wiley–Blackwell, 2002.

Vlasic, Bill, and Bradley A. Stertz. *Taken for a Ride: How Daimler–Benz Drove off with Chrysler.* Collingdale, PA: Diane Publishing, 2001.

About the Author

Dennis Gazarek graduated in 1972 from the University of Windsor with a Bachelor of Commerce in Honours Business Administration and has spent almost his entire life immersed in the auto business. His father, uncle, brother, and cousins all were employed in the automotive industry.

An individual of many diverse tastes and interests, he has been a former record-holder in the *Guinness Book of Records*, an expert skier and motorcyclist, successful youth football coach, amateur saxophonist, and a lifelong learner and student of history, human behaviour, ethics, and values.

Dennis has written articles for magazines, the Web, and corporate use. He also has a patent for a unique, tilting three-wheel motorcycle.

Dennis lives with his wife, Janet, in Ajax, Ontario, further developing his motorcycle invention and working on his next book. Gazarek has three grown sons from a previous marriage.

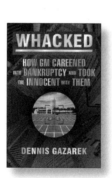

TO ORDER MORE COPIES:

GENERAL STORE PUBLISHING HOUSE
499 O'Brien Road, Box 415, Renfrew, Ontario, Canada K7V 4A6
Tel 1.800.465.6072 • Fax 1.613.432.7184
www.gsph.com